REAPING
THE
HARVEST

REAPING
THE
HARVEST

The Bounty of
Abundant-Life Homeschooling

DIANA WARING

Published by Diana Waring—History Alive!, P.O. Box 378, Spearfish, SD 57783.

Unless otherwise indicated, all Scripture quotations are taken from the Holy Bible, New King James Version, Copyright © 1982, 1994 by Thomas Nelson, Inc. Used by permission.

Library of Congress Control Number: 2002092742

Printed in the United States of America
1 2 3 4 5 6 7 8 — 07 06 05 04 03 02

There are times when a person's life so impacts us, our vision is forever changed. In New Zealand, I met a woman whose understanding of God's design in creating each one unique opened my eyes to a deeper comprehension of how He delights in us.

It has helped me see my children with fresh eyes and has immeasurably contributed to my understanding of homeschooling. With gratitude, I dedicate this book to her.

To Rosalie Pedder
My teacher, mentor, and friend

Table of Contents

Acknowledgements

Many people have contributed to this book. I would like to thank:

- The ladies of the Monday night Bible study—Laura, Lori, Kim, Ginger, Karen, Deb, Theresa, Jamie, and Cheri—who prayed chapter by chapter, week by week;

- Our small group from Countryside Community Church—Rick and Vicki, John and Liz, John and Roxie, Scott and Dawn, Lornie and Hollie—who prayed while we were home and while we travelled;

- Our YWAM school leaders in New Zealand—Bruce and Fay Settle and Cecil and Denise Lowe—who oversaw a great healing and new foundations in my life;

- Loren Cunningham, for graciously granting me time for an interview during his hectic visit to New Zealand;

- Rod and Alexis Wilson, who have blessed us with an unexpectedly delightful friendship and who have diligently prayed from afar for this book project;

- Our YWAM Pub/Emerald Books friends—Tom Bragg, Warren Walsh, Jim Drake—who have encouraged us through the years and opened doors for our message;

- The many, many people who shared how *Beyond Survival* blessed them, and who encouraged me to continue on;

- My special friends—Debra Bell, Becky Bishop, Sally Clarkson, Vivian Doublestein, Cathy Duffy, Tina Farewell, Bonnie Ferguson, Sharon Grimes, Maxine Harris, Miriam Heppner, Maggie Hogan, Susie Kemmerer, Jane Lambert, Cam Leedahl, Shirley Quine, Nancy Robins, Julie Ross, Linda Schneider, Barbara Smith, Joan Veach, and Cindy Wiggers—who have all spent hours in insightful conversation, which has helped me process this amazing adventure of parenting teens;

- Our editors, business consultants, and friends—Len and Heather Armstrong—whose strengths and giftings in the area of business and publishing have allowed us to grow AND keep our sanity;

- My children—Isaac, Michael, and Melody—who have given me the best years of my life and allowed me to know the joy of belonging to a healthy, loving, zany family;

- My best friend, co-parent, business partner, fellow world traveler, and beloved husband—Bill Waring—who not only dreamed with me but had the courage to live it out; and

- Jesus, the One and Only. In reality, this is not about us; it's about Him. May He be glorified!

Introduction

This can be the most wonderful time of all for a parent, holding the richest moments, the greatest opportunities, and the best growing seasons. Everything we have been working on as parents up to this point has been mere preparation for the really good stuff: TEENAGERS!

You know, I am not sure how it happened. One day I was wondering if diapers would ever be a thing of the past, and just a few days later (or so it seemed) my children were driving their own cars! The questions about how to teach reading and writing, how to give them pride in a bed well-made, how to use a fork and knife, how to share their toys, and how to get to sleep at a decent time have morphed into how to prepare for the SAT's, how to help them find a part-time job, how to keep enough food in the house for their never-ending hunger, how to deal with members of the opposite sex calling on the phone, and . . . how to get them to sleep at a decent time (some things NEVER change)!

It seems, too, that the pace has picked up considerably from when they were little. For example, our three children are spinning like tops in their different arenas of interest: music, ballet, writing, photography, world missions, sound recording, graphics, politics . . . The list is never ending and always expanding. The opportunities to learn and grow in these areas are diverse and multifaceted: everything from reading about it in a book at home to traveling to the ends of the earth. Trying to stay up-to-date with my teenagers feels like riding on one of those brightly-colored, lovingly-fashioned merry-go-rounds—filled with continuous sight and sound and movement. It's a fabulous ride, but I am often dizzy!

When we began homeschooling, the question often was, "How long will you keep doing this?" The answer was clear, "I am homeschooling now while they are little so I CAN homeschool when they are teenagers!" I so looked forward to the day we could talk about the real things of life. Now, I revel in the long talks, the future planning, the tougher questions. We have seen it work for others, too. Families we meet who are launching prepared, excited, motivated young adults give us so much hope and encouragement.

Forget the nay-sayers, the down-trodders, the ne'er-do-enjoyers who advise you to "close your eyes and hope to survive." Forget the media, the movies, the meddlers who tell you that your teens are going to destroy your sanity, your checkbook, and your home. Instead, we can reap the harvest!

We can enjoy our teenagers, listen to our teenagers, love our teenagers, and watch them grow (sometimes literally)! This book is partly a description of our own experience during this fertile time period in our children's lives. It is also what we have gleaned from many others who have walked this rich path before us, informing us along the way of the wonders and wildness of homeschooling teens. *Reaping the Harvest* is intended to provoke thought, insight, laughter, and tears and is meant to be read by both parents and teens. We believe that our teens need to be as involved in their own growth and development as we are, and this book can provide a platform for many eye-opening, ear-listening, heart-widening discussions.

If you are considering the remote possibility of teenagers in your future, read on. If you stand on the brink of teenagers in your home, read on. If you are in the midst of teenagers right now, read on. If the question in the back of your mind is whether you can survive the teenage years, my encouragement to you is that you can go beyond survival and into the bounty of abundant-life homeschooling! For a moment, take the time to lay aside your fears and join with me in discovering the wondrous possibilities that lie ahead. All you have to do is turn the page.

PART ONE
TILLING THE GROUND

got teens?

You think you've got teenagers? I would like to introduce you to a family that probably holds the record for the fastest-growing: from one to four in just days! Roger and Christine Whetton of New Zealand began as a somewhat normal homeschooling family. When their son, Evan, was ten years old, they discussed with him the idea of enlarging their family by adopting a little girl from Russia. He thought it was a great idea, as long as the child was younger. Roger and Christine were happy to oblige, as they were thinking in terms of a four-year-old child. So, united in this family-enlargement quest, they began the long process of overseas adoption. After a taxing year, they were ready to go to Russia for their soon-to-be adopted daughter, Anya. Since there was a Russian law requiring siblings to be adopted together, the adoption agent in New Zealand was certain that Anya must be an only child. After all, the Russian agency had approved her adoption.

When they met Anya in Russia for the first time, she was in the hospital. As they spent the allotted half-hour with her, their hearts were captivated by this sunny, lovely child. Though she was seven and a half, slightly old for adoption, Roger and Christine felt that this precious girl was their daughter selected by the Lord. In great joy, they promised to adopt her immediately. However, later that same day, they learned to their great astonishment that Anya had an older brother and sister in the same orphanage, both of them older than Evan! What on earth could they do? Adopting Anya's siblings would not only be breaking their word to Evan, it was financially impossible. Perhaps the most difficult barrier to cross was that Roger and Christine were not at all sure they would be able to integrate that many older children into the Whetton family. But they could not start over with some other young, no-siblings-attached girl—they had given their promise to Anya and had seen her nearly burst with happiness.

REAPING THE HARVEST

As Roger and Christine prayed and sought counsel, they were told by the Russian workers that the older children did not have to be adopted, since one was much older and the other was not available for adoption due to mental retardation. The Whettons then decided that all they could do at the present was to carry on and adopt Anya. The day before the adoption hearing, they visited Anya at her orphanage, where her brother, Dima, and sister, Yulia, hovered close by. It was obvious that Yulia had a strong, motherly attachment to her little sister, which gave rise to some obvious concerns about the impact this adoption would have on each of the siblings.

The director of the orphanage assured them that there was nothing to worry about, since orphanage children were more attached to their peers than to their siblings. In a separate interview with the social worker, they were told that each of these Dodonov children were very bright. Mixed signals, contradictory comments, and sibling relationships all remained unfinished business that would eventually change the landscape of this homeschool family.

When they returned with Anya to New Zealand, they were told by a visiting Russian official not to worry about the issue of leaving siblings behind but instead to have Anya write to them in Russia. Thus began a painful time of correspondence as Anya's brother and sister pleaded through the mail for her new parents to adopt them as well. Roger and Christine were able to have a translator write a Russian letter to these two young people, explaining that they applied to adopt Anya believing her to be an only child and that they were not in a position financially to adopt them, too. It stopped the pleading letters, but it brought Roger and Christine no peace.

Evan was now fourteen, and they decided to talk the matter over with him. How would he feel about having a brother and sister older than he was? They shared with him their dilemma, the pros and cons, and asked him to think and pray about it.

Roger suddenly thought of a route to try: bring the children to New Zealand on work permits when they were old enough. Though his idea was turned down, the official to whom he had spoken put him in touch with another government agency in New Zealand. Even though this agency had strong opinions against bringing children to another culture, they were very supportive of family reunifications—which was Roger and Christine's mission. Amazingly enough, through this agency, an affordable way was found to adopt these two children.

As Christine says, *"When the Lord made us willing to welcome those two teenagers into our family as long as He found the way, things started to happen."*

First, Evan came to his parents and said, *"Go for it!"*

Secondly, a letter arrived from Dima and Yulia. They thanked Anya for sending photos, commenting on how much she had grown. Then they casually mentioned that they had forwarded the photos on to their brother, Sergei, who was in Safonova.

Roger and Christine were stunned! Another brother?

Quickly they pulled out Anya's adoption papers, which had never been translated into English. Sure enough, there was a fourth sibling listed on the paperwork—older than Anya, younger than Yulia.

In for a penny, in for a pound. They couldn't leave him behind, could they?

"There are many plans in a man's heart, Nevertheless the LORD's counsel—that will stand."   *—Proverbs 19:21*

Thirdly, God opened peoples' hearts to spontaneously give to the Whetton family—clothes, money, even bicycles! It was an amazing experience of every need being met, every difficulty being resolved.

When we visited the Whetton's a few months after their second trip to Russia, there were three, new, family members: Dima (15), Yulia (14), and Sergei (13). They nicely rounded out the complement of Whetton young people, along with Evan (14) and Anya (11). As we met these three, bright, interesting, Russian teens, they were in the midst of learning English and beginning to homeschool. Sergei's first words to us as we drove up in a borrowed, Russian-made car (a *Lada*) were, *"Russian car, piece of junk . . ."* We could tell we were meeting a live wire! It was extraordinary to spend the day with them, watching the family trying to learn how to communicate with each other, seeing them try to understand what the others needed. It was not easy for any of them . . . but it was certainly worth it. That day was one of the most emotionally moving days of my life. Roger and Christine have opened their home, their hearts, and their family to these teenagers whom God has brought to them. Teenagers? What a blessing!

OUR JOURNAL

THE FIRST "AHA!" MOMENT ON THE ROAD TO TEENS

Have you ever had one of those "defining moments?" Something that came your way and changed everything that came after? I have. It happened on a bright, summer day, when the heat of the sun slows everything to a moseying pace. It was 1981, and I was hugely pregnant with our first child. My close friend, Becky, came over to commiserate with me about our hugeness and the heat, as she was also expecting her first child. She had brought me a gift, something to take my mind off my labors. It was a hard-bound book that Becky described as "absolutely riveting!"

As moms-to-be, we had been in constant dialogue about pregnancy, labor, newborns, and all that would come after delivery. In fact, a few months prior to this, we had shared an eye-opening discussion about what we would do with these little ones when they reached school age.

"Oh, we are definitely going to send our children to a Christian school," Becky told me.

I was astonished. *"Why would you do that?"* I queried.

It was her turn to look astonished. *"What are YOU going to do?"*

"Send them to public school, of course! Let them have a chance to impact the world with their vibrant Christian witness!!"

Her pitying expression came as a result of knowing a whole lot more about child development (her major in college) than I did. But, as a true friend and compatriot, she sought to discover a gentle way to educate me about the true nature of children and their needs.

It was shortly after this discussion that she ran across the "riveting" book she was now giving to me and that would change both of our lives forever. It was the homeschool classic, *Home Grown Kids* by Dr. Raymond Moore.

I sat down on that summer day and read the book in two hours. When I finished, it was a done deal: we would homeschool our children. Defining moment. Period. The End. Change of entire life. That determination came, I might add, as a bit of a shock to my husband, Bill, who was then a public school teacher! Actually, we dialogued at length, and eventually, with his day by day experiences in the classroom, he became a greater proponent of homeschooling than I.

So, what was so captivating, so convincing, so enlightening about this book? For me, it was the lightning-bolt revelation that one could actually have a healthy relationship with one's teenage children—that homeschooling provided a platform for an ongoing, interactive, vital relationship between parents and teenagers.

I was stunned! I had never, ever seen healthy, friendly relationships between parents and teens. Let me say that once again: I had never, EVER seen healthy, friendly relationships between parents and teens. As we were growing up, we all heard that a "generation gap" was part and parcel of life, something that could not be avoided, but which we somehow hoped to survive. If you were like me, you probably remember the way you walked three or four steps behind your parents on outings so no one would know you were together. You may have tried, as I did, to identify more with your peers than with your parents.

Suddenly, at age twenty-six, someone rocked my boat. In this book, *Home Grown Kids*, I saw a man taking completely the opposite viewpoint: it is possible to have healthy relationships with your teenagers IF you spend enough time (quality and quantity) and IF you hold a place of influence in their lives by teaching them yourself. In other words, you could hold a place of influence in the lives of and build relationships with your teens IF you homeschooled them.

My mind began to repeat the litany:
"Homeschool, homeschool, homeschool."

THE SECOND "AHA!" MOMENT ON THE ROAD TO TEENS

In a magazine interview with Edith Schaeffer, I once read the comment that her husband AND her children were her best friends. I was captivated by the thought that my children could become my best friends. Teacher, chauffeur, laundress, nurse, chef, loan officer, and police sergeant, yes, but BEST FRIENDS? How on earth does one do that? How do you move from these other roles to the easy-going, understanding, give-and-take relationship of best friends? What are the necessary steps to get there?

It seemed pretty obvious that this would require some thoughtful planning, some long-term decisions, and some creative efforts. It would require spending the kind of time together that is necessary in order to become best friends, making time for listening, sharing, and dreaming; time for just hanging out like friends do; and time that was not "get this done, finish that task, pick this up, take that out!"

By homeschooling, thankfully, we already had the "quantity of time" issue resolved. Now, if we could just take steps to begin to turn at least some of it into "best-friend-quality time."

My mind added to the above litany:
"Best friends, best friends, best friends."

THE THIRD "AHA!" MOMENT ON THE ROAD TO TEENS

When Isaac, our oldest child, was about five years old, Bill and I attended a Gregg Harris seminar. He said something that grabbed me by the shoulders and shook some sense into me! It went like this:

"Do you know the greatest blessing in your life? It's a TEENAGER!
"Do you know the greatest curse in your life? It's a TEENAGER!
"Do you know what makes the difference between whether your child will be the greatest blessing in your life or the greatest curse in your life? It's what you do with them from here on out—how you raise them everyday from now on."

Hmmm. Obviously, we wanted our teenagers to be the greatest blessing in our lives, not the other (ahem!) possibility. But, this is easier said than done. What were the routes to relationships that would open up this amazing potential?

The third and final litany began:
"How you raise them, how you raise them, how you raise them."

ROUTE #1—TIME WITH THEM

As I talked with friends about educating and caring for children who would someday become teens, the whole litany just kept coming out over and over: *"Homeschooling!" "Best friends!" "How you raise them!"* This was clearly where we should be heading, but it was like a maze rather than a map. In other words, I wasn't sure how to get there from here! So, I put up my antennae and began to listen for some clear signals.

Watching others successfully find their way gave us great hope that we, too, could successfully navigate these teens years. Seeking the Lord for His enormous wisdom and creativity was like petrol in never-ending supply for our journey. And walking this out with our children, day by day, has resulted in a greater understanding of the fact that no matter where you go, there you are! No matter where we are on the map, we are all there together. Which brings us to the first route we discovered.

Spending time together—fun time together—as a family is absolutely, without-a-doubt, one of the most important legs of the journey. With teens, you ask? You bet! Time together as a family is as important and as appropriate now as it was when they were wee ones, even if *they* don't realize it. In fact, you may have noticed that as children become teenagers, they will wilt and grow distant without special times spent together with the family.

"What's wrong with Johnny, Gertrude?"
"Oh, nothing that a little family time won't cure."
"Good enough. Get out the Pass the Pigs *game."*

Time together, with teens, certainly needs to be scheduled in. I remember reading in *Reader's Digest* when my children were younger that a large percentage of American families ate only one meal per week together. I scoffed in my homeschool state of righteousness, since we consistently ate together twenty-one times per week. You just don't get any better than 3/7!

Enter the teen years.

"Mom, sorry, but I have to work tonight. Save some dinner for me, will you?"
"Mom, sorry, but we have a hike planned all day Saturday. Won't be home till late."
"Mom, sorry, but my dance class lasts till nine. I'll grab some fast food."

And so it goes. Hence the absolute necessity of scheduling special time together with your teens.

One of our main scheduled, set-apart times is on Sunday evening. The standard fare is buttermilk waffles and a great book read aloud. Bill reads, while I hover over the waffle iron and the children take turns spreading yogurt, strawberries, and maple syrup over these golden works of art. It's easy; it's a no-brainer (since we need the same ingredients each week); and it's fun. The book is one we all agree to (not always easy to find!). We have especially enjoyed Gene Stratton-Porter and J.R.R. Tolkien.

If waffles and hobbits leave you dry, here are some other ideas. Maybe you love to go to museums, or concerts, or flea markets together. Your family's taste may run to bicycling, frisbee throwing, or horse fairs. Perhaps your set-apart time should be skiing together, like our friends Bruce and Barb West. They meticulously plan family ski trips during each winter, which is the highlight of their family's year. (Having grown up in Miami, Florida, I never acquired a taste for nor had the experience of hurtling myself down a mountain on two skinny boards . . . ah, well, to each his own.) It doesn't matter what the activity is, as long

11

as it is something the whole family (especially the teenagers) think is absolutely FUN to do—something that creates the sense of "family-ish-ness" and something that everyone looks forward to with great expectation.

We have found that travelling together is a MARVELOUS way to stay connected and to maintain an extraordinary sense of family-ish-ness. Just picture it: all of you snug as a bug in a rug in the car together. Imagine, if you can, an auto trip where no phones are allowed, no headphones are used, and no videos are played. Instead, in this imaginary scene, you spend time looking out the window at lovely vistas, visiting contentedly with each other, and listening to the classical music playing on the car stereo.

Wait! Don't throw the book away yet!! That was only an imaginary scene, though certain parts could shape your vision of the next family car trip. Go somewhere that will be fun for the family. Enjoy the scenery, and bring lots of tasty snacks. (Rule #1: When teens are onboard, double the portions of food and triple the drinks!) Though I seldom succeed in being this organized, the "with-it" mom will have made healthy, low-cost, delicious snacks or picnic lunches for the trip. Go with an expectation of something special to be experienced.

Perhaps, you might want to try creating memories and good times (and tall tales) by camping together. There is nothing like the smell of a smoking campfire—especially when it permeates all of your clothes and bedding. These shared moments—mosquitoes, rain, burned hot dogs, lumpy sleeping bags, the whole nine yards—if accompanied by laughter and good-natured groans are a priceless commodity in taking you where you want to go in relationships with your teenagers.

We have heard such fun stories from other homeschooling families who have hit the open road with the idea of creating fun family times that we know it is really a winner. Whether it is just down the road to the local campground or on the other side of the world with a backpack, getting away together is a fabulous route to take, even though it requires effort.

Years ago, I heard one woman's amazing story. She described how she and her husband had a plan all along: teach the family how to sail, buy a sailboat, then take a year's leave of absence from work, rent out the house, and sail to the South Pacific! Can you believe it?! They actually accomplished it!! The children, all married with children now, told their parents that it had absolutely been the most wonderful year of their lives. Their reason? The "togetherness" of the family.

Aha! Homeschool, homeschool, homeschool becomes:
Time with them, time with them, time with them.
So, the first route on the road to teens: Time with them.

ROUTE #2—ENJOY THEM!

A few months ago, Bill had to go out of town for several days. Can I tell you honestly that this is not my favorite scenario? Extra pressure, responsibility, and juggled schedules weigh heavily on the single parent, whether long-term or temporary! So, I was doing my best to keep everyone on task, fed, and in their right minds . . . when suddenly Melody called out, *"Mom, the water coming out of the faucet is blue!"*

What on earth?!! I ran downstairs to the kitchen, and sure enough, the water was a weird, bluish-greenish color, though it was getting lighter and lighter the longer the water ran. Thoughts of chemical spills in our city water system raged through my mind while panic grabbed my pumping heart. Newspaper headlines appeared before my eyes—"Toxic Waste Discovered In Sink!"

"Don't drink anything! I'll call the city water department right away!!"

The lady on the other end of the line was a little puzzled but said she would send someone right over. In the meantime, I ran to all of our other sinks to see what color water they were producing.

Hmmm. Everything else was normal. Weird, weird, weird.

A few minutes later, a polite man from the city showed up at our door. I showed him the evidence—saved in a Mason jar—while describing the horror I felt at what was certainly a bizarre chemical situation. He looked quite concerned and asked me about our outside water faucets. As I took him around to check our garden hoses, Michael, my eighteen-year-old son, poked his head around the corner of the house, where he was painting the trim.

"Michael, do you know anything about blue water coming out of the faucet?" I approached in panicked concern, trailed by the equally concerned, city-water man.

The moment I saw his surprised, deer-caught-in-the-headlights expression, the jig was up.

"Uh, yeah, Mom, I do. It's food coloring!"

My jaw fell to the ground in disbelief.

"It was YOU??!!"

A what-will-happen-to-me-if-I-tell-you-the-answer grin was on face.

"Why did you put food coloring in the faucet, Michael?"

"Just wanting to surprise you and Melody . . ."

I turned to the polite, city-water man and saw his huge grin. *Well,* I thought, *let's make it grins all around.* I smiled at Michael. I smiled at the man and said, *"Oops."* The man was still smiling as he walked away.

13

I turned to Michael and said with amused amazement, *"I can't believe you did that."* Michael looked at me with a sheepish grin and said, *"I can't believe you called the city water guys!!"* With that, we both burst out laughing and went inside to tell Melody all that had transpired.

What route to relationships with teens did I discover in this situation? Relax! Chill out! Grin and enjoy 'em!

Enjoy them. Enjoy their quirky sense of humor. Enjoy their ideas of how to spend vacation time. Enjoy their discussions of what is being studied together. Enjoy their driving—EEEK! That one's easier said than done!! Enjoy their room design and decor (though suggestions may be quite appropriate from time to time: *"You know, I have found that life looks better when your bed is made and your clothes are put away. . ."*). Enjoy their hair style and clothing selection. (I must confess that I still add my two cents if we are going on a family outing.) We are currently going through an orange phase with Melody—orange blouses, orange skirts, orange sweatshirts, orange lipstick. And, as much as it pains me to admit this, I am actually beginning to enjoy the color.

We are finding that we don't always agree about their style or their decisions (big decisions, yes, little decisions, no). It may not be easy for us to stop being the decider of clothing style, fashion, and color. It may not be easy for us to appreciate a hairstyle that reminds us of a baboon. It may not be easy for us to enjoy the room decor our teens find attractive. BUT, as they are making the transition to adulthood, it becomes increasingly important for us to live graciously with these changing teenagers. We must give them space to develop and grow into the individuals God has created them each to be. And to do that requires an attitude of enjoyment for the uniqueness of each one.

> *Aha! Best friends, best friends, best friends becomes:*
> *Enjoy them, enjoy them, enjoy them.*
> *First route on the road to teens: Time with them.*
> *Second route on the road to teens: Enjoy them.*

ROUTE #3—LISTEN TO THEM!

The third route on our road to relationships with our teens is to listen to them. Now, I am not talking about the listening that I do while my mind is engaged elsewhere and I occasionally grunt, *"Uhuh . . . Yep . . . Mmm, mmm . . ."* Instead, it is the pivotal listening where you feel like your ear and mind are both straining to catch every nuance of meaning that your teenager is communicating. It is listening to them like you listen to a friend. It is learning the gentle art of querying without pushing. It is creating the atmosphere and the attitude where hearts, dreams, and concerns can safely be revealed.

You know what can really hinder this kind of communication? When we have an attitude of anger, disapproval, or uptightness. Many's the time when my teenagers' attempts to share with me have been completely shut off by my glaring eyes or my one word comebacks, usually delivered in sarcasm.

Proverbs 14:1 says, *"The wise woman builds her house, but the foolish pulls it down with her hands."*

Ouch! I could almost feel that house falling down around my ears! What's a mother to do? Become a wise woman. How? For me, the antidote was to humble myself and to go ask for their forgiveness. Ouch! Double Ouch!! Each and every time I reacted improperly, I had to humble myself and ask for forgiveness until the ouches taught me to keep a civil tongue. Really and truly there is no other way to restore the relationship with your teen.

There was the day when Isaac, who was about sixteen at the time, walked into my room and announced, *"Mom, I really hate school."* He was perfectly serious.

Stop the world . . . I'm getting off here . . .

"Well, Isaac, just stab me in the heart right now and get it over with." It felt like people all over the U.S. and Canada were listening to me tell them how to get "beyond survival and into the abundant life of homeschooling!" . . . and here was my very own son telling me that I had failed miserably with him. You might say I was *some* upset!

After a few minutes of uncomfortable emotion, it seemed that maybe I should stop reacting and start listening. So, I asked him to forgive me for my outburst and to tell me more.

Slowly, hesitantly, Isaac began to share what was bothering him. It turned out that I had forgotten the cardinal rule of Isaac's learning style. He is a "feeler," a "people person," and I had sent him, a capable high school student, off to his own room to do his studies alone—all by himself. It wasn't that he was not able to do the work on his own; it was simply that he had a hard time always looking at a book without getting to discuss what he was learning. He finally looked at me and said, *"Mom, could you just do a few of these classes with me?"*

Ah, yes—a parent engaging in her child's homeschooling, or more accurately, in his personality. Problem solved.

REAPING THE HARVEST

Listening, this third route, is critical because it allows us to enter our teenager's own world of hopes, dreams, understanding, and intentions. When we enter into their world, we discover the most wondrous insights about these young people created in the very image of God. I have been astonished to find courage beyond my ken, a passion to serve, visions of creative productions, and much, much more. These young people whom I have known all their lives, and the ones in your home whom you have known all their lives are the most amazing creatures! God has been at work in them—in the deep and hidden places of their hearts, and we will never know anything about it if we don't shut our mouths, quit directing their EVERY step, and just listen to them.

If you hear some strange comment from your teenager, pursue it with your ears. Let me give you an example of what we can hear if we will listen. At the beginning of her junior year, Melody told me she wanted to do volunteer work at the hospital. I wondered what had put this thought into her head after all the other plans and activities she had already prepared for that year.

On her own, she called the hospital and talked to several people, each one promising to call her back. I thought, *OK, you've done your thing, let's get back to work!*

But Melody kept mentioning it at odd moments. *"Why do you think they haven't called me back?"*

It was frustrating me that she kept bringing it up. Why couldn't she just be satisfied with the killer schedule she already had? Why did she want anything else? Hmmm.

Finally one day, during a quiet mother-daughter moment of cooking dinner, Melody explained to me that the Lord had really stirred her heart about serving others—that it was a passion of her heart to help people who couldn't help themselves, that she had been reading books about servants of the Lord who had blessed other people through service, and that she really wanted to walk that walk.

I was shocked. I had seen this as a crazy idea disrupting her life, while all along it had been the Lord motivating her heart to be more like Him. It completely changed my attitude about this unusual request, because now it was obvious that this was a step of obedience and service to the Lord.

Amazing people, teens. Don't miss out on this incredible time of their lives by not listening to them! It is in the listening to them that you may very well discover the "Y" in the road, the bend in the route that is essential in raising them.

Aha! How you raise them, how you raise them, how you raise them becomes:
Listen to them, listen to them, listen to them.

First route on the road to teens: Time with them.
Second route on the road to teens: Enjoy them.
Third route on the road to teens: Listen to them.

THE GRANDDADDY OF
ALL ROUTES—LOVE THEM!

The final route to relationships with your teenagers is really the sum total of all these and all of the best aspects of parenting and homeschooling: Love them! Love them fiercely; love them freely; love them with laughter; love them with tears; love them with prayers; love them with encouragement. What a simple yet profound route: easy to see on the map, more difficult to follow on the road.

Love in action, tangible love, costs us something, but it provides such benefit, such help, and such joy to the receiving teen, that it is eminently worthwhile. How do we start showing this kind of love? I've discovered one way is to neither give them everything they want nor withhold good things that would bless them. For instance, a few years ago, Melody announced that she wanted to own a dog.

"We already have a dog, dear." Our beloved, bizarre dachshund, Miggy, has been the source of much laughter in our family, and I was amazed that she was not satisfied.

"No, Mom, you don't understand. I want a REAL dog!"

Hmpf! Sputter, sputter. *"What do you mean, a REAL dog? Miggy is a REAL dog!"*

"No, he's not. He's a small lapdog, and a dachshund to boot. I want a BIG dog, a REAL dog."

"Oh, really? And who would take care of this REAL dog?"

"I would, honestly and truly, I would."

Silence. *"But we travel several months of the year, Melody. What would we do with a big dog?"*

"He could sit with me, on my seat!" Triumphant smile.

Sigh. *"We'll see."*

Well, this refrain continued to circulate around my house and in my head: *"I want a REAL dog . . . I want a REAL dog."*

Bill and I considered what it would mean to us—a hassle—and what it would mean to Melody—a blessing. So, what's a parent to do? Get the girl a dog, of course.

"OK, Mel, find a dog."

Rustle, rustle went the newspapers and the local ads.

"Eureka!" she shouted a few days later. *"Here is an ad for lab/cross puppies—for FREE!"* *Free* was in our price range, so we called the advertising family and made an appointment to see these pups.

They really were adorable. Melody and I chose the cutest one—he kept coming to hang out with us—and we took him home. Melody promptly named him "Wimsey" after Dorothy Sayers's unforgettable detective, Lord Peter Wimsey. And so began the saga of a growing dog.

I am not kidding. This dog grew . . . and grew . . . and grew some more. He was, in a word, HUMONGOUS, and he was filled with more energy than a nuclear reactor. He loved, no, he craved running—anywhere, anytime. And things began to fall—things such as chairs, plants, and people—as he raced through the entire house.

As our travelling/homeschool convention season drew closer, we began to talk to Melody about the reality of trying to take this mammoth marathoner in a van around the country. The handwriting on the wall was obvious to us, but difficult for her to see. Finally, an opportunity presented itself for Wimsey to move to my sister-in-law's farm. Amid tears (and relief!), we parted ways with this dog. (Side note: Wimsey is still alive and running every day on the farm—he's been clocked at over 30 mph. We think he was crossed with a greyhound!!)

Well, at least we tried. End of story. Dachshunds forever!

After some months, the refrain began again. *"Please, may I have a REAL dog?"*

Sigh.

Our circumstances while travelling had changed quite a bit since we were now hauling a travel trailer. This not only meant that we travelled with our own food and our own beds, but we could possibly have another dog along on our cross-country excursions.

Double sigh. What's a mother to do?

Proverbs 3:27 says, *"Do not withhold good from those to whom it is due, When it is in the power of your hand to do so."*

Well, it was within the power of our hands to do this thing now, and it would be really, REALLY good for Melody's heart.

"OK. But we need a SMALLER real dog this time!!"

Off to the animal shelter we went. We rescued a gorgeous, two-year-old, REAL dog named "Marble." She has settled in quite nicely, is a great traveller, and has blessed the socks off Melody.

On this granddaddy of all routes—love—Bill and I had to start considering why we were always saying, "No" and ask ourselves when we could start saying, "Yes." *Selah.*

The routes on the road to teens—to a bounteous harvest of friendship with these amazing young people—took time to discover. As we went from trying to get out of the maze of the "generation gap" to the map of joyous relationships, we unearthed a few simple principles that have proven astonishingly successful. We learned that we had to spend time listening to our teens to begin to know HOW we could show love to them. We needed to develop an attitude of enjoyment of who they are in their special moment of "teenager-ness"—their jokes, their styles, their interests. And they needed to see and understand that we DID enjoy them. Finally, we needed time together laughing and playing and talking and discussing and camping and travelling in order to grow together.

Got teens? You lucky dogs. Spend time with them; enjoy them; listen to them; and love them. They are the most incredible people, these emerging adults, and they can become the best friends you'll ever have.

RECOMMENDED RESOURCES

Age of Opportunity: A Biblical Guide to Parenting Teens by Paul Tripp
This book is a wonderful, insightful book devoted to helping us understand that God did not intend for us to look at the teenage years as something to merely "survive," but it is, in fact, the most incredible opportunity for us as parents to pour ourselves into our teens' lives. This is not a book for lazy parents!

Five Love Languages for Teens by Gary Chapman
The principles of showing love to others in a way THEY can receive has profound implications for families, especially for this time in your teenager's life. Read it and learn.

The Gift of the Blessing by Gary Smalley and John Trent
Parental blessing given to children is both a Biblical model and a powerful tool. This book gives incredible encouragement and practical insights into how to truly bless our children.

Resisting the Snapshot Mentality

One year we had the opportunity to spend a whole day at Camp Snoopy in the Mall of America. That is the most amazing place—a theme park, complete with roller coaster and ferris wheel, in the middle of a mall! We took our three youngsters to all the best rides and activities we could find. (My personal favorite was the one where I tried to bash the plastic alligator head to make it yell, "OW!")

Toward the end of the day, we took our courage in our hands and bought the ticket for the log-in-the-water ride. All day long we had been observing folks careening down a long, steep waterfall in logs, screaming and holding on for dear life. I think, once you're a mom, your enthusiasm for riding the wildest rides fades, along with your cravings for cotton candy. But, our children were begging, so, with a sigh, I agreed.

The first part of the ride was kind of fun, kind of slow and boatish. But I knew we were heading into deeper water, so to say, when the chain under our log began lurching us heavenward. We travelled, amused, through a scary scene with Paul Bunyan and Babe the Blue Ox to emerge at the last possible moment into the light of day at the top of the waterfall. Oh, no! This was the moment I had been dreading—zoom, scream, zoom, spla-a-a-a-sh, SOAKED!

Aha. Well, that was it—a moment of sheer terror, then the fading memory of wetness and laughter.

But, wait, what's this? In a little hut to the side, there was a further development. These enterprising theme park people had set up a camera right at the brink of the waterfall. And they took candid camera pictures of the folks in the logs to sell to said folks. We found our snapshot and looked at it disbelievingly. Captured in this moment of time, the photo displayed all five of us frozen somewhere between wild-eyed terror and a bad-hair day. We bought the picture at our children's request; however, we did not set it up on the mantle for all to see. Why not? It's simple: our appearance has dramatically improved since the moment that snapshot was taken.

OUR JOURNAL

Attending a dozen or so homeschool conventions every year has given us the opportunity to observe the children of homeschool vendors year after year after year. We have several weeks of intense visiting-all-around and then nothing until the following spring. As all of our children have grown from little ones to teenagers, we have felt akin to fond aunts and uncles in the extended family chain, overseeing their growth from time to time. Our on-again-off-again view of these young people has provided long hours of fascinating discussion about their social growth and development.

"Did you see what so-and-so was doing this weekend?"
"Uh, no, not really."
"Did you see who so-and-so was hanging out with this weekend?"
"Uh, no, not really."
"Did you see what so-and-so was wearing this weekend?"
"Uh, no, not really."

Hmmm. Well, I was watching. I was remembering actions and attitudes, impressing them indelibly on my mind. And, unfortunately, I was forming unhappy, uncharitable opinions about who this or that teenager was going to become in just a few years.

Imagine my surprise to meet these same young people the following spring and to discover that they were maturing, growing in their faith, and walking out their Christian witness.

Huh? What had happened here? I was SURE that I had correctly observed these young people in action and that I had truly perceived their state of being and had formed logical conclusions about what that was going to mean in their lives.

Double Huh? As I prayed and pondered about what I had determined previously and what I was seeing now, the Lord showed me that, like a little tourist clicking away, I had been taking mental "shapshots" of individuals during a moment of time and had continued to see them in that particular snapshot. But, the Lord does not see people that way. He sees them as a work of art in progress, a Michelangelo-like sculpture, a work that HE is doing. Under the masterful hand of God, young people change from glory to glory into His image. Like the song says, "He makes all things beautiful in His time." Now I try to forget still shots and simply keep the video rolling.

MORPH TO MATURITY

As parents, we need to be aware that our teens go through a tremendous upheaval in body, mind, and emotions. Just about the time you think you know and understand who these children are, they suddenly *morph* into unknown aliens with entirely different responses, sleep patterns, eating habits, and vocabularies.

When Isaac was about thirteen years old, he went from a sweet, helpful, kind boy to an animal (as my husband says): he began hibernating; he grunted when spoken to and, generally, turned into a grouchy, growly bear. After enduring several months of his primordial behavior, I began to wonder if we were experiencing a real-life "invasion of the body-snatchers!"

Where had our little helper gone?
Why was he sleeping all of the time?
What was happening to all of our food?
Why was he in continual conflict with all of us?
How much more do we put up with before he becomes an endangered species?

And then, one day, as if by magic, the bear was gone, and Isaac had returned. But this Isaac was different. He was more of an adult with barely a trace of boyhood remaining. He was once again sweet, helpful, kind, but in a mature way.

Whew! We wiped our foreheads with relief. It was just one of those growing phases of a child's life. Wish we had recognized earlier what was going on for that year!!

When Michael turned thirteen and bearish, it took us a while to remember what Isaac had gone through. This time, however, we walked through this period of change with a lot more grace and mercy toward the "changee."

Melody went through this change in her own way, quite different from the boys—just when you think you have this whole thing figured out! But we were expecting the greater sleep, the greater hunger, the greater emotions, the greater conflicts as she, butterfly-like, emerged from her chrysalis.

REAPING THE HARVEST

We must, as parents, walk with our children through this time of physical, emotional, and mental change with kindness, gentleness, and a healthy dose of humor. Our transforming teens often have no clue what is happening to them—they're just grasping for a rope and trying to hold on. If we can encourage them, if we can change the schedule a bit to let them sleep more, if we can finance their eating habits, and if we can pray for grace to live through the tempest, the family will come through the experience intact and even closer than before.

What was that song? *You got to try a little kindness, show a little kindness . . .*

This process of maturing and growing and developing means that our children are going to change. We should expect the changes and have the open-handed mentality to allow for a few twists in the road, a few awkward moments and struggles. Have confidence that your teenager will grow up and get on with life. Resist the snapshot mentality!

If we get too anxious about that perfect behavior and poised response that we think we should expect, there will be disappointment. Then, while we impatiently demand instant maturity, we stop to take that snapshot and begin to label them:

"Oh, you know Isaac, he's our absent-minded professor . . ."
"Yeah, he forgets his possessions everywhere we go . . ."
"Jackets, books, socks . . . scattered across the country!"

"Absent-minded professor. Absent-minded professor. Absent-minded professor." It became our perspective on Isaac. And, because we forgot that children grow up and mature and change wonderfully, we kept him stuck—in our minds—in that mold.

"Get your driver's license? I don't think so. You might forget where you left your car!" We were actually serious about that concern. After all, he had forgotten clothes and possessions in crazy places at various times. Replacing a coat was not all that expensive, but a car?! Things could not stay frozen in time forever, especially when we had a raring-to-go teenager who wanted his driver's license! Realizing that he had indeed matured, that he was no longer a ten-year-old boy but an increasingly responsible teenager helped us to recognize that our concerns were probably not valid. He enthusiastically applied for his driver's license, and I am happy to report that he has never, ever, lost the car! In fact, I prefer to have Isaac drive me on my errands rather than drive myself—I hate trying to remember where I've parked . . .

We must beware the trap of identifying a child with a negative, defeatist attitude. Sometimes, childish actions are merely part of the process of learning and growing, and will, if given the right encouragement and environment, change into healthy, thoughtful adult responsibility. Admittedly, there must be changes from childhood to adulthood. But if we have *labeled* them "lazy," "stupid," "thoughtless," "mean," "selfish," and continue to think of them and speak to them in that light, it will be as if we have wrapped chains around them and bound them to that action. How much better, how much healthier, how much more like our Lord to see the possibilities in these soon-to-be adults and, therefore, to set them free from these labels.

Do you remember the scene in John 8:1–11 when the woman caught in the act of adultery was brought before Jesus? Her accusers were quick to point out her actions in their despising tones and to demand the satisfaction of seeing her punished according to the law. What did Jesus do? After a pointed statement to the accusers, *"He who is without sin among you, let him throw a stone at her first,"* which revealed to the men that they were also guilty of shame and sinfulness, He turned to the woman and asked her, *"'Woman, where are those accusers of yours? Has no one condemned you?' She replied, 'No one, Lord.' And Jesus said to her, 'Neither do I condemn you; go and sin no more.'"* He did not brand her forehead or label her with a scarlet letter "A" so that all would know she was an adulteress. No, not even a little. He released her from the label, he forgave her sin, and set her free to grow in godliness.

It's an important lesson for us to learn as the parents of teenagers. Let us walk without the labels, without the accusing attitudes. We must forgive AND forget. May we be very, very careful not to brand their foreheads so that all the world will know what they have done in the past. Let us be the liberators, not the jailers, of our teenagers.

(By the way, lest you think I have branded Isaac an absent-minded professor through this written word, I asked permission to tell his story about the driver's license. He enthusiastically gave it for your edification. What a guy!)

NIX THE NAG

When a child is very young, parents need to assert control in various situations.

"No, Honey, don't touch the wood stove."
"Sweetie, you need to share your toys with your brother."
"Little one, you must drink your milk today."

And so on, and so forth.

However, children grow up. In this process of growing, they must also learn to assert SELF-control in their own lives.

"I must get out of bed now!"
"I will practice piano now!"
"I have to do my algebra problems now!"

And so on, and so forth.

If parents continue to provide the outside control by telling their growing children every single thing they must do, children will not have the opportunity to develop and use self-control. Makes sense, doesn't it? But it's far easier said than done . . . especially for homeschooling parents who are ALWAYS with their children and can see all of the things that should be getting done but are not.

One area where this shows up clearly is in the area of practicing a musical instrument. As parents, we figure that if we are shelling out all of this dough for private lessons and for an instrument to boot, we need to see some pretty impressive results. And, just to protect our investment, we remind our children to practice.

"Honey, have you practiced piano yet?"
"Honey, don't you need to practice piano now?"
"Honey, I'm getting a little steamed here . . . You need to sit down right this minute and practice piano!"

Granted, it is a natural thing to do, but nagging and applying outward control won't help your teenagers become passionate about playing piano (or whatever else you are nagging them about), nor is it going to teach them self-control.

Talking about self-control, years ago we went to visit David and Shirley Quine, fellow homeschooling-and-children enthusiasts. Their second-born son, Ben, was playing the piano as we walked in the door. As we visited, he kept playing . . . and playing . . . and playing! After a few hours of hearing him practice, I mentioned to Shirley how impressive it was to hear him practice this much.

"Boy, you must have found some pretty powerful motivators!"

"Well, actually Ben is self-motivated to play the piano. He took lessons when he was little but decided to give it up for baseball when he got older. We

didn't want to push him when he wasn't interested. And do you know, after a few years of baseball, he decided on his own that he really wanted to play piano instead. So, now he practices hours and hours, all from his own desire."

Hmmm. That is pretty powerful stuff. Parents: DO try this at home!

We tried it and have watched our own teenage daughter move from having fun playing music to becoming a very serious piano student. In the summer of 2001, she attended a piano camp at the University of Kansas and talked about her goals with a piano professor. He told her that if she truly wanted to attend a conservatory, she needed to begin practicing four hours per day. When she told us she intended to do it, I must confess I gulped significantly. That is an awful lot of piano playing.

"I know, Mom. What I thought I should do is to try practicing four hours a day for the rest of the summer. That way, I can discover if I really like playing that much. If not, I'll find a different interest to pursue. If I do like it, then I'll go for it."

It worked. Though I can not imagine sitting down to play an instrument for four hours per day, Melody took to it like a duck to water. It is completely self-controlled, and because there is joy in the playing and goals for the future, we have no need to coerce her to play.

Self-control. What a powerful agent it is in a person's life. How does one light that particular fire in one's teenager? It comes partly by not nagging, pushing, or prodding; partly through finding the areas and subjects that are the child's deep interests, where their natural love of learning or doing will propel them into working hard (thus is born self-control); and partly through the means in this next section.

CAUGHT BETWEEN
A STUMP AND A SLICK PLACE

An important aid in parenting is the system of utilizing natural consequences: if children do something wrong, or don't do something they should do, allow the *natural* consequences of their actions to bring about the needed correction.

For instance, a child was supposed to have written a report for a 4-H project. It is due in the morning, and it's not done, so, the natural consequence would simply be disqualification from the contest. However, many of us, the night before, would say, *"Let's get that report done . . . I know you don't have time to do it on your own now, but if I help you, we can surely finish it."*

Sounds good to help out, doesn't it? And in some cases, there might be a perfectly legitimate reason for the paper not being written, which would benefit from a healthy dose of grace and mercy (i.e., helping them to get the paper done). But so many times, it is a matter of put-it-off-itis, and the child needs to feel the weight of that mistake. That would be utilizing natural consequences.

This is even more important when our children become teenagers, though the consequences can be more costly or more painful, because this is really the final opportunity to learn how to be self-controlled before they hit the "big time" of adult responsibilities. If we were not offering to help the night before, it would be accurate to say that most of us were nagging every day from the time the paper was assigned, simply to make sure it got done. So, the paper was written because we kept asserting outside control.

"You can not move from this table UNTIL you write that paper!!"

At some point in this journey to adulthood, we absolutely must let them make their own decisions about when and where they will write the paper and to let them suffer the consequences of not writing the paper. Remember, this is the kind of stuff they will experience when they are on their own living as adults in the real world. How much better for them, how much easier to bear the consequences and learn the realities of the effects of poor self-control in the safety and love of your home.

Of course, we are still their parents. We still love them, nurture them, and counsel them. Offering counsel goes something like this: "Here is the wisdom of adulthood, and I recommend you listen to it." As opposed to outward control, which says: "Here is the wisdom of adulthood, and I will MAKE you live by it!" Huge difference, isn't there?

And it is amazing how much more they will listen to our counsel if it is given with an attitude of respect and compassion.

"You know, I appreciate the difficult spot you are in. I know it's a tough decision, but I have found that things work out far better when you take care of your responsibilities, like writing this paper, before doing the things that

*you would prefer to do. I'll be happy to lend a listening ear if you get stuck
and need someone to bounce ideas off of."*

This use of natural consequences, "nixing the nag," is not something that
comes naturally to me, but I am learning—as you will see from this next story.

Last spring, we had the joy of hosting two young people from New
Zealand, Genevieve and Zach Smith, for about three months. Much of that
time was spent travelling to conventions, but there were a few weeks at
home. Zach and Michael had become fast friends, and they were always looking
around for something interesting to do in the Black Hills of South Dakota (where
we live).

The Black Hills are a veritable treasure trove for the outdoor enthusiast—
hiking trails, climbing peaks, bicycling, and more. No matter that it was April,
and the snow was just leaving the ground; Zach and Michael were eager to go out
exploring on their own. They took our old pick-up truck and went off on a great
adventure—a hike, a camp, a climb, dinner cooked over a hiker's stove—it was all
in the plans.

What they had not foreseen was the slipperiness of the off-the-road slope they
turned onto. Realizing that they could not keep going up without sliding down,
they attempted to turn around. Unfortunately, that put them into an even more
precarious position, since they could neither go in reverse up the slope on the
slippery grass, nor could they go forward down the slope. It seems they had not
seen the tree stump just in front of the bumper. Going backward was impossible;
going forward was even worse.

What does an enterprising teen do at this point? Dial home on his cell phone,
of course! What does his mother do? Panic! And what does his father do? Tells
him to figure it out: *"You got the truck in there, Mike; you can find a way to get it out
again."* Bill offered several suggestions, such as gravel under the back tires, etc.

The phone rang again.

"Dad, it's not working!"
"Mike, keep trying."
"OK."

The background sounds were of a mother begging a father to please call AAA
for a tow. In a few minutes, the phone rang again.

"Dad, it's not working!"

"Mike, keep trying."
"OK."

The background sounds were of a mother with increasing intensity, begging a father to please call AAA for a tow . . . *"My baby!!"*

Bill patiently explained to me that many was the time he had managed to unstick a stuck vehicle, and it was good for Michael to learn that if he got in a mess, he needed to figure a way out of it. Bill was doing an excellent job of cheerleading on the sidelines, offering the boys several ideas of things to try.

Finally, a triumphant voice on the last phone call:

"Dad, you'll never believe it!"
"What?"
"Zach and I took the tire iron and hacked the tree stump enough for us to drive over it!"

Ah, those ingenious teens.

"Cool. Be careful where you drive the truck."
"Oh, yes, Dad, I'll be REAL careful!!"

With joyous smiles bursting through the phone lines, the enthused and victorious teens drove off into the sunset of an April evening. Meanwhile, back at the ranch, the mother learned two important lessons: let them experience natural consequences—it is good for them, and listen to the father—he was once a teenage boy!

Too Many Rules

For many years, our children had one main rule to live by:

"Build one another up in love."

It covered most situations, most of the time, providing a standard of behavior that was just and right. In a wrestling bout when they were entering teenager-hood, someone's nose got significantly tweaked. Thus was born the second main rule of our family:

"Don't touch the schnoz."

This one helped preserve sensitive facial features.

The final rule(s) was (were) added when all three of them grew taller than my five-foot, six-inch height:

❶ *Mom is always right.*
❷ *When Mom is wrong, refer to rule #1.*

I seldom have to invoke this one (er, two), but when my stature is not up to the job, I remind them with a glint of steel in my eye and a glimmer of laughter in my face that they need to remember: *Mom is always right.*

This limited rule making was born in my husband's significant understanding of children and teenagers. When I was tempted to create a different rule for every situation, he would challenge me patiently:

"Too many rules, Diana."
"Uhuh. What does that mean?"
"It means that you are trying to control their every action by imposing all these rules. They don't need that."
"Uhuh. Why not?"
"They need to know the principle 'build one another up in love,' and they need to learn to apply it. You don't need more rules; you need to help them learn to utilize the ones they have."

Aha. This was an entirely different way of looking at life. I came from the school of jump-to-it military respect *(When I say "jump," your reply is, "Sir, how high?")* where rules were the stuff of life: rules in the classroom, the playground, the workplace, the church. They taught me rules covering every action—don't run, don't fidget, don't wear a hat, don't shout, don't breathe through your mouth, don't scratch out your mistake (erase it), don't use pen, don't use pencil, don't wear pants (unless it is under 55 degrees—I grew up in Miami), etc.

I thought that was the way it was supposed to be. Not a lot of fun, nor a place of dignity or self-expression; nevertheless, the way it was. Deal with it, Diana.

Living by principles rather than rules was a window to a whole new world. A world governed by well-thought-out principles is a world of grace and truth, a world of freedom and dignity for each one—with liberty and justice for all!

Have you ever experienced listening to a speaker or reading a book and saying to your family, *"That's it! From now on, these are the rules we are going to live by?"* As parents, we figure, *"If that speaker or author was able to obtain such fantastic results from those rules, then this will be the magic key to similar results in our children."* You know, of course, that that is wishful thinking. If raising teenagers was just a matter of finding the right rules and making them live by those rules, successful parenting would be a snap, a breeze, a no-brainer, a no-pray-er.

Perhaps our attraction to all of these rules comes from our desire to be in control of our teenagers' actions. You see, there is a direct connection between rule making and control. The more rules imposed, the increasing control being asserted. We have all heard the term "control freak," and this is a large part of that out-of-control control. What does it do to the "controllee?" It puts them into an increasingly small, rigid box where they have no freedom to grow, to learn, to express, to create.

For our teenagers, this kind of controlling, rules-oriented, rigid restraint results in one of two possibilities once they leave home: they either explode outwardly into out-of-control wildness, rebellion, and destruction, OR they implode into even more rigidly boxed-in, control freaks than their parents, unless by God's grace they come into the glorious liberty of the sons of God.

When Jesus was asked by a Jewish lawyer (one who was really into following all of the rules!) what was the most important commandment in the law, He answered, *"'You shall love the LORD your God with all your heart, with all your soul, and with all your mind.' This is the first and great commandment. And the second is like it: 'You shall love your neighbor as yourself.' On these two commandments hang ALL the LAW and the Prophets."*

What is happening in this scene? A person who is totally immersed in rules and rule keeping wants to trip Jesus up by having Him choose one rule over another, at which point this rule-knowing lawyer will be able to quote some rabbi or some tradition or some law to show that Jesus was wrong. However, Jesus bypassed all of the nit-picky, legalistic rules and behaviors and went right to the heart of the matter (and the heart of God): He said that we are to love God with everything in us (which results in a walk that delights the heart of God) and to love our neighbors as our very selves (which results in a walk that delights our neighbors).

In the same way that delighting the heart of God is not about obeying a myriad of nit-picky, legalistic, make-yourself-perfect-type rules, this parenting of teenagers is not about issuing a myriad of nit-picky, legalistic, make-yourself-perfect-type rules. It is not, in the very heart of it, about quotas, curfews, or clothing choices. Those issues need to be considered but always within the overall context of love. If there are problems, issues, or mistakes to be dealt with, it requires love to resolve said problems, issues, and mistakes. More and more rigid rules to deal with every possible situation will only bring about greater frustration, distance, and destruction of the relationship. Rather than those nit-picky, legalistic, make-yourself-perfect-type rules, we need love—love which takes the time to listen rather than merely react, love displayed by wise decisions and careful actions, love shown by the parents, and love shown by the teenagers.

At the end of Chapter One, we talked about loving our teens, and now, here we are, in a separate discussion about rules coming right back to love again. That's right! I know that parents want to have the most effective list of rules to guide their job of parenting, but issuing a myriad of rules will not accomplish what you desire. It all comes back to love. Whether we are speaking of maturing and changing teenagers, self-control, natural consequences, or rules, it all comes back to love. We need the wisdom God's love gives in order to parent our teenagers rightly. We need to love them as we love ourselves:

- *granting them the dignity of understanding and communication as they are going through physical, emotional, and mental changes;*
- *allowing them freedom to try out their self-controlled wings of emerging adulthood;*
- *freeing them to experience the natural consequences of their actions (in either their successes or failures) that they might learn deep lessons while we cheer them on; and*
- *teaching them to live by the principles of God's love rather than by rigid, unyielding rules.*

RECOMMENDED RESOURCE

Families Where Grace is in Place by Jeff Van Vonderen

This book will change your life. It is the opposite of rule-making, rigid, legalistic parenting. Rather, the author gives vision and practical out workings of releasing God's grace into our families.

Ordering Off the Same Menu

Once while visiting friends in Delaware, Bill recounted a radio interview in which Zig Ziglar had described the importance of treating your children with honor and respect. Ziglar had described several opportunities to show your children just what that respect looks like in real life. That led our friends, Len and Heather Armstrong, to offer a fascinating comment.

"We have always allowed our children to order off the same menu as we do."

As I looked at them quizzically, they continued: *"It is a way to show our children that we respect them. We treat them the same way we treat ourselves. You know, those children's menus don't often have very interesting food options!"*

I sat calculating how much it would have cost, when our children were younger, to have let them order off the same menu. The dollar signs (and the accompanying astonishment) must have been showing in my eyes, because Heather continued:

"When our children order off the adult menu, the wait staff seem to treat them with an extra amount of respect as well. Our kids really enjoy the whole thing."

Hmmm. It turns out that, if Len and Heather could only afford to have Len and Heather order off the tasty adult menu, while their children were expected to order off the limited children's menu, they stayed home!

Giving honor and respect—applying the "do-unto-others-as-you-would-have-them-do-unto-you" to real-life parenting—requires an expenditure on our part, a giving of something of ourselves, an attitude of service. It's a far cry from using our position to demean, belittle, and indenture our children.

OUR JOURNAL

In September, 1999, our family had the most amazing adventure: seven months in the unbelievably beautiful and fascinatingly intriguing nation of New Zealand. Five months were spent as students in a <u>Y</u>outh <u>W</u>ith <u>A</u> <u>M</u>ission Discipleship Training School in Auckland, while the other two months were given to a whirlwind tour of the gorgeous islands with frequent stops to encourage local homeschoolers.

During the school (DTS), we were taught weekly by different outstanding Christian teachers from all over the world. It was life-changing and eye-opening! One of our absolute favorite teachers was a dynamo named Rosalie Pedder. Her specialty is teaching about how wonderfully God has created every person—in all of our tremendous variety—each one displaying through our personality, style of learning, creativity, and character the many different facets of the infinite beauty of God Himself.

She covered all kinds of learning issues during that fascinating week. We discovered that many of us had believed lies about our inability to learn or try or accomplish because some teachers, parents, and other authority figures had communicated that we were:

"stupid" . . .

or "worthless" . . .

or "lazy" . . .

or "brainless" . . .

or "idiotic" . . .

or "hopeless" . . .

or "non-intellectual" . . .

or "non-athletic" . . .

or "non-musical" . . .

or "non-artistic" . . .

or "non-mathematical" . . .

or "non-communicative" . . .

We learned that the teachers, parents, and others who said these things did so because we did not fit into their miniscule parameters of intelligent behavior— their itsy-bitsy field of vision about what was acceptable and good. Some people said these things because they were using their superior power to keep us in our places; some were controllers making sure we "danced only to their tune;" some were driven by their pride to show what outstanding students (or children) they could create—only we didn't make them look as good as they felt they deserved. Ick! Double Ick!!

However, Rosalie helped us to see that, because God has created each one of us in His image—think of it, created in the image of God Himself!—each one is worthy of honor and respect. As we spent time chewing on that concept, old lies came bobbing to the surface. "You're not really worthy of honor and respect because you're a loser." "There really is something wrong with you." "God can't use you because you're not smart enough." And on and on.

As students began to share those thoughts, these lies were exposed to the truth of God's Word, and the power of the lies was gloriously broken! Can I tell you that at this point in the teaching there were a lot of tears in our classroom? At least, I think there were—my eyes were so heavy with unexpected humidity that I couldn't really see anyone else!! Great healing for minds, hearts, and spirits flowed that week—and a restoration of hope that we could learn and try and accomplish whatever God gave us to do.

Our one week with Rosalie Pedder and this teaching has impressed upon us for life the awareness of God's earnest desire that we would treat every person with the honor and respect due His creation. And, I might add, it has impacted the way we parent our teens!

BRING ME A COKE!

When Bill and I were first married, we met a family with a farm-dachshund. What's a farm-dachshund, you ask? It a dachshund who lives on a farm with regular farm dogs and believes himself to be one of the gang. (Author's note: It all works fairly well until he decides to come into the house and jump on your lap!)

Anyway, we newlyweds would visit this long-established family, swapping dachshund anecdotes and sharing a meal. Very early in our acquaintance with them, we observed the way these parents utilized their teenage children:

"Hey, get me a Coke."
"Hey, bring me the paper."
"Hey, turn the channel." (early form of remote control!)
"Hey, get me another Coke."

We watched the teens, scurrying here and there, serving us like we were royalty and they were servants. It was a bit unsettling. It was obvious from various comments and actions that these parents loved their children. It was also obvious that they saw their own position as the "servees" and their children as the "servers." Never did we see the roles reverse.

The experience gave rise to some interesting discussions between Bill and me:

"Hmmm. Is THAT what parenting looks like?"
"I hope not!"
"Were you uncomfortable back there?"
"Yup. You?"
"Yup."

Hmmm. Something must be missing from the equation. The question was, *"What's missing?"*

Some time later, we were visiting with a family from church. As the conversation swirled hither and yon, they communicated to us through various words and actions that they served their children . . . all the time. They made their children's beds (even though said children were heading toward teenage years), they did all of the chores around the house, they took their children wherever they wanted to go, bought them pretty much whatever they wanted. Their children displayed an attitude of disrespect toward their parents that we found unsettling.

This experience, too, gave rise to another interesting discussion between Bill and me:

"Hmmm. Is THAT what parenting looks like?"
"I hope not!"
"Were you uncomfortable back there?"
"Yup. You?"
"Yup."

Hmmm. Something was missing from this equation also. Again, the question was, *"What?"*

This time, however, we had the benefit of being able to compare and contrast two families. Though they were entirely different in some respects, in one area they were just alike: serving was only on one side of the equation. Serving must be present on both sides or the equation will not balance. The first family's children served the parents; the second family's parents served the children. Though most would quickly agree that the first family had a problem, it may not be as obvious that the parents of our second family also had a problem.

38

They were not training those children to be servants. These parents were not mentoring servants; they were not increasing the children's skills in serving; they were not allowing them to experience both sides of the equation—serving and being served. The children were learning how to be served, and that most ungraciously. Children need training in order to serve well, so parents must model serving. For some, demanding service is easier than modeling or explaining it. For others, serving wordlessly is easier than training. It requires effort both to serve others respectfully and to train children to serve graciously.

The Bible reveals God's wisdom in this situation:

"For you, brethren, have been called to liberty; only do not use liberty as an opportunity for the flesh, but through LOVE SERVE ONE ANOTHER."
—Galatians 5:13

Jesus, in the Gospel of Mark, said:

"You know that those who are considered rulers over the Gentiles lord it over them, and their great ones exercise authority over them. Yet it shall not be so among you; but whoever desires to become great among you shall be your servant . . ."

These two verses of Scripture show us how to handle this issue of who serves whom. The answer is BOTH! Serve one another: parents serve children, children serve parents, children serve each other, husbands serve wives, wives serve husbands, families serve others.

We have found that it is important to remind ourselves and our children of this principle from time to time.

"Michael, I'm having a difficult day. Would you please serve me by cooking dinner tonight?"
"Sure thing, Mom!"
"Isaac, I saw your laundry waiting to be folded, and I knew you were too busy with school today to take care of it . . . so, TA DAH! I folded it . . ."
"THANKS!"
"Mom, I just heard about a family that's really struggling right now. Will you help me put together a basket of homemade goodies so we can serve them with kindness?"
"Great idea, Melody."

May I say it again? Giving honor and respect—applying the "do-unto-others-as-you-would-have-them-do-unto-you" to real-life parenting—requires an expenditure on our part, a giving of something of ourselves, an attitude of service (and a training of our children for service). It's a far cry from using our position to demean, belittle, and indenture our children.

TACOBLIVION

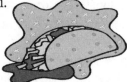

One of the most embarrassing memories of my childhood was the night my parents invited a neighboring couple over for tacos. Now, I have to tell you that my mom made a mean taco—she was from Texas, after all—and they were fairly famous around the neighborhood. It was incredibly easy to eat oneself into oblivion on Mom's tacos, and that is basically what happened that night. Though I was only about eleven at the time, I ate six huge tacos with great abandon. Evidently, our visiting neighbors ALSO ate a significant portion of the delectable entrée.

Later that night, in the manner of days gone by, we walked our neighbors back to their home, visiting as we ambled. The gracious lady, our visiting neighbor, made this remark:

"Oh, Joyce, I cannot tell you how good those tacos were! You know, I just made a PIG of myself!!"

In my eleven-year-old brain, I completely agreed with the sentiment of having made a pig of myself. Unfortunately, my brain was not quite conversant with HOW one expressed what one thought. What came out of my mouth was:

"Boy, you can say THAT again!!"

Stunned silence. Then gasps of outrage on the part of my parents and stuttering apologies, while I tried to figure out what had just happened. Hmmm. A definite doghouse experience.

This incident came back to me vividly when Isaac was eleven. We were spending a weekend on the coast of Washington, and a fine, convivial family time it was—swimming, beach walking, sandcastle building, and more. We made sure to also celebrate this mini-vacation by eating fabulous food fixed in fascinating fashions.

One evening, during dinner, I made a remark that, if I ate much more of this kind of rich food, I would have to waddle back home. Isaac chimed in with:

"Man, Mom, I was just thinking the same thing!"

Yeow!! Instantly, I turned into a fire-breathing, mad-as-a-hatter, tiger-by-the-tail mother, especially because I had a continuous struggle with weight gain.

"Isaac, come with me! We are going to have a SERIOUS talk!!"

I was so offended and so hurt by his comment that I could hardly sit down and have a calm discussion with him. Doing my best, I asked him why on earth he would try to hurt his mother with such a spiteful comment. He looked at me in tearful amazement and said:

"But, Mom, I wasn't talking about you . . . I was talking about ME!"

Ah. Well, ahem . . . light bulb flash in the old memory banks.

Slowly, with increasing moment-by-moment understanding, I began to tell Isaac of my own childhood inexperience with communicating and how the words which made sense in my brain morphed as they came out of my mouth into something totally surprising and unsuspectingly offensive.

As we considered one another with the mutual admiration shared only by survivors, we began to get the giggles over the whole thing. Tee . . . Hee . . . Tee, Hee . . . Haw! . . . Haw, Haw!! Upstairs, the rest of the family—who had been waiting in great suspense—breathed a sigh of relief over joy restored, happy resolution of conflict, and let's-get-on-with-the-vacation smiles all around.

Grace was needed in this situation. God's grace was extended and received. It is so amazing how His grace in our lives changes one's perspective. In the book of Colossians, it says this:

"Therefore, as the elect of God, holy and beloved, put on tender mercies, kindness, humility, meekness, longsuffering; bearing with one another, and forgiving one another, if anyone has a complaint against another; even as Christ forgave you, so you also must do."

You know, parenting provides us with NUMEROUS opportunities to live out this particular scripture. Whether bloopers, misunderstandings, or larger infractions, this scripture teaches us how to respond.

Here it is again. Giving honor and respect—applying the "do-unto-others-as-you-would-have-them-do-unto-you" to real-life parenting—requires an expenditure on our part, a giving of something of ourselves, an attitude of service, and an attitude of mutual grace. It's a far cry from using our position to demean, belittle, and indenture our children.

THE BEST IS NOT ALWAYS NORMAL

Growing up in a military family, I believed that honor and respect flowed one way—upward! The younger gives honor to the older; the child respects the parent ("Yes, sir!" . . . "No, sir!" . . . "How high, sir?!" . . .). In other words, the "lesser" gives it all to the "greater" and the "greater" receives it as their due. Consider this pertinent (and highly challenging) Scripture:

"No, much rather, those members of the body which seem to be weaker are necessary. And those members of the body which we think to be less honorable, on these we bestow greater honor . . ."

—1 Corinthians 12:22–23

What does that mean? How does that affect our parenting? Have the rules of honor and respect been changed without our knowing? Well, if you are working with an approach that focuses more on conduct and behavior than on the motivations of the heart, then, yes, the rules have changed.

They changed because God's ways are certainly not our ways, and His thoughts are not our thoughts. Even in our parenting, old ways must pass away, and all things must become new. There are Biblical patterns for us to follow in relating to children. His standard for people-to-people interaction is quite different from the latest bestseller on parenting. When He speaks, we need to listen.

I learned this rather dramatically when Isaac was about six years old. At this point in my mothering life, I was very concerned about having others compliment me and say, *"Oh, what WONDERFUL children you have!"* My effort was to make my kids seem wonderful by making their behavior conform to what other adults approved of and expected. Anything that caused others to look at me or my children with arched or condemning eyebrows struck terror in my heart and resulted in crabby, mean-spirited, control-style parenting. Unfortunately (or, perhaps, in the wisdom of God, fortunately), my oldest son often did things that raised those eyebrows of judgment. It wasn't that Isaac sought to wreak havoc with my plans for being considered the world's best mother of six-year-olds. It was simply that he saw the world differently than most adults. And in the creative, curious mind of a six-year-old, little boy, he found unusual ways to express that difference.

"Diana, do you know what your son was doing?"
"Diana, do you know what your son was saying?"
"Diana . . . Diana . . . Diana . . ."

With eyebrows raised, various people wasted no time communicating what they thought of my parenting skills and my son. So, I did what I thought was necessary to control Isaac's marching to different drumbeats.

"Isaac, stop that!"
"Isaac, be quiet!"
"Isaac . . . Isaac . . . Isaac . . ."

Now, there was nothing rebellious, disrespectful, or wrong in what he was doing. It was merely unusual, different from the norm, not following the herd. But I didn't want to be the mother of an unusual, different child—not when it caused raised eyebrows!

Mercifully, I was awakened to God's perspective on my attitude. We were at a carnival, and Isaac was enjoying it immensely. He had given his ticket to ride the carousel, and I stood watching him, thankful that at least on this ride he wouldn't have the opportunity to do anything weird or attract attention. However, much to my astonishment, I saw him go up to the man working the carousel and begin to ask him questions about how the ride was put together.

"Oh, no. Can't he just ride the stupid machine without asking questions?
I'll have to stop him!"

At that point, God stopped me! It was not audible, but it was as clear as anything I've ever heard in my life.

"Diana! I have created that boy in MY image! You have been treating
him with disrespect, trying to form him into another image. But I have plans
for him and have created him just the way he needs to be to fulfill My plan.
Cease and desist!"

REAPING THE HARVEST

Though I have used all of these words to convey what God spoke to my heart that night, it took only a moment of time to understand that God had stopped me in my parenting tracks and turned me around. He was requiring me to do something I had never before considered: to honor and respect Isaac in all his creative ways BECAUSE he was created in the image of God, for His plans and purposes. Boy, was I shook up! I stood, rooted to that spot by the carousel, and asked God for forgiveness for my controlling, disrespectful attitude. As soon as Isaac finished his carousel ride, I asked him for forgiveness as well.

From that day on, I worked to treat Isaac with respect and honor. It can be difficult to sort out bad behavior that must be corrected from innocent behavior that must be respected. Though I didn't always do it right, I stayed committed to trying because that command from God echoed in my mind and heart through the years of Isaac's childhood. What was the result? Was it worth the work and effort? Was it beneficial to change my whole way of viewing my children?

Fourteen years after the carousel ride, various people of various ages from various walks of life in various countries have told me how wonderful Isaac is, how amazingly talented he is, how his artistry in music has touched them deeply, wondering where they can get one like him! You see, Isaac WAS created by God in the way that God planned, for the purposes He has in mind. My ceasing to control him allowed God to work deep in his heart, below behavior. As the mother, I just needed to get with the program and cooperate.

Here is the kicker: EVERY child marches to the beat of a different drummer. EACH of your children is unique. EVERY child is created in the image of God, for His plans and purposes. That means that EVERY parent needs to honor and respect what God has done in the unique creation of EACH child. It will take effort; it may take changing one's thinking; it will certainly seem unusual to the rank and file. And it is important to hold this concept in a sort of tension: just like serving one another and just like extending grace to one another, this honoring and respecting business is a two-way street. There is nothing that breaks my heart more than seeing children be disrespectful of their parents, unless it is seeing parents be disrespectful of their children. So, allow this precious, God-given attitude to flow in both directions. It will bring such lavish dividends that you'll stand in amazement.

Here it is again: Giving honor and respect—applying the "do-unto-others-as-you-would-have-them-do-unto-you" to real-life parenting—requires an expenditure on our part, a giving of something of ourselves, an attitude of service, and a willingness to bless our children even if others think they're weird. It's a far cry from using our position to demean, belittle, and indenture our children.

LOVE IS MESSY

There seems to be an attitude in much of Christian homeschool-dom concerning what is proper, what is acceptable, what is allowable. It might be said, "We don't smoke; we don't chew; we don't *court* homeschool girls that do." Have you noticed that there are unwritten rules of:

- *fashion (denim jumpers vs. denim jeans),*
- *acceptable curriculum*
  (classical vs. unit study vs. traditional vs. unschooling),
- *family size (who decided that ten children is the right number?),*
- *proper hair length (boys AND girls, head AND face),*
- *what makes appropriate music*
  (choruses vs. hymns, a cappella vs. instruments),
- *suitable cars for homeschoolers (mini vans rule!),*
- *church attendance (or NON church attendance!),*
- *boy meets girl . . . and likes her*
  (the betrothal vs. courting vs. dating issue),
- *where babies are born*
  ("You went to the HOSPITAL?! How heathen . . ."),
- *how to train your children to have correct behavior*
  ("We don't smoke; we don't chew . . ."),
- *who should go to college*
  (and which ones are acceptable for homeschoolers),
- *acceptable activities for your daughters when they finish homeschooling*
  (ARE they supposed to stay home till they marry?
  What about college . . . or a career?),
- *. . . and so on.*

Where did these rules come from? What happens if you don't obey them? More importantly, what happens to your children if you don't obey them? Here's my concern: what happens to your children if you DO obey them? Though many would try to give "chapter and verse" from the Holy Writ concerning each dot and tittle, the truth is that these are manmade rules.

Aha. Manmade rules of acceptable behavior—manmade rules that many of us are mindlessly living by—manmade rules which are used to decide if we "measure up"—manmade rules that the latest homeschooling guru will teach you so that you know every moment of every day, situation by situation, family by family EXACTLY what you are supposed to do!

Does this remind you of anything in the Bible? Do you remember the interesting conversations Jesus had with the rule-keeping, rule-making folks of His day?

> *"Then the scribes and Pharisees who were from Jerusalem came to Jesus, saying, 'Why do Your disciples transgress the tradition of the elders? For they do not wash their hands when they eat bread.'*
>
> *"He answered and said to them, 'Why do you also transgress the commandment of God because of your tradition? . . . Hypocrites! Well did Isaiah prophesy about you, saying: "These people draw near to Me with their mouth, And honor Me with their lips, But their heart is far from Me. And in vain they worship Me, Teaching as doctrines the commandments of men."''*
>
> —Matthew 15:1–3,7–9

"Teaching as *doctrines* the commandments of *men* . . ." That seems pertinent to our discussion, doesn't it? Rules, manmade rules, that take on the power of "doctrines" gain a powerful hold on people. They keep us from the blessed, blood-bought freedom we have in Christ.

Rules focus on the outward, external, what-others-can-see behavior:

> *"Don't run in church."* Grrrr . . .
> *"Don't open your eyes when we pray."* Grrrr . . .
> *"Don't speak unless spoken to."* Grrrr . . .
> *"Don't buy from people who discount!"* Grrrr . . .
> *"Don't . . . Don't . . . Don't . . ."* Grrrr . . . Grrrr . . . Grrrr . . .

What other words did Jesus have for those who were concerned about rule making, about the outward appearance of religious behavior?

> *"Woe to you, scribes and Pharisees, hypocrites! For you cleanse the outside of the cup and dish, but inside they are full of extortion and self-indulgence. Blind Pharisee, first cleanse the inside of the cup and dish, that the outside of them may be clean also. Woe to you scribes and Pharisees, hypocrites! For you are like whitewashed tombs which indeed appear beautiful outwardly, but inside are full of dead men's bones and all uncleanness. Even so you*

also outwardly appear righteous to men, but inside you are full of hypocrisy and lawlessness."

—*Matthew 23:25–28*

Ouch! How many times have I been concerned with cleaning up the outside appearance of my family, but inside I was full of anger?

"Just get your socks and shoes on right now! I don't care what your brother did to you; we're not going to be late to CHURCH!!" Grumble, grumble, grumble, grinch, grinch, grinch. And then we appear on time, every hair in place, smiles pasted on the faces, but we're seething inside.

Now, let me hasten to assure you that there was nothing WRONG with telling my child to get his socks and shoes on. There was nothing WRONG with us having every hair in place (somewhat miraculous, in fact!). There was nothing WRONG with having smiles. The problem was that it was all on the outside—it was not true to the conflict raging inside of us. We all know that people can not live with that kind of frustration. Children with that pressure are going to act up again somewhere. If I had taken the extra few minutes to deal with the conflict, until there was a point of reconciliation between brothers, and THEN had them get their shoes and socks on, there would have been TRULY happy smiles on our faces. We might have made a late entrance to church, but our insides and outsides would have matched (far more important than matching socks!). We will work on punctuality next Sunday.

Of course, we have rules. We have getting-along-with-others rules (mentioned in the previous chapter) and getting-along-with-life rules. These kind of rules make life easier for our family:

Make your bed in the morning.
Wear clean clothes.
Brush your teeth.
Be polite.
Eat your broccoli. (My husband breaks this one every time!)
. . . and there are more.

We DO have expectations that each family member will accomplish these rules. If they don't, there are consequences: messy rooms, stinky bodies, bad breath, no friends, lack of nasty disease protection provided by cruciferous vegetables. When our children were young, we enforced these rules so that they would build healthy habits. As our children became teenagers, we allowed the natural consequences to help remind them of these healthy habits. However, these kinds of rules are not the issue. These rules are not the back-breaking, spirit-numbing, heart-depressing rules that Jesus condemned the rule-keepers for enforcing.

The story of Jesus healing the man with the withered hand on the Sabbath shows us the contrast between what rule-keepers want and what God (the Law Maker) wants:

> *"Now when He had departed from there, He went into their synagogue. And behold, there was a man who had a withered hand. And they asked Him, saying, 'Is it lawful to heal on the Sabbath?'—that they might accuse Him. Then He said to them, 'What man is there among you who has one sheep, and if it falls into a pit on the Sabbath, will not lay hold of it and lift it out? Of how much more value then is a man than a sheep? Therefore it is lawful to do good on the Sabbath.' Then He said to the man, 'Stretch out your hand.' And he stretched it out, and it was restored as whole as the other. Then the Pharisees went out and plotted against Him, how they might destroy Him."*
>
> *—Matthew 12:9–14*

The rules that were being "broken" on this Sabbath day were not rules of the "make your bed" and "eat your broccoli" variety. They were "this is how to live a perfect life," or "this is how to make sure you do everything right," or "this is how truly godly people live" kinds of rules. And, as we can see from the above Scripture, the rule-keepers completely missed the point.

Rule-keepers in Jesus' time were concerned with keeping rules religiously— with keeping one's outward behavior correct—but they misunderstood the heart of God. In this scene, Jesus was revealing God's heart to the people, which caused a strong reaction from the rule-keepers. They then sought to destroy Him—God in the flesh!

Rule-keepers in our time are concerned with keeping the rules properly— with keeping children's outward behavior correct—but they are STILL misunderstanding the *heart* of God. In fact, the manmade rules that we adapt and put to work in our families may help us control behavior but, in their unyielding, rigid legalism these rules will wound our children and will eventually bring about those explosions or implosions mentioned earlier.

So, what is God's heart for us? What does He want for us? What motivated Jesus to heal that man's withered hand? Love . . . God's love expressed in a practical, personal, healing moment . . . God's love freely given in the midst of antagonistic, religious rule-keepers . . . God's love richly bestowed and utterly undeserved. The interesting thing is that God's heart for us, His "rule," if you will, is that we would have this same kind of love for each other.

"Beloved, let us love one another, for love is of God; And everyone who loves is born of God and knows God. He who does not love does not know God, for God is love."

—1 John 4:7–8

Love . . . love . . . love.

Hmmm. Love. Love as expressed by Jesus toward that man with the withered hand was somewhat unconventional (healing on the Sabbath?!). In fact, you might say it was messy—it did not remain tidy and rule-pleasing. No, it spilled out of the rule box and compassionately flowed all over that man.

Aha. God's love goes beyond our little rules. It brings healing and wholeness and freedom and liberty to those it touches. It does not stay in the box; it does not impress the rule-keepers; and it tends to be messy.

Love is messy? What on earth does that mean?

Well, for a moment, consider how Jesus described love. When challenged about what it meant to "love our neighbor," Jesus described a travelling man who was set upon by thieves and robbers, robbed, beaten, and left for dead. The first couple of folks who saw this man lying in the ditch were very religious people— a Jewish priest and a Levite. What was their response? Leave him to die. The third person to pass by, a Samaritan, was from an ethnic group despised, DESPISED, by the listening audience. And what was this man's response? You know the story. He had compassion on the beaten man, bandaged his wounds, set him on his donkey, and took him to the local hotel. There he cared for the man's needs, and when he had to depart, he paid the hotel keeper in advance to continue the care until the man was healthy enough to leave.

Wow! Who was the hero of Jesus' story? The Samaritan, a member of a totally disdained group of people. Why did Jesus do that? Wouldn't it have been tidier, more acceptable for the listeners, to have the hero be the Jewish priest or Levite? Wasn't that Samaritan "unclean" or something equally disgusting?

Hmmm. Consider that the Jewish priest and the Levite lived by a myriad of rules and regs that might have been broken if they had gone to help that beaten man. If he were to die while they were touching him, they would be unclean! Better to not run the risk, better to stay within the formulas, pre-conceived ideas, and legalistic rules in order to stay righteous . . . well, to stay "right."

Reaping the Harvest

The Samaritan, however, tossed the rules and regs book and let his compassion for the beaten man show him what to do. It didn't slow him down one whit to get his hands messy, his timetable messy, his monthly budget messy, or even his reputation messy simply by helping this poor man. And Jesus, in telling the story, showed us that in real life, dealing with real people, who have real needs and real hurts, love is indeed MESSY.

In fact, when Jesus announced in the synagogue who He was and what He was doing, He quoted from the book of Isaiah:

> *"The Spirit of the LORD is upon Me, because He has anointed Me to preach the gospel to the poor. He has sent Me to heal the brokenhearted, to proclaim liberty to the captives and recovery of sight to the blind, to set at liberty those who are oppressed; to proclaim the acceptable year of the LORD."*
>
> *—Luke 4:18–19*

Very messy concepts.

God's love takes the extravagantly fabulous news of the Gospel and gives it to poor people, brings compassionate healing to those with broken hearts, flings open prison gates and sets moldering captives free, makes the darkened eyes of the blind to see, liberates those who have been under the oppressor, and tells all who will hear that the Lord is, at this perfect moment of time, fulfilling His age-old promise of redemption.

Wow! None of these items were in the rule books of the rule-keepers!! This is God's creative power, His healing compassion, His doing-things-we-would-never-dream-of love. It sets people free, all manner of people: old people, children, men, women, Jews, Gentiles, rich, poor, loved, despised, righteous-in-the-eyes-of-the-Law folks, guilty-and-caught-in-the-act sinners. Because God's amazing love spills out freely over all (whether we think it is deserved or not), it seems messy. Because God's redemptive love does not stay neat and tidy and predictable, it looks messy. Because God's compassionate love looks on the inside of us, sees the truth, and acts upon that, it feels messy.

It was messy when:

- *Jesus spit on the man's eyes to heal them;*
- *Jesus wrote in the dirt to set the adulteress woman free of her captors;*
- *Jesus spoke to a Samaritan woman who was living in sin;*
- *Jesus healed the old woman on the Sabbath;*
- *Jesus held and blessed the little children in the midst of adults;*

- *Jesus told the Pharisee at dinner that he was an ungracious host;*
- *and on, and on, and on throughout the Gospels.*

It is messy when:

- *Our children misbehave and we correct them gently, while others arch their eyebrows in disapproval;*
- *Bad people become respectable;*
- *We invite our neighbor's child in to play because she is sick;*
- *Mean people seek forgiveness;*
- *We go to visit elderly people in a nursing home;*
- *People are changed, and we have to change our response to them;*
- *Someone dies, and we sit with their family through the initial grief;*
- *and on, and on, and on throughout our lives.*

It's all very messy, but oh, so close to the heart of God!

Now, what is God's concern: our outer behavior conforming to rules or our inner attitudes conforming to His ways?

> *"But the LORD said to Samuel, 'Do not look at his appearance or at his physical stature, because I have refused him. For the LORD does not see as man sees; for man looks at the outward appearance, but the LORD looks at the heart.'"*
>
> —1 Samuel 16:7

The heart . . . the heart . . . the heart.

Hmmm. The heart. When Jesus was confronted by the rule-keepers about his disciples eating without ceremonially washing their hands first, He said that it was not *"what enters a man from outside which can defile him; but the things which come out of him, those are the things that defile a man."* (Mark 7:15) His disciples didn't get it, so they asked him privately what on earth that meant. He explained that it was from the heart that evil, defiling thoughts, and attitudes (which lead to actions) come.

God is concerned with our heart—with what's on the inside. So, if God is concerned with heart issues, and if He wants us to love our children with His love (which, remember, is "messy"), then how on earth do we translate that into everyday parenting? Be encouraged. The following three principles can, by God's grace, settle into your mind and set your heart free.

Reaping the Harvest

❶ First, remember that God's love is unconditional.

It is not performance based at all. In the story of the prodigal son, the father's love continues to flow, which is why he was even watching for the son's return, despite the totally yucky actions of the prodigal. God's love is like that. And He wants us to love our children like that, unconditionally with a First Corinthians Thirteen-ish kind of love.

When Isaac was eighteen, I stumbled across a book about parents who only gave love and approval based on their children's performance. Reading it, I rehearsed in my mind various scenes from my own childhood, thinking about how this had affected me deeply. Suddenly, the Lord interjected into my pity party the thought that I had been treating Isaac with this same performance-based expectations. Struck to the heart, I read to him in trembling tones what the book described. I then asked him as gently as I could if that was his own experience. With tears flowing down his face, he nodded. Oh, my. My precious son had been living with the same pressure of trying to please so that acceptance would be given. I asked his forgiveness with tears flowing down MY face, and then I told him the truth: that he need never do another thing right in his life in order to be loved and accepted—it was there for eternity. Since that time, I have reminded him in the midst of discussions of actions and plans and the stuff of life that he is loved and accepted regardless of what he does.

❷ Secondly, remember that God's love is heart-oriented.

We need to listen to our children, to discover what is in their heart, what's going on inside of them. We need to not assume we know what's behind certain actions; we MUST take the time to listen gently and carefully to what they say (and what they don't say).

In our family, we have adopted an attitude of gratitude to the Lord for our hair color. (As mine grows increasingly gray, I am beginning to consider thanking God for the technology available for CHANGING back to His original plan for my hair!) In other words, we have not gotten into the "shocking color of the week" hair fashion that many young people are trying out. However, one weekend in New Zealand, Isaac and Michael were with the graduating class of their YWAM Discipleship Training School when one of the young ladies suggested that it might be fun to dye hair. Michael with his 1/4 inch hair length thought it would be a hoot because he could easily shave it after showing it to his mom and dad! So, down to the South Island he

travelled to show us his "stuff." I was some astounded when my beloved son walked in the door with yellow and dark strips of hair color—though I must admit to you that it was kind of cute! He assured us he would shave his head (his normal monthly behavior) right away. Time got away from Michael that day as the travellers had to hurry, and he ended up in a homeschool meeting that night with his unusual look. During the meeting, he spent a lot of time sharing with some of the homeschool young people (who were struggling with their walk with God) what it is to give yourself wholly to the service of God, encouraging them to love God with all of their heart, soul, mind, and strength. Unfortunately, one of the homeschool dads saw Michael and his hair colors and made a judgment about him. He phoned ahead to the next large homeschool group we were to be addressing and informed them not to bother to go hear the Warings because one of their sons was in rebellion and had a Mohawk! It was astonishing to us that this man had completely missed what Michael was sharing with these young people—that he had only looked on the exterior and missed the heart—AND that he had not even gotten his complaint right. Michael did not have a Mohawk; he had a SKUNK!!!

❸ Thirdly, recognize the dignity, worth, and respect due to our children and to each other.

If, as parents, we are about to confront a bad attitude or a wrong behavior or an explosive situation, we would do well to remember that the people involved (big or little) have been created in the image of God, and we need to honor that. It changes the way we communicate. Instead of belittling words, we will use words that are truthful yet respectful. Instead of demeaning sarcasm, we will speak with a truthful yet kind tone of voice. Instead of humiliating punishments, we will use wise disciplines.

One day, during the Wimsey stage of our family, I came to the conclusion that Melody's dog was going to destroy our home (which was now functioning as his race track), or if the home was not destroyed, one of us would end up with a broken leg (he REALLY ran fast and he REALLY ran hard!). So, I sat down with Melody to break the news to her: Wimsey had to go. It was hard—one of the hardest conversations we have ever had. It was tearful, and at times, voices were raised. But at the most tense, most emotional moment, the Lord gave me His gentle wisdom by reminding me of a time in my childhood that I had wanted a horse. As I shared with Melody my own childhood memories of a particular painted horse (with a VERY expensive price tag!), of how I had been sure that my parents were going to give it to me for my birthday, and how devastated I was when my birthday was over and no horse came forth, Melody's countenance began to soften. As I shared this story, I understood more deeply Melody's pain. As I began to cry for both of our yearning hearts for an impossible-to-have animal, Melody began to cry with me. We both cried for each other, and for ourselves. The hugs, the mutual grieving turned a difficult parental moment into a precious building block of understanding and compassion for one another.

Easier said than done? You bet. That's why, as parents, we need God's enabling help day by day, moment by moment. That's why we need to ask our children's forgiveness when we blow it. That's why we need to not take ourselves so seriously because we are not nearly as good at Biblical parenting as we think we are. (A little laughter goes a long way.)

One final thought for any of us that have been caught up in rule-keeping:

Rebellion breaks rules. Yes, it does . . . No question about it.
But, legalism MAKES rules, which is equally stinky in the nostrils of God.
And, dear ones, God's love is messy. (Go and love likewise!)

Here it is one final time: Giving honor and respect—applying the "do-unto-others-as-you-would-have-them-do-unto-you" to real-life parenting—requires an expenditure on our part, a giving of something of ourselves, an attitude of service, and a willingness to love our children even if it seems messy. It's a far cry from using our position to demean, belittle, and indenture our children.

RECOMMENDED RESOURCE

Bound by Honor: Fostering a Great Relationship with Your Teen
by Gary Smalley and Dr. Greg Smalley

This IS a book for fixing what's wrong in your relationship with your teen in a step-by-step approach that builds honor and reduces anger. It is absolutely fantastic!

Under the Influence

One sweltering Fourth of July, we attended the rodeo in Belle Fourche, South Dakota. This was the real thing, make no mistake—broncs busting, bulls wheeling, cowboys sauntering, cowgirls waving, rodeo clowns hiding in barrels. The air was thick with excitement and dust from the spectacular events taking place, and the crowd was humming with enthusiasm for the athleticism of man and beast. From moment to moment, people would hold their breath and then scream with approval when a ride was completed or moan with anguish for a fallen cowboy.

That's why I like rodeo—it's a real slice of authentic, Old West Americana. Little did I know, however, that this particular rodeo was going to contain the stuff of legends. At a break between events, I glanced out beyond the arena and saw an astonishing sight. A man, mounted on something dark and wooly, was sitting head and shoulders above all the other cowboys.

"Bill, what on earth is that behind the chutes?"
"Oh, that's Jerry Olson riding Chief."
"Who is Jerry Olson?"
"He's one of my classmates from school."
"What on earth is Chief?"
"A buffalo."
"What?! A guy you went to school with is riding a BUFFALO?!!"

At that moment, the gates swung wide, and that magnificent American bison (which locals call buffalo) galloped in, rocking Jerry on his massive back. I have never in my life seen such an amazing spectacle! Buffalo are mammoth creatures with enormous heads and shaggy beards. It is unheard of for a person to safely walk up to a buffalo, much less try to mount and ride one! In fact, there are occasional reports of unsuspecting (and incautious) tourists being killed while approaching a buffalo too closely. A buffalo is not, in the words of C.S. Lewis, "a tame lion!"

After Jerry rode in on the buffalo, he accomplished a series of incredible, don't-try-this-at-home (or-on-the-ranch-either!) maneuvers, including letting Chief lie down on him (a living buffalo robe for those cold nights!), having Chief jump into the back of a moving pick-up truck(!), and standing up on Chief's back while he was loping around the track.

> *"Uh, Bill, how does someone ever learn how to train a buffalo like that?"*
> *"Well, Jerry's dad also rode a buffalo named Chief. In fact, his granddad was the first one in the family to tame and train a buffalo. I guess they just pass their secrets down from generation to generation."*

So now you know. If you want to train a buffalo, you need to be born into Jerry Olson's family.

OUR JOURNAL

At a family camp in Matamata, New Zealand, Bill, Isaac, and I sat down for a family-style chat. There was a casual, take-all-the-time-you-need atmosphere, and it set the scene for a most amazing conversation.

During the several months of training with YWAM, Bill and I had discovered how incredibly valuable it was to have each other's gifts and strengths to help in times of decision. We had learned that Bill could keep me from making an awkward move and I could help him avoid getting into tangled circumstances—if only we would talk to each other first! What a gift from God—built-in protectors in the person who loves us best.

We were still working out the everyday practicalities of this as we shared it with an all-ears-open Isaac. His face mirrored his musings as he told us that he could sure use someone like that in his life. As he spoke this thought out loud, it suddenly dawned on him that we were uniquely suited to be his loving, advice-giving protectors. So, he asked us formally if we would help him be aware of awkward and tangled possibilities in relationships, career choices, finances, and whatever else came along.

We were awed by his request. We recognized the trust Isaac was willfully placing in us and understood that we needed to be very careful to not overstep our boundaries—after all, he was already eighteen years old! So, prayerfully and carefully, we began to walk out another dimension of parent-teen relationships. Have we done this perfectly? Not a chance. Has Isaac always come to us at critical moments? Hardly. But are we growing in this grace? Absolutely!

THE BUCK STOPS HERE

We have all heard the old saying, "Youth is wasted on the young." To that, I would like to sagely reply, "Bah, humbug!" If the parents of a youth are sharing the wisdom of their experience, the depth of understanding God has given them, and the objective vision that develops through the passing years, then the amazing energy of youth can be harnessed by their parents' wisdom, and GREAT things can be achieved! The task is, of course, to pass this parental wisdom on. Just how on earth does one do that?

Consider this analogy: when you travel to a foreign country, one of the first things to be learned is how their currency system works. When we went to New Zealand, we traded our pennies, nickels, dimes, quarters, and greenbacks for a completely different look. Though quite awkward for us at first, this currency with its beautiful colors, interesting textures (plastic), and different coins soon became an entrance into the culture. We used it to pay for Maori history books, fish and chips, sweaters, and penguin viewing. We not only had to learn about what the different denominations of dollar bills and coins looked like (it is IMPERATIVE to learn the difference between a $1,000 bill and a $10 bill), we also had to translate the value of our own country's money into the value of the New Zealand currency. Fortunately for us, our American dollar was worth two New Zealand dollars at the time—it made "shop-till-you-drop" much less painful!

Similarly, parental wisdom is like the familiar currency of one's own home country. The "coin of the realm" is experiences we've had, the knowledge we've gained, and the learning we've labored for. It is like money in the bank—money we know the value of and know confidently how to handle, money we've been acquiring for a long time. The trick, when trying to give this currency to our children, is to understand that they are from a "foreign country." They don't know automatically the value of our currency; they don't know instinctively what to do with it. We need to recognize that we have to exchange our currency into something they can actually use—something they can appreciate and receive. We must learn the exchange rate so we pay it out appropriately. We must help them learn how to handle this currency—bills and coins—with proper care.

Aha. So, we have the "money" of parental wisdom in the bank, and our task is to learn how to invest that money into our children. Our "investment" comes in all manner of denominations, large and small. The big issues—the "G notes," such as marriage, career, ministry—are essential, but we need to realize that the small issues—the "Ones" and "Fives" and "Tens," such as girls, boys, cars, clothes, girls, boys, finances, jobs, girls, boys, studies, the team, girls, boys, sibling conflict, chores, girls, boys, shampoo, deodorant, girls, boys—are equally important for us to give to our children.

OK. So what does this look like in real life? How does one give the "coin of the realm" to one's children in a way they can utilize? Which denominations of currency are necessary in which situations? How can we protect our investment?

One of the best and most effective ways to translate your parental wisdom to your children is by storytelling your life. Share the experiences of your childhood, your teen years, your college days, your first job . . . whatever is appropriate to the situation.

> *"When I was your age, I used to walk 376 miles to school barefoot in the snow—WITHOUT complaining!"*

Hmm. Maybe I haven't given enough explanation. What is required in exchanging your experiences into the currency of parental wisdom is humility, grace, and truthfulness seasoned with laughter.

> *"You know, I remember, when I was your age, it seemed like I was walking FOREVER just to get the six blocks to my school. It felt like it was nearly 376 miles, and boy, you should have heard me moan and groan to my parents!"*

All of a sudden, there is a connecting point, an exchange of your currency into theirs. They can listen to what you have to say—and even learn from it—because you employed the three H's: honesty, humility, and when appropriate, humor. From that point, your children can begin to learn from your experiences and can begin to apply them to their own situations.

Storytelling was used when some of our children (who will remain anonymous in this case) had difficulty waking up to their alarm clocks. They had CD players programmed to play soft and appreciated music at the time they needed to get up. Unfortunately, the music was lulling, and it was so easy to reach over and turn it off that it was not getting the job done. That was when my dearly beloved story-told his experience:

"When I was in high school, I had an early-morning paper route, which allowed me to have a job and still be in athletics, drama, AND music. The only, ONLY way I could drag myself out of bed at five o'clock in the morning was to set my alarm across the room and make sure it was turned on loud and obnoxious. Believe me, when that thing went off, I vaulted out of bed. And, once I got upright, my only job was to keep moving!"

Light bulbs went on in their eyeballs. So THAT is the secret. Amazing as it is to me, they have learned how to get up and get going without my early morning, motherly shaking them to wakefulness. Ah, the value of this type of currency!!

Storytelling is like letting your children peek into your past—where they can learn from what you did right and what you did wrong, from what brought you joy and what brought you pain.

Maybe it would help if I related an incident of how storytelling influenced my family. One day, as we were returning home from the Denver homeschool convention, our family was listening to a tape of one of the speakers. In the message, something was said about parenting. It sparked an interesting conversation in the van, and at the end of it, we asked our kids what they would like us to do differently as parents. After a few moments of quiet contemplation, Melody piped up with the statement that she would really like Mom to play more games with the family. Her comment was made in friendliness and respect, but it hit me very, very hard.

Like a cornered tiger, I snarled at them all: *"I don't HAVE to play games with you guys. I cook, I clean, I teach, I do all of the stuff I need to do. Why do you want me to play stupid games with you anyway? I'm a good mom without doing that . . . Grrr . . ."*

Bill looked over in concern and said, *"Diana, it's OK. Calm down."*

Silence, uneasy silence, reigned in the car. And the Lord began to speak to my heart.

"Diana, it's time to deal with this."
"No!"
"Diana, it's time to deal with this."
"NO!!!!"
"Diana . . . It's time to deal with this."
Sigh. *"OK."* (How does one argue with God and win?)
"Ummm . . . Guys, can we talk?" Tears rolled down my cheeks as I choked out the pain of being alone in my childhood.

"We didn't play games in my family. My parents had their own issues to deal with, and I had no brothers and sisters to play with. Always moving, always being the new kid on the block . . . so I turned to things I could do on my own, like reading and watching TV, where it didn't matter that I was alone. Games signify, I guess, belonging, and I never felt like I belonged."

In that moment, my husband and children reached out, put their hands on me, and prayed. Their love, their compassion, their understanding brought healing and hope. It changed my ability to play games (though it is sometimes still a struggle to say, *"Yes,"* it has become a great source of fun), AND it taught my children a bit of the value of family togetherness. I did not set out to share parental wisdom with them, but the experience of sharing my past brought a connecting point that has deepened their compassion and understanding for others.

Notice that storytelling and sharing parental wisdom in humility, honesty, and humor is a far cry from using control and manipulation to get our children to behave as we think they ought. We know of Christian homeschoolers who teach others to achieve "obedience" in their children by using shame, humiliation, threats, and other forms of control. That may result in outward obedience (at least during the time the child is in the parent's home), but it does not change their heart or their mind.

As was described in the last chapter, our children are each created in the very image of God, and we must treat them with honor and respect. That means that when a bit of parental wisdom is needed, we give it in a way that honors God. Just imagine yourself sharing your "two bits" with your kids while God sits in on the conversation. That is a very healthy picture to hold onto, as it is an entirely accurate portrayal of just exactly what is happening (Sobering, isn't it?).

One more thought on this currency of parental wisdom: try to use the right amount of money for the right situation. It is unsettling to have someone pull out a $1,000 bill to buy a pack of gum! So it is in parenting. Dole out the appropriate amounts of wisdom. When your children need a wee bit of wisdom, don't deluge them with the sum total of EVERYTHING you've ever learned!! You can tell when this is happening—their eyes roll back in their heads, and they keel over. It is not recommended.

Instead, when they say, *"Gee, Mom, should I go to the ball game or stay home?"* throw out a few one's and five's.

"Well, here are some things I did. Maybe these will help you make your decision."

The next day, your teen may come to you, totally impressed, and say, *"Wow, Mom, that was really helpful. How did you ever learn that stuff?"*

That's when you hand over the big bucks of parental wisdom. Remember, they asked for it! (Grin!)

A WINDOW ON WEALTH

The currency of parental wisdom is what you share from your past. Parental transparency is the currency of what you share in the present. Basically, parental transparency is living in a fishbowl for your kids' sake so that they may learn how adults live.

Travelling in a van for several months at a time with one's family is akin to living in a fishbowl. We know. Been there; done that; got the bumper sticker. It was very, VERY hard to have a disagreement with Bill (i.e. a *heated* disagreement) when there were three pairs of eyeballs and three sets of ears tuned in to the whole thing. Many's the time we pulled over and had our discussion outside of the van so as to be able to have a little privacy. I just thought it was one of the unmitigated hassles of travelling, something to be borne with as much fortitude as possible. Imagine my surprise when Isaac told us that it had really been a help to him to watch us handle our differences!

> *"What? You were listening?"*
> *"Uh, Mom, it was hard to miss."*
> *"Aha. But you're saying that watching us in action helped you?"*
> *"Yup. It's hard to know how adults handle things when they're always hiding the problems and the resolutions."*

Ah. Out of the mouths of teens . . . So, as we came to understand this powerful teaching tool, we began to make a concerted effort to let our children in on the issues of our current situations. What are the possibilities here? Finances, unanswered prayers, arguments, mid-life career decisions, in-laws, crisis points, church issues . . . all are areas our children will face as they become adults.

We watched this principle lived out many years ago in the family of the beloved pastor who married us, Bob Stone. He and his wife Nancy had been watching the progress of their daughter, Tanya, in the public school system and decided that she was not thriving in that environment. So, a few years before graduation, they pulled her out to homeschool. We visited them some months after this momentous event, and they happily shared some of the unexpected results.

"We realized that Tanya needed some practice in practical math applications, so we decided to be transparent with her about our finances and show her how it was done. She's gone grocery shopping with Nancy, who taught her how to use coupons and unit pricing. She's also been paying the bills with Nancy. (Author's note: Imagine letting your teenager know this much about your finances!) *When Tanya learned that one could use math to SAVE MONEY, she got really excited. It's been a blast for us all!!"*

You might be saying at this point, "So, what's the big deal anyway? How much can a teenage girl learn from the family finances??"

Good question. What Tanya learned eventually affected her so deeply that she bought a house! From the job she worked while still homeschooling, she banked all of the money except her tithe. When she was married, she brought that amazing skill and that savings nest egg into her marriage, where it has borne some incredible fruit. Within a year of marriage, Tanya and her husband were able to put a down payment on a house. That step led to more wise financial steps, which eventually allowed them to finance her husband's further education. All this from grocery shopping and paying bills with Mom. Amazing!

Of course, none of us has it together in all areas! It is just as valuable an exchange of currency when we let our kids observe our struggles to improve. It helps them see that old dogs really can learn new tricks.

We were on the other end of the spectrum from Bob and Nancy. Handling finances was always an area of complete mystery. How come there was so much month left at the end of the money? And how come some people had money left at the end of the month? What did they know that we didn't? And, since we had dug a pretty good hole financially, how on earth did we go about digging out—apart from an unexpected great uncle thrice removed leaving us untold riches? Well, Bill and I started to pray earnestly about this area. We asked the Lord to teach us His ways in the area of finances, to show us how to grow up into Christian maturity concerning how we handle our money.

Though we had great hope in God's ability to transform our understanding and change us from the inside out, we still weren't getting the hang of this money-in, money-out business. All along, our children were watching this process—eyewitnesses to real-life issues.

Finally, the Lord brought us to a willingness to make a budget (a REALISTIC budget). As Bill and I hammered out the details, we could see that, if we were careful in our spending, we could pay off our debts over a reasonable amount of time—oh, joy! However, one of the biggest hurdles for us to get over was money used for eating. You see, we eat a lot—a lot of the time. Three teenagers (especially the two sons) eat their weight in food every three hours or so! Having a budget for food meant that we had to get creative, had to look for foods that would stretch the stomach without stretching the budget.

So-o-o . . . it was time to be transparent with our children.

"Listen up, guys. This is how much money we have for food this month. We all need to pitch in and do our part—like eating the broccoli set before you. Remember, if we can succeed in this, we'll pay off our debts and have MORE money for doing fun things, like eating!
"Go! Fight! Win!!"

Because they have been a part of this process, we can openly share with them how it's going, how I'm doing in the business of learning to be careful with money. They are actually a part of the solution. Their encouragement, their cheerfulness in the face of oatmeal, their rejoicing as we pay off one bill after another, has helped us immeasurably. And, in a very practical way, it is teaching them to be wise in their handling of money—a good part of the foundation for real-life, adult living.

Another area of transparency concerns the way we treat each other as spouses. I remember hearing Josh McDowell state that the most important thing a father could do for his children was to love his wife. And the most important thing a mother could do for her children was to love her husband. Why? The love of husband and wife is foundational for the family—it brings security and safety for all the inhabitants of the home. And for our discussion, it also provides an incredible model of what healthy marriages look like. In this day and age, that is of such immense rarity, such treasured value, that it is like having gold bars stacked to the ceiling—we're talking the "Big Bucks" of parental currency now.

Since many of us grew up without such models, it seems an impossibility to provide a good example in this area. I am greatly encouraged by the Word of God, which says, *"Nothing is impossible with God."* That is truly the key. Just like my story of learning to handle finances properly (even at the age of forty-six!), we can learn, with God's help, how to love our spouses in the way that God intends. While we are learning, as much as we stay transparent, we will be modeling for our children.

When I was twenty-three, I ran across a book entitled, *What is a Family?* by Edith Schaeffer. Little did I know that this book would revolutionize my understanding of Christian marriage and family. With great transparency, Edith describes the reality of what it looks like when imperfect people who love God get married and have children. It is not perfect, but it is possible. It is not pie-in-the-sky, but it can be a real taste of heaven on earth (along with a few bites of the opposite!). Because she really allows her readers to get a glimpse into her marriage and family, her transparency gave me a truer sense of how to live as a wife and mother.

Transparency is powerful. It is not pretending to be perfect. It is not putting on a show for the sake of others. When we are transparent before our children, it is letting them into the things we do right AND into the things which we do wrong (which are much harder to be vulnerable about). The things we do wrong, if we allow God to transform them, can become the most powerful inducements for good in our children's lives.

Remember to consider how much currency is appropriate for your children in their situation. Don't drop the whole load of all your troubles on your little ones—they are not ready or able to handle it. However, as your children mature and grow, allow them to see the realities of adult life in increasing doses—living transparently before them and before God. It will bring a huge return on your investment.

HOW TO INVEST 86,400 DOLLARS

Once upon a time, there was a man greatly favored by a rich relative. This fabulously wealthy relative loved the man immensely, so, he daily bestowed upon him a portion of his own vast riches—deposited directly into the man's bank account. The man was given 86,400 dollars each and every day of his life! The only cloud on his horizon was that it had to be fully used every day because at midnight the account was completely erased. He never had more than 86,400 dollars to use, but how many of us would complain about that?! His ongoing task was to learn how to spend this sum wisely each and every day. And it is our task as well since our rich Relative also gives each of us the same 86,400 seconds to invest every day. We only have one day at a time to invest in our children, and once that day is gone, we can never get it back. *Selah.*

One of the most surprising aspects of having teens in the house is the vast quantity of my time it takes to keep them healthy and happy! When they were little, I had to read every word for them, cook all the meals for them, bandage their "owies," etc., so I expected to spend most of my waking hours tending to their needs. But why did no one ever tell me how much time teens take? Maybe it's because by the time children become teenagers, if their relationship with their parents has not been nurtured, they won't be around . . . they won't talk . . . they won't share . . . at least, not with their parents. Taking the time to listen to their dreams, to listen to their concerns, to listen to their problems, to listen to their adventures, to listen to their hurts, to listen to their joys—and considering a thoughtful response—requires a big investment of time.

❶ So the first principle of investing this currency in your children's lives is to invest early and often. Time for snuggling, time for reading books, time for sharing chores together, time for listening to their funny ideas, time for looking at their unusual paintings ("why is the horsie blue?"), time for singing silly songs . . . and all of the other things parents do with their wee ones IS time well spent.

As they get older, the time we invest might not be as large, but it must be given as often as possible in order to get the maximum return. Time for doing fun family adventures, time for reading together, time for teaching them to cook interesting meals, time for quietly chatting so they can share what is on their hearts, time for listening to what they are learning, time for hearing about relationships, time for sharing dreams of the future, time for hanging around doing what you love to do (like fishing and skiing and quilting and hunting and eating), and all of the other things wise parents do with their teens IS time well spent.

❷ The second principle of handling this currency is that it is essential to plan times together. In real life, as schedules with teens get increasingly tighter with jobs, hobbies, cars, friends, fill-in-the-blank, this can get real messy. As stated earlier, the only way to assure that you know your teenager's mind and to assure that they know you care is to plan it out—schedule in time together. Things like:

- *One-on-one lunches*
  (even if it's a sandwich in the park, it's STILL lunch!);
- *Business meetings to see how they are coming with their*
  various endeavors;
- *Shopping trips just for fun (we LOVE our hour-long trips to*
  Rapid City for shopping, as it gives lots of chat time);
- *Meals together as a family (it was easy when they were little,*
  it's a challenge when they get older);
- *Concerts, ballet, theater, museums (something interesting to talk about!);*
- *Camp outs (there is nothing like a little campfire smoke and a*
  few rocks under the sleeping bag to bring camaraderie to a family!);
- *Game night (everything from Charades to Scrablble).*

REAPING THE HARVEST

❸ The third principle in handling this vaporous currency is to make the choice. Choose to spend time with your teens, even when other choices might be easier. Remember, you get what you pay for! When people in our community have asked us what we do for a living, we describe jumping in the van and travelling for months at a time. With astonishment in their eyes and dismay in their voices, they have often said, *"You travel with your teenagers?! For months on end?! Oh, my, I'm so sorry."* Then it is our turn to look at them with astonishment and dismay because they have missed the very best part of parenting! Being together with your teens can be so incredibly fun—they bring such energy and freshness of perspective to situations that it is worth their weight in gold to have them along.

An example of this in our own life comes from the last year we were able to travel as a whole family. We were in Orlando for a homeschool convention. Because we had Zach and Genevieve from New Zealand, we thought it was probably a good idea to do some of the touristy stuff that people do in Orlando. All five of these young adults wanted to go to MGM Studios, while Bill and I were going to catch up on some much-needed rest and study. However, when we drove them to the entrance, and I saw people dressed up as the little, green soldiers from *Toy Story*, I instantly made a new choice about my day's activities.

"Oh, Bill, I HAVE to go with the kids!! This looks like FUN!!"

My beloved looked at me with a mixture of delight and amazement that I was ready to ditch resting to go run around all day, but he cheerfully recommended that I go for it. So, with my three teens and two add-ons, I entered the park. What a wonderful, exhilarating, special time it was. Not because of the rides or shows, but because it was so incredible to be sharing it with my children. While the rest of the crew went off to ride an elevator with built-in thrills, Isaac and I chose to stay back for a leisurely lunch together. It was such a magical moment—we were able to dream big dreams of the future, sharing more deeply our visions than we have ever done before. The whole day was like that—a precious moment in time spent together laughing and walking and eating and seeing. It was an investment, and it brought a richness to us that I will always treasure.

So, the principles of the currency of time with your teens are: invest early and often, plan your investment wisely, and choose to invest. Remember, time is like money in the bank, but you have to spend it today.

WHAT'S IN YOUR CUPBOARD?

Dear friends, what precious heritage do you have in your own family or culture? What treasured knowledge or passion or language or skill, like our buffalo story, are you passing on to your own children? In the richness of your own home, your relationships to your children, what are you pouring into them that they could not get anywhere else?

We have seen through the years of travel, that homeschoolers want the best for their children. That is good and commendable! However, they often want to give their children EVERYTHING that is available in a wild and wacky schedule:

MONDAY: *Piano, Drama*
TUESDAY: *Soccer, Violin*
WEDNESDAY: *Scouts, Bible Quiz*
THURSDAY: *Painting, Kazoo*
FRIDAY: *Ballet, Basket Weaving*
SATURDAY: *Anthropomorphic Cloud Viewing, Etymology of Icelandic Verbs*

Excuse me, please, but where, oh, where, is the time to be together? Where, if you can show me, is the time to pass on your own unique heritage? Exactly what do you hope your children will EXCEL in if their schedules are so incredibly full of bits of this and that?

May I show you what a homeschool mom showed me? We were invited one weekend for Sunday dinner to the home of Jack and Kristi Hall. They are a wonderful homeschooling family and good friends to us, so we looked forward with great expectation to this time. Along with the invitation came an unusual request, however. Each one of us was to bring a favorite poem. Interesting idea, no?

It was fun to consider what poem would be the most enjoyable to take to share with friends, and we came up with quite an eclectic collection— *Jabberwocky, Jest A'Fore Christmas, The Embarrassing Episode of Little Miss Muffet, Book Lice,* and *Whirligig Beetles*. It was the stuff of laughter and zaniness with a healthy dose of dramatic license. Embarrassing as it is to admit, it was also our normal poetry fare.

However, we discovered that Jack and Kristi both have truly poetic souls. They recited poems that made one reflect, that caused one to ponder deeply, that refreshed the spirit. It was a whole new world of poetry opening up to us—I felt like our hearts had been enriched at a new level by these poems and by the people who shared them. But what touched me most was the last poem recited by Kristi. In her quiet and thoughtful way, she told us how her grandmother had taught her the poem when she was a girl and how she had always cherished it.

THE DAY IS DONE
by Henry Wadsworth Longfellow

The day is done, and the darkness
Falls from the wings of Night,
As a feather is wafted downward
From an eagle in his flight.

I see the lights of the village
Gleam through the rain and the mist,
And a feeling of sadness comes o'er me
That my soul cannot resist:

A feeling of sadness and longing,
That is not akin to pain,
And resembles sorrow only
As the mist resembles the rain.

Come, read to me some poem,
Some simple and heartfelt lay,
That shall soothe this restless feeling,
And banish the thoughts of day.

Not from the grand old masters,
Not from the bards sublime,
Whose distant footsteps echo
Through the corridors of Time.

For, like strains of martial music,
Their mighty thoughts suggest
Life's endless toil and endeavor;
And to-night I long for rest.

Read from some humbler poet,
Whose songs gushed from his heart,
As showers from the clouds of summer,
Or tears from the eyelids start;

Who, through long days of labor,
And nights devoid of ease,
Still heard in his soul the music
Of wonderful melodies.

Such songs have power to quiet
The restless pulse of care,
And come like the benediction
That follows after prayer.

Then read from the treasured volume
The poem of thy choice,
And lend to the rhyme of the poet
The beauty of thy voice.

And the night shall be filled with music,
And the cares, that infest the day,
Shall fold their tents, like the Arabs,
And as silently steal away.

Listening to Kristi recite this poem was like a balm to my soul. It was a precious ending to a magical time of poetry and sharing. As we drove away from their house, I was struck by what a rich heritage Kristi had in a grandmother who taught her to love poetry. And how wonderful to see this heritage being passed on to her children—each of whom had recited their own favorite poems that day.

We each have, within our lives, something very special to give our children. If we don't:

. . . recognize it,

. . . appreciate the value of it,

. . . or take the time to pass it on, our children's lives will be the poorer for it.

How many of us had parents who were highly skilled but never taught us their skill? How many famous artists, musicians, poets, or actors never passed their passion and understanding on to their children? How many scientists, mathematicians, and engineers discovered amazing things, yet never discovered the value of passing on this ability to their children? How many Christian parents in history have neglected to pass on to their children the torch of a hunger for God (perhaps they passed on the outward forms of religion, but what of the inward heart that worships)?

❶ For a moment, take inventory in the cupboard of your own heritage. What's in there? What do you bring to this family? Believe it or not, I would request that you take the time right now to take stock and write it down. Having a written record of this insight will function like a rudder for your family—it will help give direction. Some possibilities are:

- *ethnic background, language, culture*
- *family interests*
- *learned skills*
- *sports*
- *arts and crafts*
- *music*
- *scientific pursuit*
- *mathematical knowledge*
- *literary understanding*
- *philosophy*
- *discipleship training*
- *adventures in nature or travel or friendships*
- *passions (i.e. a heart for the elderly, for internationals, for unwed moms)*

So stop now, find something special to write on, and list the inventory of your cupboard.

❷ OK. Let's examine this list of what we bring to our family. As you look at what you've written, consider the value of each area. How long did you work to learn that area? How much time have you invested in it? What is that worth? How else are your children going to learn that area if you don't model it for them, make it accessible to them, and teach them?

One of my favorite examples of family heritage being passed on to the next generation comes from our acquaintance with Jesika Shand, a young woman from New Zealand who, along with her sister, Catriona, spent a month in our home. Jesika was homeschooled by her parents, Tim and Raewyn (about whom you will hear more in Chapter Six.) She is a fabulous cook, an amazing gardener, a fantastic babysitter, an energetic musician, a creative seamstress, and an avid sailor. We had such fun when the two sisters were with us, eating and laughing and sightseeing. During a lull in our activities, Jesika told me that her favorite thing of all was to be out on the open sea in a boat.

I looked over at her in amazement.

"But Jesika, what about when those storms come up? Don't you get scared?"

"Oh, no, not scared! It's such fun when the storms come!!"

My amazement grew to shocked disbelief.

"Um, Jesika, haven't you EVER been scared in a storm?"

She pondered. *"Well, there was one time I got a bit frightened. It was the only time in my life that Dad looked nervous out on the boat. I figured if he were nervous, we were probably in big trouble!"*

So, there you have it: a lovely young lady learning extraordinary seamanship from her father. His love of the sea has been passed on to his daughter, along with his knowledge, skill, and understanding.

It all started at home. It was in the family. It was a normal part of life. Home is the place where we are safe to learn, where we can drink in the richness of our family. It is the birthplace of creativity and genius. Do we harbor in our homes a latent Michelangelo or Bach or Shakespeare or Longfellow or Baryshnikov? Perhaps we have nestled in our nest a Werner van Braun or a Frank Lloyd Wright or a Bill Gates. Maybe your child will walk in the path of Edison or Einstein or Euclid. Do they just need a bit of opportunity to try things in the safety of the family?

Think about this for a moment: how easy is it for children to learn things? It seems that children are made of absorbent material—they just soak up everything in sight. Once, when I was visiting London, a man and his son in a local shop were helping customers. It was absolutely a jaw-dropper for me to see the young boy speaking English with one customer, turning to the next and speaking German, then turning to the next and speaking French! I couldn't believe that a CHILD could learn all those languages—it was hard enough for me just trying to learn ONE new language!! What an incredible blessing it is for children to be able to learn languages, skills, and knowledge while they still have that sponge-like aspect, since it becomes a lot more time-consuming, brain-draining, and difficult when a person gets older.

❸ OK, back to work. First we take written inventory of what we bring to the family. Next we evaluate it's worth. Now we must ask ourselves how we are doing in passing this on to our children. Are we creating an environment where our heritage and background is attractive to our children? Are we taking the time to create opportunities to teach them what we know? Are we making choices to pour into them what God has placed in our lives, OR are we hoping that by paying someone else—an "expert"—to teach our children, they will be filled up with good and precious things? (Of course, it is appropriate to hire an expert when your child shows an interest in a field you don't know.)

After we returned from New Zealand, I realized that if Melody were going to really love being a creative homemaker as much as I do, then I needed to invest specific and focused time to teach her the joys and creative license homemaking allows. We made the decision that Melody and I would do a fun-filled, twice-a-week, home-economics course. As we schemed and dreamed, Melody set the pace for what she would like to learn.

"Can we make candles? Can we make soap?"

Gulp. Candles I had done. Soap seemed beyond me. However, the energy of youth was not going to be wasted this time.

"Yes! You are going to have to help me, because I don't know anything about this."

"It'll be GREAT, Mom!!"

And so began a time of taking time to pour not only candles and soap but passion and knowledge into my daughter. The time spent was time that could have been used in other endeavors. But it bore dividends far beyond the mere hours. Melody has drawn closer to my heart, and I have drawn closer to hers. Melody has learned to have fun in creative, homemaking endeavors, rather than seeing homemaking as merely a chore. She has imbibed the joy I find in creating a sense of home. And her interior decorating skills are way beyond mine!

So, in this issue of what is in your own cupboard, it behooves us to consider (and write down!) what we bring to the family, what value our background and heritage has for our children, and how we can take the time needed to pass these things on to our children. If you are feeling overwhelmed that this is being added to all of your other homeschooling responsibilities, relax. This is not another "to do" on your list; this is the fun stuff, the stuff you do at night or on weekends. This may be the stuff you do instead of the purchased curriculum entitled "Home Economics" or "Job Skills" or "Practical Life Skills." If you have the vision for it, you will discover the appropriate time for it.

Can I be brutally honest? It can be a real pain to teach your children something you know and love. It can be an enormous expenditure of time to train them to do something you can do in a fraction of the time. It can be expensive to have them ruin the canvas, burn the dinner, break the bicycle . . . So, step back and ask yourself if it is worth it. Are they worth the time and trouble?

When you come to the realization that your children are worth every bit of time, every bit of expense, every bit of effort, every bit of what you have to offer,

THEN you are ready to pour yourself and your heritage into your children. It is the work of a lifetime, the work of a master craftsman, the work worth doing.

RECOMMENDED RESOURCES

What Is a Family? by Edith Schaeffer
A life-transforming book about real-life Christianity lived out in the family. Read it and be inspired!

Graceworks Planners
Though there are many schedule planners out there, I appreciate the Christian and homeschooling emphasis of the Graceworks Company.

PART TWO
SOWING THE SEED

Yagottahavagottawanna!

One September, Isaac came in the door from having helped new students move into the university dorms and announced, "I just met a couple of girls from Jamaica who have come here to Spearfish to go to school!" Perhaps I should preface this story by telling you that around our house we love internationals. Whenever my kids meet someone from another country, they know that there is a standing invitation to bring them home. So, my first question to Isaac was how soon these two girls could come to dinner.

A few weeks later, Treshana Levy and Tanice Barnett entered our home and our lives. These lovely Jamaicans had come to our Midwest neck-of-the-woods on track scholarships and were wondering if they would be able to survive our winter Arctic blasts! They were already cold in October. It was absolutely delightful to meet them, hear their gorgeous accents, and even eat the food of their country (which they graciously consented to make the second time they visited). The friendship grew through Thanksgiving and Christmas, and we were thrilled to hear of the upcoming indoor track meets where we would finally be able to see these two "do their thing."

So, early in the season, Bill and I went to the regional conference to watch "our girls" run and jump. It was a packed house as ten colleges had sent their athletes to compete in this two-day event. The field house was filled with shot-putters and long jumpers and pole-vaulters and sprinters and joggers and stretchers and watchers . . . oh my. Buzzing activity, preparation, and excitement hung thickly in the air, along with the smell of hot dogs and popcorn. Every so often (especially when I wasn't looking), someone would fire a gun to start the next race. Off the runners would go in amazing agility and stupendous strength.

Treshana had hurt her leg a few weeks prior, so she was not able to run her race that day. However, we did get a chance to see her gracefully sail through the air in the long jump and triple jump. Tanice ran her customary "leave-them-all-in-the-dust" mile, and then she got ready for the 800-meter run.

Sitting on the bleachers, waiting for Tanice's second event, allowed us the opportunity to observe the men run the 400-meter race. I love watching trained runners—their grace, their strength, their speed—and I sat up to enjoy this race. The leader set a grueling pace and maintained it. Though a few runners made the attempt to catch him, they were not able to do it . . . that is, until the last half-lap. As the runners were giving it all they had (and running out of whatever it was at an astronomical rate!) a young man, heretofore unnoticed, suddenly jumped into the lead. As he pounded to the finish line, I was stunned by the look on his face. It almost hurt to see the pain etched in his features. But, more than pain, there was determination. This runner obviously had reached down deep inside of his being and physically pulled up the strength to make the move he was making. It was sheer grit, and it won for him first place.

Bill and I looked at each other and quipped, "Yagottahavagottawanna. . ." And that young man did!

OUR JOURNAL

Bill learned the term "yagottahavagottawanna" while playing intramural college basketball. His team had a number of somewhat out-of-shape, not-used-to-the-rigors-of-running-full-steam-up-and-down-the-court, college guys who just wanted to have fun. As their coach gathered the team halfway through one particular game where they faced an opposing team of fit-enough-to-beat-you players, he noticed that his guys were huffing and blowing and, basically, trying to decide whether they should just lie down and die at that moment or keep playing. This wise and witty coach encouraged them, "Guys, to beat this team, yagottahavagottawanna!" The interpretation of this unusual conglomeration of syllables is that "you really have to dig deep down," "give it all you've got," "no pain, no win." It was a motivator for this group of college basketball players! And it has become a motto in our lives and in our family.

When Michael approached his senior year of homeschool high school, he had a deficit of science courses. His junior year had been fascinatingly spent in New Zealand, mainly with Polynesians from all over the South Pacific. It had been a time of significant growth and learning—cultures, languages, geography, ethnic dancing, ethnic music, ethnic food, Bible study, research, and more. What a fabulous opportunity it had been. However, it did not provide any high school science courses. This bothered him not a whit—until he came face to face with our graduation requirements.

Since we want all our children to have the opportunity to attend a university if they choose to do so, we have college-prep requirements for graduation from our homeschool. We were not sure whether Michael would go on for further academic study after high school, as he was planning to go as soon as possible to the mission field. Because of that, we were even more stringent on his requirements, knowing that he might not ever have a further chance to be exposed to this information and that it might prove valuable in a far-flung country. So, try as he might, there was no wiggling out of these requirements. It was definitely a case of "heads, I win; tails, you lose."

Fortunately for us, Michael is a gracious loser. He smiled gallantly and agreed to study two years of science in one year of school. His main motivation? Graduation!! He had wanted to go to the mission field since he was seven years old, and the time was fast approaching for this dream to materialize into reality. We saw a definite spark of "yagottahavagottawanna" in his eyes and knew that, even though the trek was formidable, he would conquer it.

The science courses he chose to pursue that year were biology and anatomy. Using Dr. Jay Wile's Apologia curriculum, Michael dove into the waters of biology. Do you know what he discovered? That biology is absolutely riveting! He would study biology three to four hours per day and then come out to the living room and regale us all with tales of micro-organisms and nasty things living in our mattresses. Eeywww!

After three months, the course was finished. Then, he approached a friend (a local chiropractor) about teaching him anatomy. Our friend, Dr. John Chaney, was delighted to comply with this request. His only condition was that they study anatomy at the university level! *Let's do it!* thought Michael. So he resumed the regimen of several hours of science per day for months, learning the most amazing facts about the human body—not your basic high school science program. Again, Michael described to us at every opportunity, in microbial detail, the various functions of our bodies. He learned it all with a zest (and a lot of hard work!). In fact, his joy in learning biology and anatomy prompted us to encourage Michael to pursue more advanced training in medicine—always a valuable skill on the mission field.

Graduation day was a triumph for Michael. He had jumped through all of the hoops and had enjoyed an unexpectedly fabulous learning time during the hoop jumping. Genuinely overcoming the deficit of science courses had required lots of internal motivation. As Michael learned very experientially—when facing a huge obstacle, yagottahavagottawanna.

A YOUNG PERSON'S GUIDE TO SELF-MOTIVATION

(This section is meant to be read by teens AND parents!)

Though in Chapter Seven we will look at the different kinds of intelligences, it is important to note at the beginning of this section that self-motivation is part of the intelligence labeled "intrapersonal." This wonderfully helpful way that God makes us smart is "naturally" stronger in some people than in others. Hmmm. Sounds like bad news, doesn't it? Or maybe a good excuse!

"Oh, Mother, dearest, you know I can't possibly get that done. Extensive field tests have shown that I am not naturally strong in my intrapersonal intelligence, and therefore, must be excused from anything requiring self-motivation."

Nice try. May I share with you some good news? Based upon the latest research on the way the brain works, we know that, apart from physical damage to that section of the brain, every one of us can grow in our abilities. That means that, even if you have difficulty motivating yourself to crawl to the table for dinner, you can, over time, increase your personal self-motivation. Yagottahavagottawanna!

So, now that we have removed the excuses and leveled the playing field, let's consider ways one can increase self-motivation.

❶ *First thing to do: pick a passion.*

Consider the things that are most important to you. What is it that you really want to do? What goals do you have? What do you desire so much that you are willing to work hard to accomplish it or to acquire it? Possibilities include:

- *A car, motorcycle, or fancy mountain bike;*
- *First-round draft choice of the NBA;*
- *A home, spouse, and children (homeschooled, naturally!);*
- *Travel around the world;*

- *A Dove Award for your first CD;*
- *A scholarship to a brand-name university;*
- *An opportunity to work on a Mercy Ship in Africa;*
- *Graduate from high school when you're sixteen;*
- *Play guitar so well that Phil Keaggy is nervous;*
- *Start your own web-design business;*
- *Serve the Lord on the mission field;*
- *Be elected as President of the United States;*
- *A gold medal for downhill skiing at the Olympics;*
- *Help your parents in their home-based business.*

What is it that moves you? Are there two or three dreams in your heart . . . four or five or six? Take your time, consider carefully, and then write them down. Once they are on paper, take more time to consider what you have written. Do you possess the giftings, talents, disposition, and background that bring this dream/passion into your orbit? Would you call any of them totally remote and unlikely; potential, though doubtful; attainable; very possible? (A very valuable goal, even if remote, could be worth pursuing.) A bit of realistic assessment can save you a world of disappointment down the road.

For instance, though I may dream of being elected President of the United States, I am personally disqualified before I even begin campaigning because I was born in Germany. It would be far healthier for me to examine what I can do and work toward that goal than to pine after a goal for which I do not qualify.

OK. Pick and assess. *Remember: Identifying your goals will help you grow your motivation.*

❷ *Second thing to do: examine your education.*

Are you taking educational steps in the right direction? For instance, if you want to live in a Russian-speaking nation, are you studying the Russian language? If you want to get a good scholarship to an expensive university, are you studying college-prep courses? If you would love to play the guitar professionally, are you taking lessons with an accomplished musician? If you can't wait to own a car, are you studying how to take care of it (oil changes are NOT optional!)? If you want to be a world-class homeschool mom, are you studying nutrition, learning styles, home finances, and child development?

Once it is determined that you *are* taking educational steps in the right direction, next evaluate whether you are getting all you can from your studies.

REAPING THE HARVEST

Are you aiming for mastery of the material? Are you seeking to mine all of the treasures out of a course of study? Are you giving it your best shot, or are you merely skating superficially over the subject matter? If you have a goal really worth pursuing, then just getting by isn't good enough! However, once you recognize that your course work will take you where you want to go, you'll be set free to pursue it with all of your might. Yagottahavagottawanna!

One day, Michael walked in the door from his university class. He looked at me with amazement and said,

> *"Mom, do you know what the difference is between homeschooled students and public school students?"*
> *"Well . . . I give up. What is the difference?"*
> *"Homeschooled students talk about what they've learned in a class. Public school students talk about their grade."*

Hmmm. Ain't it the truth?

If you are just "doing time," filling in the blanks so you can finish the course, working as little as possible to pass Mom's inspection, waiting until graduation sets you free, then you are cheating yourself and your future. I know. That's how I spent virtually all of my high school years—just trying to get by. I didn't dig down and really learn much of anything. Four years of possibilities—of growth and learning and reaching for the stars—went down the drain. What a waste.

Is it hard to dig in, work diligently, and go for the extra effort? You bet. What is the old saying:

> *"Anything worth having is worth working for"?*

So, the question must be asked, "Is it worth it?" Well, that depends on whether you want to live a life of mediocrity and dissatisfaction OR a life of really accomplishing what is on your heart to achieve.

Consider what the Bible has to say about this subject:

> *"**Whatever** you do, do it heartily, as to the Lord and not to men, knowing that from the Lord you will receive the reward of the inheritance; for you serve the Lord Christ."*
>
> *—Colossians 3:23–24*

Does "whatever" include studying? I'll let you look it up and decide.

In essence, examine not only your educational steps, but evaluate whether you are really studying "heartily." *Remember: Evaluating your education and effort will help you increase your motivation.*

OK. Pick and assess. Examine and evaluate.

❸ *The third thing to do: focus and purge.*

The brutal reality of life is (prepare yourself!) **you cannot do everything.** Shock! Stunned amazement! Disbelief!

I know. It *is* really tempting to try. However, since we are finite, we have a limited amount of time, a limited amount of energy, a limited amount of brain power, a limited amount of money, and a limited number of directions we can go at the same time.

So, what does this mean in light of our discussion?

First, it does NOT mean that you eliminate all the fun, all the rest, all the "try something new" opportunities. You are not a robot. You require rest, relaxation, and refreshment along with hard work.

All work and no play make Jack (and Jill) very dull.
(And I am convinced God did not create us to be dull!)

For example, though Melody is working very hard toward her goal of becoming a concert pianist, this year she also wanted to take dance from a local dance studio. For that one evening per week (and several short practice sessions at home), she does NOT play piano—she dances for fun and exercise. She also babysits for a few Bible studies, plays violin, studies biology, geometry, English literature, and world history. She also plays with her dog, reads interesting books for fun, and plans trips with friends. "Focus and purge" for Melody does not mean that she ONLY plays piano.

OK. So, we know what it does NOT mean. Now, what DOES "focus and purge" actually mean for our goals, our education, and our self-motivation? It means making choices . . . choices based on our goals . . . choices which are wisely considered.

Right now, for instance, I have the goal of writing this book. In order to actually turn that goal into reality, it requires that I choose to sit at the computer morning after morning, afternoon after afternoon. It means that, rather than talking on the phone to a friend, or reading a fascinating book, or sleeping in, or going window shopping, I choose to sit myself down in front of the computer and stare at a blank screen. "Focus and purge" for me right now means that I don't have the time to be as spontaneous as I might like to be.

Often, it's a choice between good and better. Again, what are you trying to accomplish? With each choice that comes up, you must evaluate whether this choice will take you where you want to go. Will it help to refresh you, reanimate you? Or is it simply a good choice to which you need to say "no" because there is a better choice?

Focus and purge. Make careful choices instead of drifting through the week. Be self-disciplined in order to accomplish your goals.

A pithy proverb says it perfectly:

"The soul of a lazy man desires, and has nothing; But the soul of the diligent shall be made rich."   *—Proverbs 13:4*

Remember:
Yagottahavagottawanna!

THE PARENTS' MANUAL TO SELF-MOTIVATION

One of the questions we hear most often as we speak at homeschool conventions and support groups is:

"How do I get my child to be self-motivated?"

Though the answers are as individual and unique as each child, there are a few principles that will help us in our quest to enable our children to develop their own self-motivation.

The first principle is this:

❶ *Children get far more from what is caught than what is taught.*

Uh, oh. Here it comes. The ball is in OUR court on this one. We have to consider ourselves. How self-motivated are we as adults? What kind of example do we set before our children? Are we asking them to do something we are not willing to do? It is vital that we put ourselves under the microscope momentarily and examine what we find there. Lest you think I am asking you to become a workaholic in order to help your children become self-motivated (which is definitely NOT the case!), here are some simple questions to guide you in considering your own self-motivation.

What method do you use for goal setting?

- *Do you set daily goals? —weekly goals? —monthly goals? —yearly goals?*
- *Do you set personal goals? —family goals? —spiritual goals? —financial goals?*
- *Do you converse with your children about your goals?*
- *Do you evaluate your goals? —Daily? —Weekly? —Monthly? —Yearly?*

What is the latest hobby or skill you have learned?

- *Have you explained your motivation for learning it?*
- *Have your children watched you strive to learn it?*
- *Have you moaned, groaned, and given up before learning it?*
- *Have you been enthusiastic about what you're learning?*

How well do you "focus and purge" in your own life?

- *Are you the butterfly—whirling around in constant motion but not accomplishing much?*
- *Are you the bog—overwhelmed, so you sit and do as little as possible?*
- *Are you the ant—setting attainable goals and steadfastly pursuing them?*

What do you see? Are you a positive example of self-motivation for your children (not a positive *lecture*, but a positive action)?

"It is enough for a disciple that he be like his teacher, and a servant like his master . . ."   *—Matthew 10:25*

Is this an area that you have submitted to the Lordship of Jesus? If so, yahoo! You are doing something extremely wonderful and motivational for your children, which will help them to develop their own self-motivation.

If not, start growing your own self-motivation now. Pick and assess your passion(s), examine and evaluate your education, and focus and purge. As parents, we don't have to be perfect in order to positively impact our children; we just need to keep changing, maturing, and growing up. They will learn as much (or more) from watching us grow into an increasingly mature adult as they would if we had started out doing it all right. So be encouraged, and be motivated! Remember:

"In all labor there is profit, But idle chatter leads only to poverty."
—Proverbs 14:23

In other words, don't just talk about it; do it! Ask the Lord for His help, and begin today.

The second principle:

❷ *Touch their palate.*

In Proverbs, we are told:

"Train up a child in the way he should go, And when he is old he will not depart from it."
—Proverbs 22:6

One of the meanings of this verse has to do with "touching the palate" of a child. The Hebrew mother in ancient times would take a wee bit of food, chew it up very well (the *original* baby food grinders!), and touch the baby's palate. Evidently, this gave baby the first opportunity to develop a taste for such interesting foods as gefelte fish and matzoh balls!

Have you ever wondered how on earth French people learn to eat snails . . . and enjoy the experience? How about Filipino connoisseurs who salivate over decaying duck eggs? Or what about Pennsylvania Dutch folks who love to eat scrapple (which I refuse to define!)? Or all the other exotic, specialty foods from various cultures—how on earth do these people learn to eat this stuff?

The answer is very simple: they keep offering their young children that food until they develop a love for it.

I watched this in action when I spent a summer in Belgium with a French-Swiss family. Every morning the father would make coffee with chicory (a novel taste), boil milk until it was frothy, and set out the big coffee mugs. Each adult at the table was served a large portion of café au lait (half milk, half coffee), while the two-year-old son was given a portion of hot chocolate and a little bit of coffee.

Hmmm. That was interesting to observe. So, I asked in my inquiring American fashion, *"Why are you putting coffee in his hot chocolate?"*

The father willingly shared the Swiss prescription for developing a nation of coffee drinkers: start the children off with hot chocolate as soon as they can hold a mug, then begin adding a little coffee to the mixture, gradually making it more coffee than chocolate until, finally, it is strictly café au lait!

Ta Dah! Let's apply this incredibly effective recipe to our own lives. How can we give our children a hunger for learning, for self-motivation? By giving them a taste for it. By showing them how much we enjoy learning and being self-motivated. By starting when they are young with a small portion, mixing in a bit of self-motivation with parental motivation, and then gradually increasing the mix until they are fully self-motivated.

What does that look like in real life? *Ask* your children what they would like to learn. This is always an eye-opening adventure!! If your children are anything like mine, you may have to reject the subjects which are impossible due to the million dollar lab required. However, surely there will be possibilities in at least one or two areas of interest that your child could pursue regardless of what your curriculum says they are supposed to learn this year!

Perhaps it is kite-flying. OK. Your child is highly motivated with the whirling of the spring winds, to learn how to fly a kite. This is the *beginning* of self-motivation. However, as every parent knows, children and adults often begin to lag behind when the actual work is in progress. This is where you can add in the mixture of parental motivation: play happy music while you are all building the kite together, pack a fun picnic lunch, talk up the adventure with great joy and delight, and have a blast with your kids while everyone flies the kites! Your support, your parental motivation underneath their own motivation, your encouragement all help give your child a *taste* for what motivation can do. It helps them experience the wonder of actually accomplishing something they were somewhat motivated to do.

From that platform, you begin to build. Little by little, your children become increasingly responsible for carrying out their own ideas, using their own self-motivation, until your part is mainly that of cheerleader and audience.

What if your children are teens already, and you see no evidence of self-motivation? The principle is the same—find out what their passions are and get behind them to help motivate them into action. Be patient. Pray earnestly. Don't give up on them. When your teens discover that you are really serious about supporting *their* interests, *their* passions, *their* projects, you might see an absolute turn-around in this area of self-motivation.

The third principle:

❸ *Train up children in the way THEY should go.*

One of the other meanings behind Proverbs 22:6 is that each child has been uniquely created by God for His purpose and His good pleasure. We, as parents, need to discover how to nurture what God has already placed inside of them—we need to train them up in the way God has specifically designed them to go.

What does that mean? For example, if your child has been created by God with a love for people and people-related issues, but you are constantly requiring them to sit all alone and do math, science, history, literature, or grammar, it will create frustration in their hearts. If, as they grow older, you try to push them into accounting (where they will be surrounded by mostly numbers and not people), even if they try to please you and study for an MBA degree, they will NOT be trained up in the way they should go.

Do you remember the children's song:

"Oh, be careful little ears what you hear . . .
Oh, be careful little eyes what you see . . ."

That very same sentiment applies to us as parents in a profoundly significant way:

"Oh, be careful how you train them to go . . ."

Walk in the awesome fear of God in this matter. Do not assume that you are smart enough to control your children's futures, to decide their educational paths when they are older, to know what they have been created by God to do. Instead, humble yourself and listen; listen to God in prayer and to your children in conversation. Observe how they have been made—what excites them, what motivates them, what causes them to sit and weep in frustration, what discourages them. Be careful to not use your power and authority as parents in a matter that binds them into a life that they were *not* uniquely designed by God to live. Rather, discover the wondrous design, bless and nurture it, support and encourage it. Work *with* God's plan, not against it—and watch self-motivation bloom into fruition.

Brothers and sisters, train your children up in the wondrously unique way God has created for *them* to go . . . and when they are old, they will not depart from it.

 HOW TO EAT AN ELEPHANT

Have you ever watched an Olympic athlete, a world-class ballet dancer, a virtuoso violinist? Have you ever asked yourself, *"How DO those people do that?"*

Does it seem impossible? Does anyone who is a mere mortal ever learn how to do that stuff?

I am about to let you in on a little-known secret: those folks are real people with much in common with the rest of us! They started off as infants, progressed to toddlers, tots, tweens, teens, and finally adults. However, the difference between these amazingly able people and the rest of us is that they have learned . . . *to eat an elephant.*

They have worked harder, worked longer, worked smarter, at a greater cost than most of us are willing to pay. They worked breathtakingly hard at their task. They devoted their time, energy, and lives to the endeavor. They said "no" to worthy activities that would have taken them away from their goal. But remember this vital point: They learned to do absolutely breathtaking, world-class accomplishments *one step at a time.*

That, of course, is how any of us eats an elephant. The only possible way to devour something *that* big is by taking it one bite at a time. Don't look at the over-all size and say it is impossible! Instead, take one bite, then the next, then the next. Several years later, you will have accomplished what others say is impossible. Notice, that the elephant doesn't disappear in one bite: poof! Hardly. If I may skew an oft-quoted quote, "Anything worth eating is worth eating long."

Isn't that what homeschooling high school students is all about? Many of us look at that elephant and say, *"It's IMPOSSIBLE!"* But the truth is that day by day, class by class, bite by bite, we can accomplish something so magnificent, so world class that others will look at our family and wonder, *"How on earth did they do that?!"*

Yagottahavagottawanna!!

Whatever your goal, you must look it square in the eye, straighten your shoulders, open your mouth, brace yourself, and take a bite. Once that bite is consumed, take the next one. And so on. Eventually, you will have finished it, attained it, accomplished it.

(Author's note: Remember to consider carefully what your goals should be in light of the information in Chapter Nine, "Who's in Charge Here?" and Chapter Seven, "How God Made You Smart!")

Michael, my 6'5" son, is devouring classical ballet. He studies fifteen hours per week in Rapid City (sixty miles from our home). He watches videos of the great ballet performers doing *pas de deux*, male ballet dancers doing jumps and turns—and he watches these in slow motion! He is constantly stretching and working his muscles—even teaching me how to do it (who says you can't teach an older dog new tricks?). He has viewed several movies with ballet dancers in order to see how they accomplish their movements so gracefully. He's chewing quickly, but it is still one bite at a time.

During one of the movies, a dance instructor made a comment to a student which grabbed my attention: *"I want to see the movement, not the effort behind it."* How do you do that? How do you display only the movement without showing all of the effort it requires to perform it? The answer is practice, practice, practice—practice hard, practice well, practice often—bite by bite by bite. Our problem is that we so often stop too soon.

For instance, as a child, I played clarinet and then oboe in the school band. I must truthfully tell you that an oboe, before it is played proficiently, sounds like a dying cow in its last excruciating moments—very painful indeed. My father was so proud of my playing this difficult instrument, that, whenever anyone chanced by our home, he would have me play. These poor, unsuspecting guests were treated not only to the movement, but all of the effort behind it. However, if I had continued to practice, practice, practice . . . if I had studied with excellent teachers and practiced, practiced, practiced . . . if I had devoted myself to this instrument and practiced, practiced, practiced . . . it would have eventually been an incredible pleasure for guests to hear me play. In fact, they would have probably paid money to do so, which is the whole idea behind professional concerts. Unfortunately, I stopped too soon.

Why do people pay $100 or more per ticket to go to a Broadway show when they could get in for free to a high school performance? Hmmm. Good question. My answer? The level of performance is significantly different.

So, where do you want to "perform?" Are you content to live on the level of a high school performance, or do you want to be on the level of a Broadway performer? If the answer is "Broadway," then you have to work very, very hard to get there. Is it worth it? Only you can answer that. My strong encouragement for you is that as Christians we need to not be "addicted to mediocrity."

"Whatever your hand finds to do, do it with your might . . ." —Ecclesiastes 9:10

So, with goals in hand, let's consider how to eat an elephant.

❶ First, you need to be practical. Ask yourself, *"What is required to eat this particular elephant?"*

- *Instruction?*
- *Finances?*
- *Time?*
- *Other people?*
- *Place?*
- *Opportunities to practice?*

The Shand family of Port Ligar, New Zealand, give an example of someone who sorted out the practical needs. Jesika and Catriona Shand, whom you briefly met in Chapter Four, decided that they wanted to travel around the world. Boy, there's an elephant for you! Many dream of travelling around the world, but very few of us actually do it.

Look at what these girls needed in order to accomplish this goal:

- *They needed a considerable amount of money for planes, trains, and a few tours.*
- *They needed a whole lot of friends around the world to stay with, eat with, live with, so that it would not only cost less, but be more instructional.*
- *They needed to devote several months for travelling (see above need).*
- *They needed to decide where they wanted to go, based on their interests and on their family, friends, and connections.*
- *They needed a reliable system of communicating with their parents while they were travelling!*

OK. First, be very practical and figure out what you need in order to eat this elephant.

❷ Secondly, start taking bites.

Jesika and Catriona each found jobs where they could earn the money needed for travel. That was obviously the first bite which needed to be accomplished, or else the rest of the plan would be defunct from the very get-go (Kind of like letting an elephant rot!).

Next, they began contacting people in different parts of the world. The family sent out e-mails several months before the girls began their journey. These e-mails listed the approximate date of their arrival and when they would depart, and each host was invited to respond back as to whether that would work for their schedule.

Not only did the girls need to know where they could stay, they also needed to know a bit about the climate (in order to pack appropriate clothing) and possibilities (bring a camera and a cookbook). So, you see, they did homework to prepare for each possible family and location.

Next, Jesika and Catriona had to get all appropriate visas, shots, etc. One has to pay attention to the details! If you plan to go to a country where a visa is required, you can't get in without it. If you want to fly a plane, you need to get the required number of hours with an instructor. If you want to play baseball, get a glove. Pay attention to the details!

The next practical part of their schedule was to book the tickets. Then pack. Then say good-bye to family and friends in New Zealand for a year and a half. Then get on the plane.

❸ Thirdly, be committed to continue, even when it gets difficult.

Once the adventure began in earnest, Jesika and Catriona had to decide whether to continue, even when it got hard, or cold, or expensive. To travel around the world is not only difficult to plan for, it is difficult to accomplish. The girls had to have the deep and abiding "yagottahavagottawanna" to finish the trip. However, it was a deeply challenging, wonderfully changing, fabulous opportunity that they will cherish for the rest of their lives.

That is how Jesika and Catriona ate their particular elephant.

Now, how about you?

STAND BEFORE KINGS

There is one final area I would like to have us consider in the subject of Yagottahavagottawanna. If you intend to do something with your life, you might consider this proverb:

"Do you see a man who excels in his work? He will stand before kings; He will not stand before unknown men."   —Proverbs 22:29

Talk about excellence in education! If we do something to the point of excelling, if we schedule and goal-set and work hard enough (if we eat the elephant), then the Bible tells us that our work is going to have an impact; it's going to be noticed; it will have an enormous value. Not only will our work stand before kings, but we will, as well.

Let's define excellence for a moment. The dictionary says, "of unusually good quality; better than others; superior." The working definition for me is: "giving my very best, not just a pretty good effort." Doing something to the point of excellence means paying attention to the details, taking enough time to be a true craftsman, being willing to go over and over and over to make sure it is done right. It is the opposite of just throwing a few words on a piece of paper and calling it good . . . or sewing a seam imperfectly and saying to yourself, "No one will see that seam" . . . or practicing a tune on the saxophone but not working to correct those few wrong notes . . . Excellence is the opposite of doing what it takes to *just get by*, or to *get the grade*, or to *pass the course*, or to *barely graduate.*

If you think about it, you will realize that the difference between mediocrity and excellence is often a matter of effort. How much time did you invest? How hard did you work? How focused were you?

Excellence requires hard work. Excellence takes time, a lot of time. Excellence demands the very best effort you can give—sometimes requiring many days, weeks, months, or even years of effort. Excellence only comes to those willing to pay the price. But look at the result: standing before kings is no small thing! Actually, to stand before kings is an incredible place of influence. You could actually change the world from that spot! Remember, yagottahavagottawanna.

For example, in September, 1998, my then fourteen-year-old daughter, Melody, decided to enter the national VFW (Veterans of Foreign Wars) Youth Essay competition. She loves to write and has practiced writing stories, songs, letters, and more for years, so entering this contest made perfect sense to all of us. As she began to work on her 300-400 word essay, we frequently noticed a mulling expression on her face. Periodically, she would pull encyclopedias out of the bookshelf and make notes. In her room, she wrote and rewrote and rewrote her essay. One day, in great frustration, she came to her dad and said, *"I have 402 words—two words too many!!"* Bill read through her essay and helped her to remove those two words—end of parental involvement in writing said essay.

She submitted it to our local VFW that fall. We were so delighted to learn a few weeks later that she had won first place in the local competition. Yahoo! She read her essay on Veteran's Day during a potluck dinner and was awarded $50 for her time and trouble. Not bad for a fourteen-year-old. We were somewhat surprised when we learned a month later that Melody's essay had won first place in the district level. That is much harder to do, as there are many more students competing at that level. But, we were immensely glad to go to the dinner and listen to our daughter read her award-winning essay and watch her collect her check.

When Melody was informed that she had won the state VFW award for her essay, we were really, really excited. However, because we were travelling to homeschool conventions at the appointed date for receiving her state award, she was unable to read the essay before the assembled veterans. Ah, well.

Then one day, while I was suffering from a migraine headache, Melody took a phone call. I was lying down, trying to escape from the pain, when I suddenly heard Melody begin to scream, *"I won? I won? I won!!"* Zoom—up from the bed I flew. Melody took one quick break from the phone to tell me, *"I won NATIONAL!!!"*

End of migraine!! Unbelievable exuberance!! Long-distance phone calls to every relative!! Absolute joy!! Melody competed against 75,000 other seventh, eighth, and ninth grade students—and won—the *first* homeschooler to do so.

In August of 1999, the VFW hosted our family during their 100th anniversary celebration in Kansas City. Just imagine, if you can, our incredible delight and amazement at watching our own daughter stand before 8,000 veterans of foreign wars to read her essay. She spoke with such astonishing poise as she both read the words of her essay and thanked the VFW for their granting her this honor. After the standing ovation, she graciously received her silver eagle trophy and her savings bond in the amount of $10,000. Excellence in action.

And, as that proverb promised, just a few minutes later Melody was shaking hands with the President of the United States.

The Bible is true. We *will* stand before kings. But *yagottahavagottawanna.*

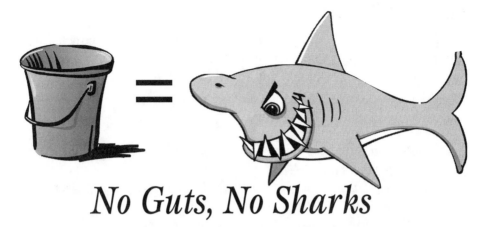

No Guts, No Sharks

Imagine, if you will, a peaceful spot with an abundance of beauty everywhere you look: gorgeous flowers, steep hills descending into a beautifully colored, salt-water bay, sheep dotting the hillsides, and children catching fresh fish. Add to that the delightful fellowship of Tim and Raewyn Shand—folks who are quintessentially Kiwi (hospitable, humorous, and heartwarming). I should describe it as a close cousin to the Garden of Eden. We loved it there.

During ten, long, lazy days of New Zealand summer we rested, while our children frolicked in the warm water around the dock jutting out from the Shand's front yard into the bay. From the dock, we saw two, huge sting rays swim past and a large octopus clamber across the bottom, looking for edibles. Every day, the Shand children would collect our children, jump into the boat, and take off for some hidden cove where the fishing was good. The catch of the day was quickly filleted right by the dock and tossed on the grill—what indescribably good flavor!

After dinner on the last night of our visit, the adults sat and swapped final stories. Tim mentioned in passing several of the sharks he had caught in the bay.

"Sharks?!"

I knew about sharks. I developed a deep-seated fear of the critters as a child living in Miami. They turned up at the worst moments: while I was swimming in Key Largo; while we were fishing off the Florida coast; in scary movies like *Jaws!* Dun Duh, Dun Duh, Dun Duh! To defuse my fear, I had actually written a ten-page report on sharks for school, but the more I learned, the scarier they became.

"Sharks! Tim, you caught sharks around here?"

In his easy-going way, Tim looked over at me and smiled. *"Oh, yes, Diana, I caught a couple of huge sharks right off the dock."*

Gulp. Double gulp. The serpent just showed up in the Garden! *"The dock our children have been jumping off for the past ten days?"* Even as we spoke, the Shand's youngest son, Nathan, and the older children were swimming right by the dock.

Gulp. Double gulp. Triple gulp!!

"That's right. I caught a twelve-foot, 300-pound Bronze Whaler while I was fishing right on that dock—a real man-eater."

"Um, Tim, if you caught a shark off the dock, then WHY ARE OUR CHILDREN SWIMMING THERE?!"

"Oh . . . no worries, Diana. You see, when I was nineteen, I made a little policy change—we haven't had a huge shark by the dock since then."

"I'm all ears, Tim. What little policy change did you make?"

"Well, the workers helping with the sheep used to fish from the dock, fillet their fish right where they caught them, and throw the fish guts off the end of the dock. Now, fish guts, as you might imagine, are quite "fragrant"—in the water or out. Sharks have a keen sense of smell when it comes to blood, and these huge sharks, miles out in the ocean, smelled a feast on a daily basis. They figured out from the constant smell that it was an easy, tasty source of food, so they came into our bay and hung around the dock regularly.

"When I was nineteen, I decided that we should make a small change. So the new policy said when you filleted your fish, you put the fish guts into a pail. Next time anyone took the boat out, it was their responsibility to take the pail way out into the bay and dump it miles from our dock. We haven't seen a shark here since then."

As Tim displayed pictures and an actual jaw of one of those huge sharks, I was amazed at the Hollywood-sized monsters he had caught while standing on his dock. Watching our children lazily swimming next to that dock years after the *little* policy change, I pondered what Tim had shared. Who would have ever thought that such a small action could have such a huge consequence?

OUR JOURNAL

I have never been one of those fit, athletic, in-shape, exercising-for-fun, eat-whatever-you-like-and-never-gain-a-pound kind of people. When I would drive past some poor schmuck riding a bicycle up a hill, I would think pitying thoughts about him not having the sense to take a car. Watching sweat-stained runners in the summer as I sat in air-conditioned comfort brought not a whit of desire to join in the frolic. I think you've got the picture.

Reality, however, has a nasty way of catching up. At forty-six years of age, the body was beginning to show unpleasant signs of deterioration. Out of shape, overweight, and increasingly unhealthy, at my last doctor's visit I heard the wake-up call to do something significant.

"Um . . . Diana, your EKG shows a slight abnormality, and your cholesterol reading is up by the ozone layer! You need to take some significant steps to protect your heart."

Lose weight. Exercise. Get in shape. Live longer.
Yeah, right.
All of the quick-fix things that overweight, out-of-shape people do—diets of all sizes and styles, taking the dachshund for a daily stroll through the park, half-hearted attempts to eat healthy—I had tried. Wasn't that enough? Evidently not.

So, about the same time I started writing this book, I took a plunge never before tried in my life: I went with a friend to a women's gym in our town.

"Oh, Diana, it's so much fun! You'll love it! All of these ladies working out together, we all just chat and do the machines. Since we're all so busy talking, we hardly even notice the workout! You'll see!"

Ignoring the incredible discomfort of entering a place I obviously didn't belong (seeing all of the fit folks), I focused on how much fun it would be to spend 30 seconds on a machine, then switch to another machine, all the while visiting with my neighbor so that the PAIN would not even be noticed!

Unfortunately, I was so out of shape that first morning, I nearly died. At least, they all thought I was about to. My heart rate zoomed beyond the chart, my face turned bright red, my lungs couldn't catch air, and I thought the world was spinning way faster than normal.

Aha. I was right—I didn't belong. Yet.

Since keeping up with a class of fit, in-shape women was not a good place for me to start, the trainer set up an individual program tailored just for me. My ongoing motivation was in knowing that there would be great rewards if I changed my lifestyle AND grave consequences if I didn't. Remembering the truth I discovered at the Shand's place—that those little, seemingly inconsequential actions have great repercussions over time—made it much easier to start. The issues were: would I be faithful to do this unnatural thing every day, and if I did, would it cease being unnatural and become the norm? Much to my amazement and delight, I did and it did. Through the wee step of going to the gym regularly, I developed the exercise habit. The high cholesterol sharks and the overweight sharks are swimming away from my dock.

DIANA'S MAXIM: Little actions done daily have great consequences.

If I had only known this when I was young . . .

PREVENTION, NOT PRESCRIPTION

Have you ever suffered a wretchedly violent case of the flu, only to have your doctor point out that a flu shot would have allowed you to miss most if not all of the misery? When you are in the grips of the flu, that is the last thing you want to know—that you could have avoided the whole episode.

Life is like that. There are aspects of life that are way beyond our control, and for those things we need to pray for God's grace and mercy. However, many parts of our lives are within our sphere of control. For those aspects of our lives, it is much better to follow a philosophy of prevention rather than prescription—flu shots in October rather than the flu in February, if you will.

What areas of life fall within this "prevention" ability? Health, finances, and morality are three aspects of life in which we can develop wise, godly, healthy habits. Think about it for a moment.

If you are wise in taking care of your body, you won't end up thinking that aerobic exercise is reaching for the remote control.
"For bodily exercise profits a little . . ."

If you are wise in your financial dealings, you won't end up with seventeen credit cards maxed out and a collection service at your door.
"Owe no one anything except to love one another . . ."

If you are wise in morality, you won't end up in a wedding presided over by a shotgun.
"Flee also youthful lusts . . ."

Deuteronomy 28 gives us quite a picture of this principle:

"Now it shall come to pass, if you diligently obey the voice of the LORD your God, to observe carefully all His commandments which I command you today, that the LORD your God will set you high above all nations of the earth. And all these blessings shall come upon you and overtake you, because you obey the voice of the LORD your God ... But it shall come to pass, if you do not obey the voice of the LORD your God, to observe carefully all His commandments and His statutes which I command you today, that all these curses will come upon you and overtake you ... " —*Deuteronomy 28:1–2, 15*

You see, God told the people the way to live that would bring blessing and joy to them, but they had a choice to make. If they chose to live in obedience to God's ways, blessing would "overtake them," and they would experience the goodness God intended for them to have. But, if they chose to live in disobedience to God's ways, they would experience the consequence of sin and disobedience—which is much worse than a nasty case of the flu!

To phrase it through the opening story, if we are careful to put the fish guts in the pail, we will be blessed with a wonderfully beautiful and safe dock to swim by. If we toss the fish guts off the dock, the curse is that we'll be swimming with 300-pound sharks—a consequence too terrible to contemplate!

If you are a teenager reading this, welcome to adulthood! Being an adult includes being responsible in your own life for where the fish guts end up. This means that a person's behaviors, their attitudes, their actions can all be proactive, which is like using care and thoughtfulness to place the fish guts in a pail. On the other hand, a person's behaviors, attitudes, and actions can be reactive, which is like taking no care about where the fish guts go. For better or worse, we can take no vacation from this responsible living. Remember, if you start throwing the fish guts off the end of the dock for just a day or two, those ocean-going sharks will be drawn like bees to a fragrant flower. You will suddenly be reacting to the consequences: man-eaters at the dock! Guys, it's better to use proactive prevention than to need a prescription for shark infestation!

What does that look like in real life? In the last chapter, we talked about how a person needs "Yagottahavagottawanna," or, in other words, motivation. In this chapter, the focus is on the habits, habitual behaviors, and attitudes which will bring great benefits to our lives through small, regular actions.

In our "instant," "microwavable," "fast-food" culture, it is critically important to learn that, if we want to enjoy the good consequences of godly living, we need proactive prevention. We need to start living responsibly now and watch the gradual impact of God's blessings come into our lives. It is like the farmer who plants a kernel of corn in the ground. There is a certain amount of delay from the moment of planting the corn until the harvest. So, if you want to enjoy the harvest, you need to start planting months earlier. If you want to swim off the dock this spring, you need to stop throwing the fish guts now. These things take time. If you have ever looked at someone's life and thought, "Man, how did they ever get all of this good stuff in their lives?" then this is the chapter for you.

Now, let's take a look at three areas—maintenance, money, and Mr. & Miss—in which wise, godly habits will bring great blessing over time. Though the list is not exhaustive, it will certainly get you started in the right direction.

DAILY MAINTENANCE PROCEDURES

Jerry and Pam are precious friends from our past. Though Jerry was brilliant in business, some practical aspects of life had escaped him. He sheepishly described to us one day what had happened with his first new car:

"I just kept on driving and driving it, adding oil from time to time. But I did not believe the owner's manual when it described having the oil changed at regular intervals. Eventually, the engine went kerplunk. When I had it towed to the dealership, they told me that, instead of clean oil lubricating the engine, I had sludge. The sludge had infiltrated all the way through. My beautiful car was defunct. Oh, well. Live and learn."

Hmmm. Amazing what a lack of attention to maintenance can cause.

What does that have to do with us? Regardless of your income, education, or background, I can absolutely guarantee that each person reading this owns something of far greater value than a brand new car. Your precious possession also requires a certain amount of daily maintenance in order to perform up to specification. Do you know what I am talking about?

Your body! That wonderfully magnificent, miraculous combination of flesh and bone is your home for this life. How are you doing in it's upkeep? How faithful are you to perform the little actions that have great consequences over time? There are many aspects to consider, but the short list is only three:

- *sleep*
- *food*
- *exercise*

HEALTHY HABIT #1: GET ENOUGH SLEEP!

Sleep is to a healthy body what a sewing machine is to torn jeans. It helps renew, refresh, restore, revive us for the next wearing. The trick is to get an adequate quantity at the appropriate time. Somehow, with the incredible energy of youth, teens think that sleep is more of a condiment than a main course. However, good sleep is as critical to still-growing bodies (with accompanying minds and emotions) as it is to older, less-energetic adults.

All right, what are the daily maintenance procedures for sleep? First, go to bed before midnight. Research has shown that every hour of sleep one gets before midnight counts double! So, if you go to bed at 10:00 and get up at 6:00, your body will feel like it had ten hours of sleep instead of eight. If one is always tired, consider moving bedtime up. Second, sleep long enough. It's ludicrous to get up before your body is ready and then spend the entire day yawning and fighting to stay awake. If your schedule requires you to get up in the wee hours of the morning, reread the first procedure!

Obviously, every one has momentary blips in the schedule that prevent adequate sleep. When that happens, the occasional ten-minute cat nap can help you make it through. But, ASAP, get back on a regular daily maintenance sleep schedule.

HEALTHY HABIT #2: EAT THE RIGHT BALANCE OF FOOD!

Food is something we can all relate to. Regardless of what strange foods we consider to be delicacies (my studies in French language and culture yielded up the interesting habit of eating snails whenever possible!), we can all agree that food is a sublime delight to our senses. Perhaps your idea of a good food is freshly-caught tuna from the coast of Hawaii eaten with seaweed and rice. Or, maybe you would prefer asparagus straight from the garden served with Hollandaise sauce. You may yearn for sukiyaki, or barbecued beans, or clam chowder, or lobster drenched in clarified butter. All of these offer a panorama of flavor, texture, aroma, and color. Food is a blessing—a gladsome gift of God.

All right, so there's no disagreement about the "value of food." However, "food values" are an entirely different discussion. Face it, some food that we may habitually eat provides about the same benefit to our body as eating cardboard layered with lard. Yum, yum. You can almost see those sharks swimming around the dock while you munch on that stuff promiscuously called food. We think that somehow, someway, we can eat whatever comes along, willy nilly, and our body *engines* will maintain factory-new health.

I beg to disagree. And I should know. I have eaten fast food from coast to coast, sea to shining sea. And, sure enough, little actions done daily have great consequences. Eating the burger and fries, drinking the soda, crunching the chips and cookies and candy on a regular basis DID have great consequences: poor health and extra weight—sludge in the engine.

So, what are the options? If we are going to break away from the whole stream of culturally-deprived eating, what is left on our plate?

Let's go Egyptian. Pyramids. Consider the daily food pyramid:

GRAINS—*breads, rice, pasta, oatmeal (6–11 servings)*
VEGETABLES—*eat a rainbow of colors every day*
    (yellow, red, green, purple) (3–5 servings)
FRUITS—*eat a rainbow of colors every day (2–4 servings)*
DAIRY—*milk, yogurt, cheese (2–3 servings)*
PROTEINS—*red meat, poultry, seafood, legumes (dried beans), nuts*
    (2–3 servings)
OTHER—*fats and sugars (eat sparingly!)*

Most of us have no problem getting enough grains, dairy, proteins, and *other* in our daily food. In fact, we major on *other* and minor on the rest of the pyramid. Fruits and vegetables are rare guests, hardly ever seen on our plates. If we want to get a healthy habit that will pay BIG dividends over the course of our lives, we need to change the way we eat. It is recommended you become very well acquainted with fruits and veggies—fresh, frozen, canned, dried. Sweet potato chips, star fruit salads, grated beets on coleslaw, jicama slices, pineapple smoothies, and more are all part of the fabulous smorgasbord God has set before us. Don't just settle for plain-ol'-plain-ol' since it will bore your mouth to tears. Live a little! Take a little fruit and veggie taste test every day. There are all kinds of fascinating flavors of these health providers just waiting to tantalize your taste buds! Dig in!!

HEALTHY HABIT #3: GET REGULAR EXERCISE!

Exercise. Some of you can't imagine why I would need to write about something so obviously good for you and enjoyable to do. Others simply can't imagine why I would want to write about something so obviously difficult and unpleasant to do. To both I would say again, "Little actions done daily have great consequences!"

If you are not a "natural" in this department, the goal is to simply move your body. Move it down the path toward the playground. Move it on the bicycle. Move it on roller blades, or in a swimming pool, or on a horse, or in a dance class. Just move.

Got it? Good.

Now that you are moving, try sweating. Move a little faster, a little harder. I know that means showering every day, but hey, "Little actions done daily have great consequences!"

So, the first area of ridding the dock of sharks is to take care of our bodies by giving them enough sleep, the right kind of food, and enjoyable exercise. This will affect your energy, emotions, thoughts, motivations, spirit, *everything*. These daily maintenance routines will ensure that you don't end up with sludge all through your engine!

SPEND LIKE A MILLIONAIRE

During college days, some friends pointed out a couple in our church and whispered to me, *"Those guys are bona fide millionaires!"*

Wow! Was I impressed! I had never been this close to a real-live millionaire, and it was an opportunity to find out what made them tick. Fortunately, this couple (whom I will call Sam and Sally for privacy's sake) were very friendly, easy-going people who loved college students. They often invited me up to their house perched on the side of a mountain.

One day, Sally and I were sorting through some of her things, and I came across a picture of a beautiful, young woman sitting regally on a gorgeous stallion. I asked Sally who it was.

"Oh, that was me when I was doing equestrian studies."
"Equestrian studies? Where on earth did you do that?"
"In England."
"ENGLAND? Wow! Was it fun, wonderful, cool, exciting, etc.?"
"Oh, yes. England was a delightful place, and I'd absolutely love to go back some day."
I looked at her with a somewhat puzzled expression. "Um, I know you guys can afford to go. Why don't you just call your travel agent and book a trip?"

"Diana, that's not how it works."
"OK, enlighten me. I am a poor, college student, and if I had the money, I'd go in a flash. You have the money, yet you're not going. I don't get it."
"But, the money isn't ours. It belongs to God. We are His stewards, entrusted with the responsibility of using the money in the way He desires. If He wants us to go to England, then we will go, but apart from that, I'll just keep my fond memories of that country and stay home."

Stunned student sat silently. I couldn't even begin to fathom what she was saying. It had never dawned on me that if you had money, you shouldn't spend it on anything you want. But, in fact, that was one of the secrets of their being millionaires. They did NOT consume all of the money that came their way but saw themselves merely as caretakers of God's resources and responsible for wise investments.

Hmmm. I knew that Sam and Sally were quick to give to others, and now I had learned that they were slow to spend on themselves. What an amazing combination! It was obvious that God's financial provision in their lives was being blessed remarkably. Could it have anything to do with these two practices, these two habits of finance? Proverbs 11:24–25 says:

"There is one who scatters, yet increases more; And there is one who withholds more than is right, but it leads to poverty. The generous soul will be made rich, and he who waters will also be watered himself."

HEALTHY HABIT #1: GIVE GENEROUSLY TO OTHERS!

We are told over and over and over again in Scripture to give—regularly, generously, and cheerfully. We are told to give to those who labor in the Scriptures on our behalf, to give to those who ask, to give to those who can not repay, to give to those who are in need. Giving is a habit we need to nurture because it so richly reflects the One who gave the greatest Gift of all. Giving is a reflection of our Father's ways, and it brings us closer to His heart. Giving was described by Jesus as an action which has an equal and opposite reaction in Luke 6:38:

"Give, and it will be given to you: good measure, pressed down, shaken together, and running over will be put into your bosom. For with the same measure that you use, it will be measured back to you."

The kicker is, of course, that in order to give, we must not consume all of our finances upon ourselves. There has to be something left or we cannot give, which leads us to our next habit.

HEALTHY HABIT #2: SAVE!

Just because you have it doesn't mean you should spend it!

Early in our marriage, I was fascinated to hear a financial analyst say that it doesn't matter how much people earn; they still tend to live beyond their means. In those early days, living beyond our means meant buying two bottles of Pepsi rather than sharing one. However, living to the max financially wasn't solely a problem for those with our financial limitations. This analyst could point out doctors in our area, making multiplied times more salary than we were, who were also in debt up to their eyebrows.

> *DIANA'S MAXIM: It's not how much you make that's important, it's how much you have left.*

How does one do this abnormal thing? How does one refrain from spending every last cent (and then some)? Sam and Sally's millionaire attitude can teach us a lot. If we begin to see ourselves as stewards of God's resources, then we can begin to break away from the attitude that says, "I deserve it;" "I want it;" "I earned it." Instead, we can begin to ask:

> *"Lord, how would you have me budget my finances?"*
> *"Lord, whom would you have me give to, above and beyond my tithe?"*
> *"Lord, show me what the real needs are this month and help me not give in to greeds."*

Giving and saving are inescapably good financial habits to learn. With time, the little actions we take in this area will have great consequences.

DOWN PERISCOPE!

As we consider the third area, let me pose a question. Have you ever watched single young people walk into a crowd? They hoist that periscope right up, scanning the crowd, wondering if Mr. or Miss Right is going to show up at last.

Hmmm. She looks promising. Or, *Hmmm. He looks good.*

Then the maneuvering begins.

Blow the tanks!
Aye, aye, Captain.
Surface close to that good-looking one.
Aye, aye, Captain.
Make it look natural.
Aye, aye, Captain.

The rest of the evening is spent in trying to capture the object. Forget serving one another in love. Forget looking on the heart instead of the outward appearance. Forget trusting that God is able to do exceedingly abundantly above all we can ask or even imagine. The hunt is on; the periscope is up; the soul is at battle stations.

Is this the best way to "love one another as I have loved you?" Is this the best way to control our thought life? Is this the best way to get to know members of the opposite gender? Is this the best way to build healthy best friends who become beloved spouses? Is this the best way to acquire a life-long love? Or is there a better way?

Bill and I have talked with our children long and often about the importance of thinking according to Biblical wisdom in this area of "boy meets girl." According to Jesus, it all begins in the mind:

"Whoever looks at a woman to lust for her has already committed adultery with her in his heart."

So, in this very first battle zone of the sexes, we must learn to control our thinking. How do you do that? It is certainly NOT by trying to NOT think about the opposite gender.

Have you ever tried this mind game?

"Whatever you do, DON'T think of pink elephants!"

What is the result? All you can think of for the first several minutes is pink elephants. Or, what about diets, where you are forbidden to eat certain foods like chocolate? What do you think about non-stop? *Chocolate!!*

One of the best ways to focus concentration on something is to try to NOT think about it. So, let's deep-six that method.

All right then, how is it done? How do you avoid thinking of every one you meet as "a possibility?" Instead of trying to keep your mind a blank, fill it up with God's thoughts about each one you meet, both male and female.

"Thank you, Lord, for what You are doing in this person. Please bring blessing and goodness into their life. Father, show me in what ways I can serve this person, how I can be Your hands extended to them. Please bring a richness of friendships to this person, that they may have a deep sense of the fellowship of the Body of Christ. In Jesus' name. Amen."

HEALTHY HABIT #1: LOVE OTHERS WITH GOD'S AGAPE LOVE!

Remember we are family—brothers and sisters. You need to prepare yourself ahead of time, so that you don't view each other as "fresh meat" but as those whom Jesus died for and whom we are called to love with agape love. In advance, prepare words or acts of service that will be encouraging and helpful, as in Hebrews 10:24, rather than stirring their emotional responses. Be a blessing through godly expressions of agape in obedience to the Word, rather than seeking to receive someone's attention for your selfish concerns.

Do you know what's amazing? The effort you put into learning healthy habits of thinking about the opposite gender pays dividends not only in your singleness but even more greatly in your marriage. It is as important, if not more important, to keep your heart and mind in Christ Jesus when you have married Mr. or Miss Right and they have become Mr. or Mrs. Right. So, all this effort you are putting out now will be a blessing for the rest of your life.

Go, team, go!

The second habit is necessary for one's entire life—not just in this area of the opposite gender.

HEALTHY HABIT #2: COMMIT YOUR WAY TO THE LORD!

"Trust also in Him, and He shall bring it to pass" (in His way and His timing!).

Here is one of many glorious, successful examples of someone who waited for the Lord's timing. Back in my college days, one of my roommates was Marilyn. She was a wonderful, beautiful, Christian, young woman who felt called of the

Lord to go to the mission field—first as a medical worker, next as a missionary. Marilyn remained single all through the time of my wedding and the births of my three children, but she was always very supportive of my family, often bringing gifts to the kids when she came to visit. Sometimes, I would tentatively broach the issue of, "Um, men?" with her, and she would simply say, "There is no one, yet."

I couldn't understand it! She was an amazingly precious, lovely lady, yet here she remained—single.

Meantime, another good buddy from college was our friend, Kerry. Kerry was one of the leaders of our Christian campus fellowship, and he was a man who loved the Lord deeply. Whenever we would connect with Kerry, who had become an associate pastor at a church in Seattle, I would wonder why on earth some sweet, young thing hadn't snatched this guy up yet. He was a vibrant, masculine, healthy, Christian man with a heart to serve. The few times I tried to query him about, "Um, women?" he simply said, "There is no one, yet."

This went on for years . . . and years . . . and years.

When Bill and I were approaching forty, we received a note in the mail from Marilyn. She regularly sent newsletters to us in South Dakota about the ministry she was developing among international students in Seattle (having recently moved back to the U.S. after years abroad). So, I casually perused the letter for a few minutes before going into total shock!

"Bill, Bill, BILL!! You'll never guess; oh, my goodness, you'll never believe it; I can't even catch my breath . . ."
"Diana, calm down. What's going on?"
"Bill, you'll never believe it! Marilyn wrote that she and Kerry are getting MARRIED!!"
"What?! I didn't even know they were seeing each other."
"I know . . . I wonder what happened!"

Before you could say, "Bob's your uncle," I was on the phone to Marilyn to discover the story of how two of my most precious, single friends had come to be engaged.

Marilyn, glowing with a joy that was evident even over the phone, reminded me that, during college days, Kerry had been very instrumental in her life, clearly sharing the Gospel and praying with her at her conversion. They had been good friends during college, but they had lost touch with each other over the years. Then, after she had moved back to the U.S., they ran into each other one day in Seattle.

"It was such fun to catch up on all that God had been doing in our lives all these years, so we just kept getting together for dinner and chatting. And then, one day, Kerry asked me to go on a picnic. Right there in the park, he went down on one knee and asked me to be his wife. Two weeks after we reconnected, God showed him that I was the one he had been waiting for."

Amazing grace. Amazing God. Amazing love story.

Can I tell you that watching Kerry and Marilyn's wedding was one of the most precious, God-graced events I have ever witnessed? We continued to talk about what God had wrought, and something Marilyn said to me then has echoed in my mind the past several years.

"Diana, the only regret I have is that I did not trust God more. As I got older, I thought all the wonderful, Christian men were already married! If I had known the whole time I was single that God knew Kerry was waiting for me—Kerry, the very best my heart could ever imagine—I would have waited in joy and patience for His timing."

Dear ones, God is the same today as He has been throughout eternity. Trust Him with your deepest desires because He is trustworthy. Wait on His good gifts, on His perfect timing, and you will be able to live contentedly and joyously in your singleness.

Remember, little actions done daily have great consequences, especially in your thinking about Mr. or Miss Right.

Let's end this section with these words:

"God gives the best to those who leave the choice to Him."   *—Basilea Schlink*

RECOMMENDED RESOURCES

I Kissed Dating Goodbye by Josh Harris

A fascinating look at the new way God is leading homeschoolers in the area of "dating."

Boy Meets Girl by Josh Harris

Relating Josh's own experience of meeting the woman God had prepared for him, this is a wonderful book to read and discuss.

REAPING THE HARVEST

Emotional Purity: An Affair of the Heart by Heather Arnel Paulsen
This is a must-read book for each family. Heather deals with the issues of the heart in male/female relationships, rather than mere exterior guidelines. Her book is warm and open, easily read, and thought-provoking.

TeenVestors: The Practical Investment Guide for Teens and their Parents
by Emmanuel Modu and Andrea Walker
If you want to learn not only to save, but to save and invest wisely, this book is for you.

How God Made You Smart!

In March of 2001, we had the delightful opportunity to travel to the upper peninsula of Michigan for a homeschool convention. You could easily describe the U.P. as a place where it snows . . . in fact, driving down lanes where snow was piled up to the rooftops was an eye-popping experience! It was gorgeous; the people were friendly; and we had an altogether marvelous time there.

One of the workshops at the convention was a panel of experienced homeschooling parents answering questions posed by the audience. It was fascinating to hear the anecdotes of other veteran homeschoolers, but the hands-down winner of the most enlightening story was David Kallman. David is a homeschooling dad, an attorney in Michigan, and an excellent communicator of the realities of homeschooling. He described a recent family trip to the historic battlefield of Gettysburg, Pennsylvania, in which his teenage son, Stephen, played a starring role. As they stood atop one of the towers overlooking the battlefield, David suddenly noticed what Stephen was doing. To his horror and amazement, he witnessed his fifteen-year-old son spitting off the top of the tower. All of the parental toes in the audience and on the panel curled in shocked sympathy as we could each imagine one of our nearest and dearest pulling the same stunt. However, David did not leave us in our toe-curled posture for long. He described his somewhat curt conversation with Stephen:

"What on earth do you think you are doing?!"

"Oh, Dad, I am timing how long it takes for my spit to reach the ground. Using the average of several spits, I want to then determine the velocity with which spit travels."

Sputter, sputter, cough, cough.

"OK. Why are you doing that?"

"Well, I'm trying to apply what I've been learning in physics to the world around me. This seemed like a great opportunity to do some real-life figuring."

REAPING THE HARVEST

David related to us that, indeed, as soon as they returned to the car, Stephen pulled out his notebooks and did the calculations. One surprised parent sat in the car, and now, dozens of surprised parents sat in the audience. He presented such a profound expression of proud but befuddled amusement.

Learning just wasn't like that when we were young. Or, was it and we just didn't know it? Could that be why so few of us got very much out of our educational experience?

OUR JOURNAL

When Rosalie Pedder taught at our YWAM-DTS, Melody was allowed to participate in the class. It was life-changing for each one of us and continues to have ripples of impact for Melody, particularly in the area of learning issues on the eight intelligences. She not only discovered where her strengths and weaknesses are, but she learned that it is possible to strengthen the weak areas of intelligence in her own life.

It was obvious to both Bill and me that Melody would be strong in the areas of linguistics (words) and music. However, we hadn't really realized that the area of being "body smart" (bodily-kinesthetic) would turn out to be her main area of weakness. It made sense since she spent a lot more time reading, practicing musical instruments, and working on the computer than she did riding a bike, walking the dog, or hiking the hills.

They say, "knowledge is power," and Melody was determined to apply that power for good in her life. After we returned home from New Zealand, she started taking regular bike rides with her brothers (and occasionally her mother!). She also added a dance class to her packed school schedule. It has been a delight to watch a more balanced life emerging from that long-ago week of teaching.

Melody has not only been encouraging growth in her own life, however. She has been transmitting this information to friends. When she went to the west coast to visit her best friend, Christy, she noticed something unusual. Though Christy was very artistic in her handcrafts, her sewing, and her decorating, she was convinced that she could not draw.

Utilizing what she had learned about the eight intelligences, Melody realized that Christy's spatial intelligence was very developed and that she probably *would* find drawing a very satisfying activity, if only she could overcome the belief that she *couldn't* draw. Together, they got out a sketch pad and colored pencils and began some rudimentary steps. The light bulb suddenly went on, and, last we heard, Christy hasn't stopped drawing yet.

We have seen that this information can revolutionize not only your own life but the lives of the people around you—discovering that God has made each of us *remarkably* intelligent in a uniquely designed medley of eight different intelligences.

Isn't that *fabulous?* God does not make junk. He makes *people* in His own image. He is the Fountainhead, the very source of ALL intelligence, and He has chosen to display various aspects of His intelligence in us.

Let's jump into this life-changing information!

AN INCREDIBLY QUICK PREFACE

A hundred years ago or so, some folks came up with a system for deciding who was intelligent (thereby deserving advanced education) and who was not (thereby deserving vocational school). They came up with an "Intelligence Quotient" (otherwise known as your IQ). It is expressed as a number that stayed with you for the rest of your life. Some people had it; some people had less; and some people had no hope. Seemed like the end of the story.

However, about twenty years ago, utilizing new research on the brain, Howard Gardener of Harvard theorized in his book, *Frames of Mind,* a different way of looking at intelligence. He examined evidence from a large group of sources: "studies of prodigies, gifted individuals, brain damaged patients, idiot savants, normal children, normal adults, experts in different lines of work, and individuals from diverse cultures." From this information, he discovered that there was good evidence, good reason for recognizing intelligence not as "a number" but as a grouping of autonomous yet related areas in the brain. Gardener defined intelligence as "the ability to solve problems or to create products that are valued within one or more cultural settings."

The good news about these eight intelligences is that we all have all of them to one degree or another. The really good news about these eight intelligences is that we can grow in each area—we are no longer stuck with a single IQ for life. The *fabulous* news is that God has made each of us uniquely smart. Let's move on to these remarkably wonderful, intelligent ways He has created us.

THE GREAT EIGHT

Rosalie Pedder taught us that each of these eight intelligences is found first in God Himself. Since we know that there is nothing good in us that does not have its beginning and source in God, she says it stands to reason then, that if the information about the eight intelligences is true, it should be verifiable in Scripture. Let's briefly examine a few of the Scriptures which demonstrate how God displays these eight intelligences:

- INTRAPERSONAL INTELLIGENCE
  "I am the First and I am the Last; Besides Me there is no God."
  —*Isaiah 44:6*

- NATURALIST
  "Does the hawk fly by your wisdom, And spread its wings toward the south?"
  —*Job 39:26*

- MUSICAL
  "He will rejoice over you with singing."
  (What kind of music does He sing over you? Country? Opera? Folk?)
  —*Zephaniah 3:17*

- MATH/LOGICAL
  Come now, and let us reason together."
  —*Isaiah 1:18*

- BODILY-KINESTHETIC
  "And the LORD God formed man of the dust of the ground, and breathed into his nostrils the breath of life; and man became a living being."
  (Notice the hands-on aspect of man's creation!)
  —*Genesis 2:7*

- INTERPERSONAL
  "Fear not, for I have redeemed you; I have called you by your name; You are Mine. When you pass through the waters, I will be with you; And through the rivers, they shall not overflow you."
  —*Isaiah 43:1–2*

- LINGUISTIC
  "Then God said, 'Let there be light'; and there was light."
  —*Genesis 1:3*

- SPATIAL

"Where were you when I laid the foundations of the earth? Tell Me, if you have understanding. Who determined its measurements? Surely you know! Or who stretched the line upon it? To what were its foundations fastened? Or who laid its cornerstone, When the morning stars sang together, and all the sons of God shouted for joy?"

—Job 38:4–7

Now for a bit of explanation about what each of these intelligences look like in us.

1) INTRAPERSONAL—KNOWING YOURSELF

This intelligence could be described as being "Self Smart." It does NOT mean being self-centered, self-absorbed, or selfish. Instead, it is the ability to be alone, solitary, by yourself without being afraid or bored. The ability to spend time alone in God's Word and in prayer requires intrapersonal intelligence. It is to be aware of your own strengths and limitations, to be confident in facing personal challenges. A person who is strong intrapersonally is able to stand against the crowd and do what he knows is right. I hope you are starting to see the incredible value this intelligence plays in our lives as Christians. People who are strong in this intelligence could be counselors, pastors, philosophers, entrepreneurs, pioneers, test pilots, writers, and people who study thinking (metacognition).

Eric Liddell, the Olympian whose life is portrayed in *Chariots of Fire,* gives an excellent example of the intrapersonal intelligence. He was able to withstand the incredible pressure of the press and the royalty of Great Britain when they demanded that he run his 100-meter Olympic race regardless of his conviction against competing on Sunday. Instead, he did what he believed to be right and ended up winning the quarter-mile race, an event he had not even trained for!

Some of the characteristics of this intelligence are:
- *one who pursues hobbies or projects*
- *an entrepreneurial attitude—willing to risk*
- *able to assess and learn from the past*
- *accurate understanding of personal strong and weak points*
- *can verbalize emotions*
- *holds strong opinions even on issues with strong disagreement*

- *studies independently*
- *needs some solitude for reflection*
- *self-confident*
- *known as one who "marches to the beat of a different drummer"*
- *good at setting goals and being goal directed*
- *a pioneer spirit—displaying a healthy independence*

To capitalize on or to strengthen this intelligence in the study of core academic subjects, one could assign these projects:

- *History—Identify someone in history the student might want to trade places with, and explain why.*
- *Language Arts—Read a story and write how the characters have impacted you.*
- *Math—Study and progress at your own pace—independently.*

Hints for students (and parents!) who are strong in this intelligence:

- *Use computers, self-directed study, and independent study.*
- *Give plenty of free time for thinking, reflecting, and being alone.*
- *Support their ideas of entrepreneurial adventures.*

For people strong in the intrapersonal intelligence, **"Life is a special place."**

2) Naturalist—Loves the Outdoors

This intelligence could be described as being "Nature Smart." It is the ability to recognize varieties of trees and bushes in the woods (and which of them provide food); to observe the clouds in the sky and know what weather is coming; to spot birds in flight and know what manner of bird it is (along with their songs, colorings, nest building habits, etc.); to "read the rocks" when looking at a geological structure; to cultivate an award-winning rose; to navigate the ocean by the stars; and more. This intelligence is used by gold prospectors, farmers, sailors, zoologists, botanists, geologists, oceanographers, lion tamers, rodeo cowboys, mountain climbers, amateur gardeners, veterinarians, hunting guides, and anyone else who works with animals or in the great outdoors. In many cultures and time periods in history, this was the "make it or break it"

intelligence—without it, you had no food, no warmth, got lost in the woods or on the ocean, and died.

An excellent example of this intelligence is displayed in George Washington Carver, the celebrated African-American who revolutionized farming in the southern states through the cultivation and use of the peanut. Through his genius in this naturalist intelligence, he recognized that the peanut would restore nutrients to the depleted soil and invented dozens of commercial uses for this lowly legume.

Some of the characteristics of this intelligence are:
- *loves to bring home critters or plants to display and care for*
- *one who enjoys pets*
- *enjoys being outdoors*
- *enjoys studying subjects such as biology, zoology, botany, etc.*
- *one who shows awareness of geologic formations*
- *prefers to be outdoors hiking or collecting rocks over being cooped up*
- *one who enjoys visiting or working in gardens*
- *one who displays a concern for ecology*
- *loves to visit the zoo*
- *on their own, they might keep a journal about or a collection of plants or creatures*

To capitalize on or to strengthen this intelligence in the study of core academic subjects, one could assign these projects:

- *History—Learn about Lewis and Clark's journey while outside in a fort, classifying plants.*
- *Language Arts—Write and illustrate a story about a safari, emphasizing descriptions of the natural environment.*
- *Math—Create a math problem using pine cones, etc.*

Hints for students (and parents!) who are strong in this intelligence:

- *Go outside!*
- *Get a pet, or volunteer at a farm, zoo, or aquarium.*
- *Take instruction in hiking, mountain climbing, camping, then DO IT.*

For people strong in the naturalist intelligence, **"Life is a camping trip."**

3) MUSICAL—WORKING WITH RHYTHM AND SOUND

This intelligence could be described as being "Music Smart." People who are strong in this area enjoy listening to music, as well as making music. They might be instrumentalists, vocalists, percussionists. They could make instruments; they could play instruments. They might like classical music, country-western music, Polynesian music, jazz music, rhythm and blues, folk music, opera, twentieth century music, African music, Renaissance madrigals, or Japanese music. They might like woodwinds, brass, strings, or percussion. They could play Sousa marches on the CD player to do chores, or a Bach violin sonata to help them write an English composition. This intelligence has to do with rhythmic tapping, soft humming, original composing, guitar strumming, tuneless whistling. Someone strong in this area might very well "sing for their supper" and for any other opportunity that comes their way!

An example of a person strong in this intelligence would be Johann Sebastian Bach. He was a church organist who composed original church music on a weekly basis. Unfortunately, the people of his own time hated it! Too many new ideas!! However, many years later, Felix Mendelssohn discovered Bach's manuscripts and shared them with the rest of the world—which led to an astonishing growth in popularity of this music, which was composed for the glory of God!

Some of the characteristics of this intelligence are:
- *has strong opinions about different styles of music*
- *one who enjoys singing whether alone or in company*
- *often has the desire to play a musical instrument*
- *one who is sensitive to sounds*
- *studies more effectively with background music*
- *has a library of musical recordings*
- *rhythmically astute*
- *one who remembers melodies more firmly than lyrics*
- *may be unaware that they are rhythmically rocking or quietly humming, and may be frustrated if asked to stop*

To capitalize on or to strengthen this intelligence in the study of core academic subjects, one could assign these projects:

- *HISTORY—Sing American folk songs while learning American history—a la History Alive! Through Music.*

- *LANGUAGE ARTS—Set a poem to melody, and sing it for your family.*
- *MATH—Use rhythmic hand clapping to learn the multiplication tables.*

Hints for students (and parents!) who are strong in this intelligence:

- *Sing your way through subjects—for instance, you can actually learn the countries of the world by singing about them!*
- *Take the time, trouble, and expense to get music lessons for these folks. They will benefit in multitudes of ways, not the least of which being that it will give them the chance to "shine."*
- *Order the Sing 'N Learn catalog—they have lots of educational products that utilize this intelligence.*

Remember, for people strong in the musical intelligence, **"Life is a song."**

4) MATH/LOGICAL—WORKING WITH SEQUENCES

This intelligence could be described as being "Number Smart." People with this ability are able to think logically or grasp mathematical concepts easily. They are analytical, rational, systematic beings who wonder why the rest of us can't balance our checkbooks. Money crunchers belong to this category, as do computer programmers, engineers, math teachers, NASA scientists, CPA's, tax attorneys, research scientists, discount book sellers, and household organizers. They are the folks who know why it is better to receive interest on an IRA than to pay interest to the IRS. Accounting, systematizing, economic advising are all fueled by this intelligence. Algebra, geometry, calculus, and addition are part and parcel of this area, as is critical thinking, higher thinking skills, patterns of logic, detecting fallacies, and spotting red herrings.

A familiar example of a person strong in this intelligence is Sir Isaac Newton. Because he was able to reason mathematically and logically, he invented the shorthand mathematical system known as calculus. Through his observation and logical mind, he reasoned that the force we know as gravity held planets in their orbit and chairs to the ground. Because of his genius in this intelligence, the first astronauts who escaped the gravity of earth and flew to the moon gave the credit to "Sir Isaac Newton."

Some of the characteristics of this intelligence are:
- *uses logic to think through issues*

- *strong in computer logic and easily able to learn computer programming*
- *enjoys grouping and sorting*
- *experiments with various possibilities to better understand how systems work*
- *loves to ponder (for instance, "What causes black holes in the universe?")*
- *comfortable doing calculations without paper and pencil*
- *enjoys strategy games like Clue, Stratego, and puzzles that demand logic*
- *likes to see the sequence, the order*

To capitalize on or to strengthen this intelligence in the study of core academic subjects, one could assign these projects:

- HISTORY—*Make a timeline of a certain era in order to visualize the sequence of events.*
- LANGUAGE ARTS—*Outline a recorded story as you listen to it.*
- MATH—*Play number games.*

Hints for students (and parents!) who are strong in this intelligence:

- *Use computers.*
- *Stimulate the brain with brain teasers, logical conundrums, games such as Clue or chess.*
- *Get a catalog from Critical Thinking Skills. Their material is tailor-made for this intelligence!*

For people strong in the math-logical intelligence, **"Life is a logical experiment."**

5) BODILY-KINESTHETIC—WORKING WITH MOVEMENT

This intelligence could be described as being "Body Smart." People who have ability in this area are very aware of and are very much in control of their movements. They are able to use their bodies in ways that make the rest of us scratch our heads (if we can find the spot!). Athletes (everyone from synchronized swimmers to marathon runners), woodworkers, dancers, mechanics, sculptors, jewelers, body builders, cake decorators, calligraphers, joggers, bicyclists, and more are intelligent in this area. Some people who rate high in bodily-kinesthetic intelligence use their whole body (like dancers). Others use their hands (like jewelers). Both large and small motor skills fit within this area.

An excellent example of a person who is on the genius level of bodily-kinesthetic intelligence would be Mikhail Baryshnikov. This Russian-trained dancer does impossible things with his body and makes it look gracefully easy. Much hard work, long practicing, great strength, and the God-given gift of this intelligence have produced someone in whose performance we delight.

Some of the characteristics of this intelligence are:
- *needs to move in order to listen*
- *a kinesthetic or tactile learner*
- *physically in motion, even while standing still*
- *develops abilities in handcrafts and other small motor skill activities*
- *experiences a physical sensation which directs in problem solving*
- *learns from fiddling with stuff, i.e. disassemble, reassemble*
- *enjoys athletic competition*
- *loves activities that engage the large muscle groups, like running, etc.*

To capitalize on or to strengthen this intelligence in the study of core academic subjects, one could assign these projects:

- *HISTORY—Play Charades.*
- *LANGUAGE ARTS—Cut out words and have the student reassemble into sentences, poetry, etc.*
- *MATH—Use manipulatives, regardless of the level of math.*

Hints for students (and parents!) who are strong in this intelligence:

- *Get moving—dance, sports, biking, hands-on activities.*
- *Don't require this person to "sit still." Allow them to walk, toss a ball, sketch . . . while listening and learning.*
- *Recognize and esteem this area as a true intelligence that God has created!*

For people strong in bodily-kinesthetic intelligence, **"Life is 'touchy-feely,' and life is movement."**

6) INTERPERSONAL—KNOWING OTHERS

This intelligence could be described as being "People Smart." People who are strong in this area are often empathetic, sympathetic, compassionate, or in other words, wonderful folks to have as friends. These are the people you want around when you are in trouble or need! To borrow a line from a well-known song: "People . . . people who need people are the luckiest people in the world!" People Smart people just like to be around people . . . Folks who are strong in interpersonal intelligence are interested in—you guessed it—people: understanding them, caring for them, listening to them, helping them, advising them. Nurses, missionaries, counselors, teachers, pastors, helpful sales clerks, loving parents, church greeters are all utilizing this God-given intelligence.

One well-known person who demonstrated high interpersonal intelligence in recent history is Mother Teresa. She cared for the desperately poor, on-death's-door beggars in Calcutta. Because she saw the value in even the poorest of the poor and recognized God's heart toward those who had never known a moment of kindness, she devoted her life to simple acts of mercy for those who could never repay, who often died shortly after they arrived at her hospice. People were her focus, practical love and compassion were her actions . . . and even the governments of the world were impacted by this giant-hearted, tiny woman.

Some of the characteristics of this intelligence are:
- *one who understands people*
- *one who enjoys making friends*
- *enjoys studying with other people*
- *sensitive to the emotions of others*
- *a natural teacher or leader*
- *loves to get together in social settings*
- *involved in activities with others*
- *enjoys friendly games that involve people rather than logic*
- *lends a listening ear and gives advice*
- *able to understand both sides of a disagreement and help both parties reconcile*

To capitalize on or to strengthen this intelligence in the study of core academic subjects, one could assign these projects:

- *HISTORY—Interview someone who was in a war.*

- *Language Arts—Brainstorm ideas together on a whiteboard for a story.*
- *Math—Have your student teach someone else how to solve a math problem.*

Hints for students (and parents!) who are strong in this intelligence:

- *Do things together!*
- *Play games; have discussions; read out loud; do group projects.*

For people who are strong in interpersonal intelligence, **"Life is a party!"**

7) Linguistic—Working with Language

This intelligence could be described as being "Word Smart." People who are strong in this area have an amazing grasp of language and vocabulary. They think in terms of words (rather than pictures or numbers); they enjoy playing with words (puns, creative writing); and they tend to do better in academics where knowledge is transmitted mainly through words. In fact, when tested on standardized tests and IQ tests, people who are strong in this intelligence will probably have a very good showing because so many tests focus on interacting with words and understanding vocabulary. Speakers, authors, comedians, poets, playwrights, creators of crossword puzzles, lyricists, journalists, ad copy writers, jingle writers, the media, talk show hosts, and diplomats all display the workings of this intelligence.

One of my personal favorite authors is Jane Austen. Her linguistic ability allowed her to gently deliver a strong rebuke to the foibles of her generation and culture while telling a fascinating tale, and though our foibles have altered significantly in this day and age, her insights still hold true for us. Because she was a genius in this area, her classic stories from the 1800's are still enjoyed immensely today.

Some of the characteristics of this intelligence are:
- *enjoys reading*
- *strong command of the language*
- *enjoys creative writing*
- *plays with the language—puns, jokes, rhymes*
- *fluent memory for specifc data in words (such as names)*
- *enjoys making up yarns*
- *thought patterns are verbal rather than pictures*

- *enjoys puzzles and games that focus on words (such as Catch Phrase or Taboo)*
- *likes to listen to read-aloud stories, as well as sermons, lectures, etc.*
- *good speller*

To capitalize on or to strengthen this intelligence in the study of core academic subjects, one could assign these projects:

- HISTORY—*Write a poem, either funny or serious, about the era of history you are studying.*
- LANGUAGE ARTS—*Storytell an incident in your family's week.*
- MATH—*Have the student talk through the math problem as it is solved.*

Hints for students (and parents!) who are strong in this intelligence:

- *Utilize creative writing in most subjects.*
- *Use curriculum that utilizes linguistics to teach subjects, such as Making Math Meaningful, Five in a Row, "Digging Deeper" History curriculum guides.*
- *Play games with words, such as Scrabble.*

Remember, for people who are strong in linguistics, **"Life is a discussion."**

8) SPATIAL—WORKING WITH SPACE AND IMAGES

This intelligence could be described as being "Picture Smart." People who are strong in this ability tend to think in pictures rather than in words. They can visualize solutions to problems, can see the answers to questions, and can understand the dimensions of a possible scenario. They are brilliant when it comes to using maps, drawing diagrams, designing landscapes, loading cars, painting three-dimensional masterpieces, and more. They have a grasp of the foundational architecture and artistry of the space that surrounds us. Painters, architects, landscape designers, interior decorators, web designers, traffic engineers, design teams who create new styles for cars and trucks, map makers, draftsmen, sculptors, cabinet makers, and more all display the wonderful gift of this intelligence.

A current example of a genius in spatial intelligence is Alexandra Stoddard, author of *Creating a Beautiful Home.* Her understanding of form and flow within the rooms of a home allowed me to restructure the design of our living spaces—resulting in frequent comments of how beautifully our furniture placement fits our home. This gifted interior designer has openly shared her secrets with us, and I for one am quite thankful for her remarkable spatial intelligence.

Some of the characteristics of this intelligence are:
- *thinks in pictures rather than words*
- *learns more from the picture than the caption underneath*
- *inventive*
- *draws random images on paper while learning*
- *enjoys learning how to paint, sculpt, draw, etc.*
- *able to learn and utilize the information from maps and charts*
- *can easily picture the location of items in his environment*
- *finds lost items that have been overlooked by others*
- *has a natural ability to draw in perspective*
- *appreciates receiving information from visual sources such as photos*
- *enjoys visual games and picture puzzles*
- *loves to build elaborate structures with materials such as Legos*

To capitalize on or to strengthen this intelligence in the study of core academic subjects, one could assign these projects:

- HISTORY—*Create a collage of the different elements of an historical person's life.*
- LANGUAGE ARTS—*Keep a journal where the student draws pictures of personal events, as well as describing them briefly in words.*
- MATH—*Make a graph of your family's favorite foods and least favorite foods.*

Hints for students (and parents!) who are strong in this intelligence:

- *Drawing and painting are excellent areas to develop.*
- *Legos and other three-dimensional materials are excellent and enjoyed.*
- *Use curriculum that focuses on this area, such as Visual Manna and How Great Thou ART.*

Finally, for people who are gifted in spatial intelligence, **"Life is a painting."**

REAPING THE HARVEST

Having examined this information, we need to be reminded that these eight intelligences are as true for America as for Africa, Asia, Antarctica, and every place in between. Though in the past, we may have cynically referred to this kind of information as pop psychology, we need to understand that this research is focused on the structure and workings of the brain. It is good science based on observation and careful study, rather than Freudian-style assumptions. It is also good parenting to recognize and work with the unique combinations of intelligences God has placed in your child. We have the incredible opportunity to help our children grow in the intelligences where they are weaker and teach them utilizing the intelligences where they are strong. It is, oh, so frustrating for them (and eventually for you) when this order is reversed, and we require them to learn through their weaker areas of intelligence.

This cutting-edge research and information on how God has made us smart is one of the most useful tools we have in our homeschool toolkit. Keep it sharp, learn to use it well, and keep it handy!

RECOMMENDED RESOURCES

In Their Own Way by Thomas Armstrong
Though written by a secular author, this book is full of practical suggestions on how to teach to the different intelligences. I found it to be very helpful, very insightful, even though he makes reference a few times to Dungeons and Dragons.

Eight Ways of Teaching by David Lazear
This book is written to teachers. It shows you how to teach to the different intelligences—which homeschoolers can handily use. The charts of suggestions for teaching different academic subjects to each intelligence are worth their weight in gold!

Don't Check Your Brains at the Door!

During the mid-1970's, I attended Western Washington University in Bellingham, Washington. There are many fond memories in my brain of my time there: of making new friends; having new experiences; learning new information; of having my intellectual horizons broadened considerably through all of the fascinating subject areas to which I was exposed, like African history, anthropology, French literature, music theory, and more. One of my most vivid memories, however, concerns my astronomy class.

Being a "non-science" type, I had put off taking my required science courses until the last couple of years of college. Thus, I found myself, a senior, surrounded by freshmen in an entry-level course. When I say surrounded, I mean, surrounded! There were probably a couple hundred of us tumbled into this lecture hall, and I looked forward to the easy "A" for a 101-level class and to the anonymity of a large group.

Our professor began to introduce us to the wonders of astronomy, the "mysteries" of the heavens, the theories behind it all. As I listened to him propound on a particular theory of beginnings, I observed students all around me drinking in every word he said.

Hmmm.

"Excuse me?"
"What? Oh, uh, yes. The student in the back has a question?"
"Yes, sir. You are describing a fascinating theory here, but I am curious. Are there any other theories that would explain the phenomena we see in the heavens?"
Splutter, splutter, cough, cough.
"Uhem . . . Well, yes, of course, there are other theories."
"Would you mind telling us what these other theories are?"

Cough, cough, splutter, splutter, enraged glare toward the back of the room . . .

Most fascinating to me, beyond the fact that my professor refused to further acknowledge my raised hand, was all of the other students looking in my direction. They were stunned; their eyes were bugging out; their faces wore shocked expressions. They all seemed to have one thought:

"Who is this to buck the system? Who is this to challenge the professor, the expert, the academic? Who does she think she is to ask such disturbing questions?"

So much for anonymity, but such fond memories . . .

OUR JOURNAL

One of the many benefits of the gypsy lifestyle we have pursued—travelling months at a time to homeschool conventions in North America—has been the opportunity for our children to hear some of the best speakers in the homeschooling movement. Jeff Baldwin of Worldview Academy is one of these. Several years ago, he was invited by the S.E.A.R.C.H. convention of Pennsylvania to address the teens.

Normally, Bill and I try to hear the speakers our children hear, but on this occasion, I was busy lecturing, and Bill was busy at our booth, so the kids tramped off together to the workshop. When they returned, they were excited! Jeff, who is a fabulous speaker, had provoked some real thinking about worldview issues, and they couldn't wait to tell us all about it.

Once we had loaded everything into the van, and everyone was onboard, the discussion began.

"Hey, Mom and Dad, Jeff was talking about art and worldview."
"Really? Cool. What was he saying?"
"Well, he defined art for us as 'skilled human creativity that reflects God's truth and God's beauty.'"
"Oh, you mean he defined 'Christian art.'"
"No, he defined 'art' itself—all art, art everywhere."
"But guys, that definition will only fly for folks who hold a Christian worldview."

"It doesn't matter! You see, this is what art really is, and if it doesn't fit the definition of skilled and truth and beauty, it isn't really art!"

Hmmm. Decision time. Do we let them enjoy this new prospect or chime in with some comments that are important to us but might cause some disagreement? Hmmm. This is significant; we have to chime in.

"OK. Stop and think about this for a moment. Picasso's paintings certainly fall outside of this grid. I don't agree with Picasso's worldview or his life-style or his expression of art. However, his paintings definitely played a powerful role in the 1900's in challenging the current philosophy of art, literature, and everything else. Now, consider if you were having a discussion on the history of art with someone who is a non-believer, and you pull this definition out—skill, truth, AND beauty—which removes Picasso from the discussion, what do you think will happen?"

Silence.

"What I am trying to say is that, if you are in a dialogue with someone and you use this definition of art, not categorizing it as 'worthwhile art' or 'Christian art' or 'art that makes sense' or 'art that doesn't need a title' or something, you will be building an unnecessary wall between you and a non-believer through an argument over the use of language. Do you think an argument over the word 'art' is necessary? Won't you be communicating to others, 'I am right, end of discussion'? Remember, within the bounds of Biblical truth, we are called to build bridges not dividing walls whenever possible—like Paul did at Mars Hill ."

Our kids were somewhat frustrated with us for not simply agreeing with Jeff's definition. And we were somewhat frustrated with them that they didn't see what we were trying to say. However, we were very thankful for the opportunity to engage on a deeper level with them in thinking about what they had heard, rather than the level of a baby bird opening its mouth and swallowing whatever comes along.

A few weeks later, at another convention in another state, we had the opportunity to have dinner with Jeff and discuss this issue with him. It was a fascinating time for all of us (especially my kids!), and at the end, we congenial-ly agreed to disagree about the definition of art, since Jeff's focus incorporated some different issues for the students he was teaching than the specific issues we were concerned about for our children.

The net result of all this? My children had their own, eye-opening experience of asking questions, analyzing, and thinking on a deeper level.

BE A BEREAN—NOT A SHEEP!

Sheep—a four-legged, grass-eating animal with a thick, fleecy coat and a tendency to follow the flock.

Berean—a two-legged, first-century person who lived in Berea and who, *"searched the Scriptures daily to find out whether these things were so."*

Question: what is the difference between a Berean and a sheep? I mean—apart from the obvious physiological distinctions between the two—what sets them worlds apart? Answer: the sheep is a black-belt master of "follow the leader," while the Bereans (whom we meet in the same chapter as Paul's visit to Mars Hill) heard Paul's earthshaking words but did not fall into line and believe him UNTIL they had checked his statements against the Word of God. While a sheep mindlessly does what the rest of the flock is doing, the Bereans were not willing to accept everything they heard without thinking it through independently. The Bereans had a standard against which they measured all new information, while the sheep probably hasn't ever considered having a standard.

How does this apply to homeschooling families? When it comes to speeches and keynote addresses and sermons and ad copy and even chats around the barbeque, it does not benefit you to simply take in and believe comments just because they sound true. It is better to consider them carefully against a standard. In issues of ad copy, compare with other product labels or ask your friends. In issues of Christian living, just like the Bereans of old, compare what the Scriptures actually indicate. Likewise, for speeches and lectures, consider whether the comments are right and true. May I speak plainly? Throughout our travels, we have seen sheep-like homeschool parents following the latest fad in parenting philosophies, curriculum methods, even car selection (why *are* there so many mini-vans in that convention parking lot?). People read in a glossy curriculum brochure that this is the very best program available, so they hurry off to buy that curriculum without further examination. We hear comments, like, *"My two neighbors homeschool this way, so we better do it, too."* Some expert expounds that a curriculum MUST include their particular concerns in order to be effective, and people believe them. We have watched in amazement as a few of these Christian homeschool speakers *skew* the Word of God to fit their own agenda, and then the audience pours out the door with sheep-like comments, such as, *"Wasn't that incredible? Isn't he amazing? I never thought of it that way before!"* Bluntly, sheep-like parents seem to believe, in general, that if someone has the smarts to become a speaker or a writer or a singer or an actor or an athlete or a college professor, then he somehow is automatically qualified to be their leader. *"He must know something we don't know, or why else would he be on stage?"*

Combined with that, as if on the other side of the same coin, is an issue that compounds this problem: many of us have no confidence in our own ability to consider, to think, to analyze, to ask questions. We have been convinced in our schooling and in our families that we are not very smart, certainly not smart enough to analyze what we are being taught. So we are left in the vulnerable position of trusting others to do our thinking for us. My prayer and hope is that, by the end of this chapter, you will have tools and courage to search and study; then, when you hear a presentation or read a book, you will go and study for yourself "whether these things are so."

In order to explore more fully this adventure of thinking, we are going to pursue three quests of discovery.

Quest ❶ : *Realize that you CAN think.*
Quest ❷ : *Learn the framework of worldviews.*
Quest ❸ : *Learn and practice the skills of thinking.*

OK. The First Quest: **Realize that you CAN think.**
The Bible indicates that we were created with an ability to use our brains.

"Come now and let us reason together . . ."
—*Isaiah 1:18*
"You shall love the LORD *your God with all of your heart, with all your soul, and with all your mind."*
—*Matthew 22:37*
"One person esteems one day above another; another esteems every day alike. Let each be fully convinced in his own mind."
—*Romans 14:5*
"Now as he thus made his defense, Festus said with a loud voice, 'Paul, you are beside yourself! Much learning is driving you mad!' But he said, 'I am not mad, most noble Festus, but speak the words of truth and reason.'"
—*Acts 26:24–25*

"Oh Lord, You have searched me and known me. You know my sitting down and my rising up; You understand my thought afar off . . . I will praise You, for I am fearfully and wonderfully made . . ."

—Psalm 139:1–2,14

"These are the things you shall do: speak each man the truth to his neighbor; give judgment in your gates for truth, justice, and peace . . ."

—Zechariah 8:16

Even a cursory examination of Scripture shows us that God intends for us to be able to think clearly—to **reason** . . . to use our **mind** . . . to understand the **truth** (and be able to distinguish it from lies) . . . He knows our **thoughts** . . .

Dear ones, He is not playing games with us. He carefully designed us to have the ability to think and reason and consider. Yet many of us do not believe it.

On the one hand, we believe an author/speaker/professor is smarter.
On the other hand, we believe we are dumber.

Both of these statements probably reflect more of an absorbed attitude than an objective reality. In other words, those who are told often enough they are not bright, begin to believe it. However, we have each been gifted by God with an incredible "machine" called the brain. It has enormous ability and was designed for thinking. Rejoice and be exceedingly glad! Remember, the Word of God says that we are "fearfully and wonderfully made." Furthermore, we can strengthen our brain power through training—just like athletes strengthen their muscles. To say our brain is not "good enough" for thinking is to devalue what God Himself has done. Let me say that again:

To say our brain is not "good enough" for thinking is to devalue what God Himself has done!

In addition to this incredible brain He created us with, Jesus also promised to send us the Comforter who would lead us into all truth . . . and He wasn't kidding. So, there you go. A brain—*a thinking apparatus*—created by God Himself and the Holy Spirit who dwells inside the believer, leading us into all truth.

Will you stop for just a moment and examine yourself?
* *Do you believe that God did a good work in creating you?*
* *Did He create you with a functioning brain?*

- *Are you believing what He says about you, or do you believe lies about yourself? (Lies such as: "You are stupid;" "You cannot think;" "You cannot learn;" etc.)*

If you have believed lies about yourself and your ability to think, you need to confess that to the Lord and ask His forgiveness for disparaging His good gifts. Then reprogram the computer! Stop saying, *"Oh, I can't figure that out . . ."* or *"I am not smart enough . . ."* and start saying, *"Lord, help me figure this out . . ."* and *"Lord, You have made me smart enough, but I need some help thinking!"*

OK. Are we all on the same page now? Do we all accept that we CAN learn, think, reason, and consider? Good. Go, team, go! (If you don't accept this yet, reread Chapter Seven about the characteristics of the eight intelligences and review the above Scripture passages to meditate on the truth of God's Word.)

The Second Quest: **Learn the framework of worldviews.**

There are so many ways for people to relate to an event. For example, on a really simple level, consider the difference in perspective that we hold on summer rain: farmers look up and smile, but tourists look up and grimace. On an increasingly complex level, the greater the divide between people, the greater will be the difference in perspective.

A. *Wife and mother versus professional athlete (simple)*
B. *German versus Ecuadorean (more complex)*
C. *Christian versus Jew (still more complex)*
D. *Christian versus Hindu (hard to bridge the gulf!)*

Though the issues separating individuals in point "A" are significant, one can see that the issues separating people in point "D" are much greater. The differences between Christian and Hindu or Christian and humanist determine how a person relates to the meaning of life. The term for this is "worldview." Worldview influences the way people see things, the way they act, and the way they reason. It is the "big picture," the understanding of the *whole* rather than just the *parts*. In other words, it is not just the details—the parts—like the color of your car, your shoe size, or the items on your shopping list. It is the whole—the framework—like how you should spend your money, whether to instill patriotism or globalism, or are people good or bad.

Worldview has to do with what people think:
- *of God (is there one? is there none? are there many? am I one?),*
- *of the beginnings of the world (chance, Bang, Creation, force),*
- *of the point of their existence (none, my pleasure, God's pleasure, nonsense).*

It may have sounded intimidating in the past, but learning about worldviews does not have to be complicated. If we can begin to understand these major frameworks for seeing the world, we will have the tools to be able to evaluate what is going on in the world around us, what is being preached to us from the newspapers and television, what is being proclaimed to us as truth in seminars, what is being shared in the local coffee shop. Once you get a handle on the basic frames of reference, you will understand the differences in how people view an event, a person, elections, religion, child-rearing, a work of art, natural resources, music, and everything else in the world.

For instance, one season our family went to see a professional dance theater group that had come to our area. This group is a modern dance company, and their performance certainly displayed the veracity of the label. Just at the moment we were enjoying classical ballet moves, the music suddenly *morphed* into bizarre modern sounds, and the dancers started dancing like mischievous animals instead of people. It was a startling experience and was designed by the choreographer to be such, so that he could lead us down the path of his worldview. Unfortunately, as the people around us left the theater, they merely commented on how wonderful the dancing was. I did not hear a single question about why the dancers were portraying animals and wearing outlandish costumes nor a single comment about what they were communicating—the worldview behind the dance.

It was as if we were in the midst of the fairy tale, "The Emperor's New Clothes." While the adults stood around commenting on the finery of the night's performance, I felt like the child who loudly proclaimed, *"But the Emperor isn't wearing any clothes!"* You see, few people there were even aware that worldview issues were being displayed in the dance. They have not been taught to think about what they see or hear or read. They simply walk through life oblivious to the "big picture" issues.

Many people today have no real concept of *why* they believe what they believe. They are not aware of the worldview in which they operate—it was imbibed along with their milk at school and at home, and they simply think that the way they see the world is the right way—the way normal people view it. There is, however, a Christian worldview. It is contrary to all other worldviews, as different as God's thoughts are from our thoughts and His ways from our ways.

There is a Christian, Biblical way to see and evaluate what happens in the world, what people do, and what people think. We can learn this framework, understand this worldview, and discover how it answers the questions other worldviews cannot.

This is **great** news! This is a **great** tool! This is **great** for you! All it will take is a little bit of work, a little bit of reading, and a little bit of thinking. So don't be intimidated!! Don't say you aren't smart enough—remember the first quest?

To give you a primer-style introduction to this subject, we will use the terms used by Dr. David Noebel in his book, *Understanding the Times* (in the abridged edition):

- *Secular Humanism*
- *Marxist/Leninist Worldview*
- *Cosmic Humanism*
- *Biblical Worldview*

Briefly and simplistically defined:

- *secular humanism is an atheistic, man-centered philosophy;*
- *marxism/leninism is an atheistic, man-centered philosophy with a doctrine of equality (except that those in charge get more than anyone else!);*
- *cosmic humanism is a pantheistic (many gods), New Age, man-is-god philosophy;*
- *Biblical thinking is a God-reaching-to-man philosophy with the doctrine of sinners needing a Savior and a Kingdom where the greatest is the servant of all.*

There are many thoughtful definitions of worldview, many Christian books devoted to explaining the issues of worldview, and curriculums/camps/schools that can instruct the interested person. To get an overall historical perspective of worldviews, I highly recommend the video series and book by Dr. Francis Schaeffer entitled, *How Should We Then Live?* It will give the student (whether teen or adult) a far greater appreciation of where these ideas have come from and the far-ranging impact of these ideas.

Any amount of time you spend learning about worldviews will pay huge dividends as you read the paper, watch the news, listen to the radio, and talk with people, *because* you will be better equipped to understand the background of *what* they foundationally believe and *how* that impacts what they are saying about a particular issue. You will develop increasing skill with "power tools" in constructing defenses against faulty thinking, illogical reasoning, and irrational considerations. However, not only will you be able to build personal defenses against this kind of thinking, you will also grow in your ability to build bridges of communication toward another person who does not understand why they believe what they believe.

OK, the adventure continues:
The First Quest is to learn that you CAN think.
The Second Quest is to learn the framework of worldviews.
The Third Quest: **Learn and practice the skills of thinking.**

We will examine some higher-level thinking skills in the rest of this chapter and consider how to put them to good use in our homeschooling. Do *not* be overwhelmed, because God Himself designed you to be able to do this and to actually derive great joy and benefit from it. For now, let me encourage you that this is a *process* that we will pursue (and become better at!) for the rest of our lives. Parents AND teens need to keep on studying, keep on learning, keep on asking questions, keep on thinking. Fortunately, God has created such an amazing universe and such astounding creatures who do such astonishing things that there is plenty to think about!!

CONSIDER YOURSELF

It is important to recognize that thinking *skills* are something we do not have naturally from birth, but instead, they develop as we mature. That is a good news/bad news proposition: the good news is that everyone can get *better* at this; the bad news is that, in order to get better, one has to *work* at it!

So, what can we do to develop these thinking skills? In this section, we are going to examine several components of higher-level thinking along with strength-training exercises for the brain, which will help achieve an increasing ability to think creatively, analyze, and reason.

Higher-level thinking skills have been divided into two major groupings: creative thinking skills and critical thinking skills. Basically, creative thinking skills allow a person to look at a problem, a need, a mess, and come up with some possible solutions. Critical thinking skills, on the other hand, allow a person to look at lots of possible solutions and decide which one would best fix the problem, meet the need, or organize the mess. Do you see how incredibly valuable each of these is? In essence, we need to nurture and develop in ourselves and our children the ability to think both creatively and critically.

Researchers have discovered that, if we break down this "higher-level thinking" into bite-sized steps, anyone can improve their ability to think. So here is a *brief* list of some creative thinking skills and some critical thinking skills (there are many more you can learn about) and a few ideas of how you can practice them at home with your family. Have fun!! (Author's note: There are books available in the library that will give fuller explanations and other examples.)

CREATIVE THINKING SKILLS

There are five different types of creative thinking skills that we will consider. Each one is a normal, everyday kind of skill, but in taking the time to focus and work with each type, you will soon develop increasing facility in their use. Your fun practice sessions will eventually begin to impact your real-life situations, bringing many more creative solutions to areas of need.

Let us first consider the creative thinking skill of *originality:* the ability to come up with new or unusual ideas. Set a loaf of bread on the breakfast table and ask the members of your family to think of new uses for bread. Since originality is a difficult skill for many of us, I urge you to not squelch the outlandish ideas your children may come up with—even if they are not very practical (or edible). Right now, the goal is to come up with new or unusual ideas, not to decide whether they are practical. (Author's note: To make a decision about the practical nature of an idea is to practice a critical thinking skill. Critical thinking is obviously important, but it will stifle originality if used while ideas are being thought up. Save the evaluating of ideas until later! A little bit further along in this chapter is a section on critical thinking skills.)

With practice, you will improve, so here are two more suggestions to use in practicing originality. Consider how your family could use a lawn mower in an original way to earn money. How about an original use for a boat?

One of the best examples of this creative thinking skill is depicted in the movie *Apollo 13* when the scientists on earth have to come up with a means of filtering the air onboard the spaceship, using only the materials that are onboard.

The second creative thinking skill, one that many families utilize already, is that of *fluency (brainstorming)*, which means to create a multitude of ideas. Whenever I think of brainstorming, I remember my friend, Joan Veach, who would gather her children together when it was time to write a poem. With a whiteboard and colorful markers ready at hand, Joan would ask her children for ideas or words about airplanes, for instance. Working all together, they would call out ideas associated with the theme, and Joan would write them on the whiteboard. Once they had covered the board with the various suggestions, she would ask them to write the poem. Try brainstorming like this for various tasks, such as a creative writing project, song titles for a puppet show, "the wackiest, tastiest, messiest dinner ever." (Author's note: The same caution applies to fluency as to originality—don't evaluate the ideas at this point. The creative thinking skill you are practicing is to freely come up with a large number of ideas.)

Another creative thinking skill is that of *flexibility*—the skill of finding a variety of approaches. Did you realize that, as you have considered the different kinds of curriculum available, you have been using flexibility? Try this one: you are going to go on a missions trip to the Ukraine; the cost is $2,500; and you are not supposed to fund it all through your own bank account. What are some options? How many ways can you think of to raise the funds? Be *flexible* in your approach.

The fourth creative thinking skill that many consider to be essential to the process of creativity is that of *elaboration*—to expand or embellish an idea, to develop it in detail. Take one of the ideas for an original use of a loaf of bread at the breakfast table and elaborate on it. Add the detail to make it more interesting, more creative. Or, consider the curriculum you are using. Ask your family how, specifically, you could make aspects of it more interesting (that ought to get some ideas flowing!).

And, finally, consider the skill of *imagination*, which is the ability to think beyond what is, beyond what can actually be seen, heard, or felt. Wilbur and Orville Wright had considerable skill in this area! They *imagined* their flying machine, based on what they knew about bicycles, before they built it. Thomas Edison *imagined* using electricity to produce light. Please note: imagination is NOT a substitute for diligent research and hard work. However, it IS the precursor to something new being invented. Authors like C.S. Lewis use their imagination to write a fictional story; composers (Beethoven, for instance) use their imagination to create a symphony; ground-breaking architects, such as Frank Lloyd Wright, use their imagination to produce intriguing structures. So, how can a family practice this skill?

One thing I do for practice is to imagine what my dogs are saying to each other.

"This is my dog bowl."
"Yes, but you moved."

"That is not the issue here. This is my dog bowl."
"Yes, but you moved."
And so on . . .

Some other ideas for practicing imagination could include: imagine how we would spend $100 if it were left in our mailbox; imagine what it would be like to be on the first spaceship to Mars; imagine living in a treehouse; imagine what it would have been like to be one of Jesus' disciples while He walked on the earth; imagine living on a submarine under the polar ice cap. The sky is the limit for imagining, as long as you haven't actually had the experience.

CRITICAL THINKING SKILLS

On the other side of higher-level thinking are critical thinking skills. Critical thinking skills involve reasoning, organizing, decision-making, and evaluating. It is *not* creating new ideas; it is working with ideas that already exist. As was stated at the opening of this section, critical thinking allows one to move from a group of possibilities toward a solution, a goal, or a result.

Here, we are presenting seven forms of critical thinking for families to practice. Again, you will recognize these from daily life. Just as practice in creative thinking skills eventually leads to creative problem solving, so practice in critical thinking skills will begin to impact real-life situations.

To begin, try your hand at the skill of *planning*, which means to figure out a method for doing, making, or arranging. Think about how you can utilize this particular thinking skill in your family—plan a treasure hunt (complete with maps); plan an inexpensive vacation (always high motivation for this one); devise a plan for each one in the family to choose a family activity. Practicing a thinking skill does not have to be hard—think of something your family would enjoy *planning*! Have fun!

DIANA'S MAXIM: Thinking doesn't have to be painful!!

A valuable skill for adults (and those teens wishing to attain that state) is *prevention*: to forestall in anticipation of something, to make impossible by prior action. If you have very small children, you have already been using this thinking skill by baby-proofing your house! Other prevention exercises for you to consider are: "How to arrange my schedule so that nothing important is left out;" "How to prevent procrastination;" "How to avoid making unnecessary trips to the grocery store everyday;" "How to ensure that our family time is fun for everyone;" among others. If you open this up to family discussion, you will be amazed at how capable your children are—and how enjoyable it is to practice thinking!

Next, let us consider the critical thinking skill of *analysis*—breaking something into its component parts and examining these parts to understand their nature, function, and interrelationship. If you look for the underlying worldview, or the author's bias, or the hidden propaganda in a book, movie, interview, etc., you will be asking the questions of analysis:

- *what is new to me in this?*
- *what part of this is true?*
- *is there anything unproven or illogical in this?*
- *is there anything useful in this?*
- *is there anything harmful in this?*
- *should I discard any part of this?*
- *should I retain any part of this?*

Among my children's friends, I have developed somewhat of a reputation—many of them consider me to be a very unpopular addition to video night! Why? Because I analyze every video for worldview, purpose, propaganda, etc. One of Melody's close friends said, *"Why can't your mom just watch the movie for fun? She makes me use my brain too much when I just want to veg."*

Aha! Good question. Why should we use our brains to analyze when we read, watch, or listen? Because there is much "out there" that is illogical, irrational, unproven, unhealthy, and wrong. If we are not watching for it, we could swallow those ideas whole.

To practice analysis, try debating both sides of this question: "Homeschool teens should be required to take a GED before they can graduate." To do this, you will have to break down the issue into its various parts. What is a GED? Why do people normally take it? Why would someone want a homeschool teen to take this test? Who would want a homeschool teen to take this test? Is it a good indicator of learning? Is it a faulty indicator of learning? By examining the various parts of the issue, you are enabled to debate, which will sharpen your analyzing, which improves your thinking.

The next critical thinking skill is one of my particular favorites. *Compare and contrast* means: recognizing the similarities and differences between things. During Isaac's homeschool high school, we asked him to read Baroness Orczy's *Scarlet Pimpernel* and Charles Dickens's *A Tale of Two Cities*. Each of these books deals with the time period of the French Revolution and the Reign of Terror; however, they have quite a different flavor. So, Isaac's assignment was to compare and contrast the two. If you want to start simple, compare and contrast an orange and an apple. How are they similar? How are they different? Think about a bicycle and an airplane. How many similarities can you discover between these two? How many differences? You could actually make a game out of this for your family and give a prize for the one who comes up with the most similarities and another prize for the most differences.

Now, consider the critical thinking skill called *decision-making*—the ability to examine the various alternatives and options in order to decide on a course of action. You are using this skill when you list out the "pro's" and "con's" in order to make an informed decision about something. Try out your family's decision-making ability over acquiring a dachshund. What are some of the areas you would have to consider? Cost, care, value, rewards, and hassles are all important in this decision. (By the way, if having a dachshund leaves you cold, feel free to substitute golden retriever, Siamese cat, Tennessee Walker, goldfish, parrot, elephant, whale, etc.)

An excellent exercise in critical thinking is to watch for *propaganda*—that which is used to persuade people based on opinions and unsubstantiated ideas. Have you ever seen movie stars or athletes interviewed about their thoughts on an upcoming election? We have to stop and think about what qualifications they bring to an area. Though they might be excellent in their own field, do they know anything about politics? Are they qualified to influence our decisions? Or, is it propaganda used by a particular political party for the purposes of influencing unthinking people to vote for their candidate? There are books available in the library that will teach you how to recognize and identify propaganda.

Finally, look at the very necessary skill of *evaluation*—judging, evaluating, or appraising something based on a predetermined set of criteria. As Christians, when we are called upon to make an evaluation of something dealing with worldview, morals, or character, we have a standard, a predetermined set of criteria—the Bible. With God's Word as our standard, we have an objective, never-changing, eternal measuring rod by which to evaluate or judge.

For instance, if you watch a movie that romanticizes and glorifies adultery (such as *Out of Africa*), you can evaluate the content of the story in light of the Bible. If you see someone beating a dog, you can judge the wrongness of that action based on the Bible. If you hear a speaker describe his or her perspective (which flows out of their worldview), you can appraise the rightness or wrongness according to the standard of God's Word.

Here are some exercises for you to try as you practice evaluating: consider the ideas you found for an original use for a loaf of bread and evaluate. Evaluate these ideas based on a standard of taste buds and eye-appeal. Try reading aloud an article from a magazine and having the members of your family evaluate what they hear. You will want a standard for evaluation, so if the article has to do with child-rearing principles, evaluate it against the Bible. If it has to do with raising vegetables, consult a vegetable-growers encyclopedia and decide if the article has merit. You could watch a play, listen to a concert, visit a museum, or study a painting and then evaluate what you just experienced. Remember, evaluation requires a standard, a set of criteria.

Here are some questions to ask:

- *How professional was the technical aspect of this event, place, or thing?*
- *Do you agree with what you saw? Why or why not?*
- *How important to your family is this event, place, or thing? Why?*
- *Does this event, place, or thing have value to the Church? To the nation? To the world?*

Do you remember what your music teacher told you about improving on your instrument? It is the same principle with thinking: practice, practice, practice!

QUESTIONABLE BEHAVIOR

As homeschoolers, we should be always seeking to find balance on the continuum of *staying on target* as opposed to *exploration*. If we teach our children that they simply need to "check it off the list," that will slowly but surely deaden their lively curiosity. On the other hand, if we *only* follow their curiosity, our children will not gain basic-level proficiency in foundational subjects. So, we need to be wise in our thinking about this issue. It is imperative that our children have their questions answered, that they are allowed to explore the things they are curious about, that they seek to truly understand the *"why?"* WHILE at the same time they are practicing the art of staying on task, being diligent, and not allowing distractions to keep them from finishing.

How does one do that? If we consider a see-saw, it may give us a visual picture that will help. If we are too heavy on one side of a see-saw, we'll sit on the ground forever. If we are flighty on the other side of the see-saw, we'll stay airborne and never accomplish anything on earth. The best way is to have a bit of both. Stay fairly well-matched on the see-saw, and you can go for a flight *and* also land on earth.

In homeschooling, this means to examine yourself. Are you always saying, *"No, I don't have time for that,"* or *"I don't know the answer,"* or *"Will you please stop asking me questions and get back to work?"* Are your children content to merely answer the questions in the back of the book with no discussion, no questions, no running to you with, *"Mom, look at what I just learned!?"* If so, you MUST move toward the other side of the see-saw. You MUST rekindle their curiosity. You MUST get them asking questions.

If, on the other hand, your children never finish a page of math, never complete a history project, never finish the science experiment, never hand in the creative writing assignment, never accomplish any of the tasks because they are always off following rabbit trails, you need to move in the opposite direction on the see-saw. You MUST explain to them how real life requires finishing certain tasks. You MUST help them learn the skill of staying on target. You MUST get them balanced in their approach to learning.

Having said all that about balance, let us now turn to one of the most valuable thinking skills in our possession—*curiosity*. Curiosity is characterized by the four-year-old in his constant query, *"Why?"* If we will work with our children's natural curiosity, rather than squelching it, they will be head and shoulders above most people these days in higher-level thinking. Teach your children to ask, *"why?"* and you will have given them one of the most significant tools in the thinking trade.

So, how do we nurture that in our children and ourselves? First, look for every opportunity that comes your way to ask appropriate questions of people you meet.

"Where did you grow up?"
"What was it like to live in that part of the world?"
"What made you decide to go into that kind of business?"
"What do you enjoy most about your career?"
"What is your favorite thing to do when you have time?"

Secondly, ask questions about things you don't understand.

"Why is the flag flying at half-mast?"
"Why do the leaves change color in fall?"
"Why does oatmeal set up like cement if you leave it too long?"

"Why does God love us so much?"

Thirdly, ask questions about what you read, hear, or see.

"Why does that speaker believe that children should be under strict control?"
"Why does that author write that his academic viewpoint is the only
Biblical perspective?"
"Why does that artist consider this statue a representation of Christian art?"

If you don't know the answer, ask a question. If you disagree with the author/speaker/professor, ask a question. If you want to provoke someone to think beyond their boundaries, ask a question. A good teacher will ask questions not only to discover what the students know, but also to discover how they think, and sometimes a particularly wise teacher will ask questions to help the students think through issues and come to their own understanding. Asking the questions does not always mean finding the answers. However, when we ask questions, we will often learn something new, and we will usually think more deeply.

If we don't understand something, asking may make the difference between "getting it" or not. Make it a practice to ask, ask, ask.

Got it? Practice, practice, practice . . . ask, ask, ask. Good!

OUT OF THE BOX CURRICULUM

Here is a final thought on our subject of "Don't Check Your Brains at the Door!" Be very careful to think clearly about the kind of curriculum you are using with your children, both younger AND older. As we have travelled for the past dozen years to homeschool conventions, we have seen the tendency for parents, who have allowed their younger children to delight themselves in what they were learning to suddenly change into harsh task masters when their children get to high school years. There seems to be a fear that if they don't "get serious," their children will never make it as adults, never get into a university, or never get a good-paying job.

In order to give a standard against which you can evaluate your curriculum choices, let us consider the latest research findings on the best way to learn. First, a quick peek at how most of us were taught, which is undoubtedly the WORST way to try to learn.

- *First step: Present material through lecture or textbook*
- *Second step: Leave student to study on his own*
- *Third step: Test material*
- *Fourth step: Find out what they DON'T know, "Look, Mom, I only missed three!"*

Now take a gander at what researchers on the brain and on learning have discovered about the most effective ways to learn.

- *First step: Listening (reading, talking)*
- *Second step: Exploring (asking questions)*
- *Third step: Discovering (questions answered, Aha! moments)*
- *Fourth step: Practicing (draw it, write it, cook it, dance it, sing it, act it)*
- *Fifth step: Owning (teach it, use it)*

Regardless of the brand name of the curriculum you are using, you *must* allow the space and time and opportunity to really think through what is being learned; to really process by asking questions and experimenting; to interact with the material by writing it, dancing it, singing it; to truly own the material by using it regularly or by teaching it to someone else.

The preliminary requirement in this cutting-edge understanding of the best way to learn is time. It takes time to read, to ask questions, to explore the possible answers of the questions, to discover the answers, to interact with what is being learned, and to teach others. Time?

"But we have SO much to do!"

I know you have. Still the question is will your teens finish high school with a checklist marked off and little memory of what they learned (how much of what you learned in high school is still with you today?), OR will they finish with an amazing grasp of the materials they have studied, a voracious hunger and enthusiasm for learning, and an equipping with the knowledge and understanding necessary to pursue the next step in their lives?

Time is limited—so choose wisely and choose well! You can't do it all—so do what is best!

The first step in excellent learning is *listening*. We can listen by reading someone else's words in a book, letter, or magazine or by hearing someone speak (live or on tape). Now, when you yourself think about reading something, do you most enjoy reading a dry, boring book that puts you to sleep in five minutes, OR a fascinating, can't-put-it-down, eyewitness kind of book? When you listen to someone, do you most enjoy listening to a lecturer who speaks with a monotone, no inflections, and no eye-contact kind of approach OR a lively, enthusiastic kind of person with lots of stories?

I am assuming that you chose the second selection in each option! Your children are no different. Allow them the joy of learning through good books and good tapes. If you are using a high school English Literature textbook, and it has snippets of a classic book to dissect, go to the library and get the real book! Let your teen read the real thing, and *then* dissect or discuss or compare. Pursue other enjoyable, educational ventures as they come along. For instance, if the book happens to be *Pride and Prejudice*, watch the excellent version of it on video. If you are studying World War II, don't depend solely on the committee-written textbook version of what happened. Instead, find a veteran in your local area that your teen can interview (prepare a bit beforehand, so you'll know the right questions to ask to elicit the most information and the best stories). Adding appropriate videos such as *The Longest Day* to your World War II study will also bring this time period to life! If you are studying a foreign language, there is nothing more motivating and helpful than meeting people who speak that language as their native tongue. They will display such ease around a language that is causing you such work, which will be a model of how people really can readily and easily speak that particular language.

So, listen! Find the best sources to listen to, and then listen.

The second step is **explore**. You have been listening to books, to people, to tapes, to videos. Normally, if the books, people, tapes, and videos are interesting, the student will have all kinds of questions about what is being said.

"What if . . . ?" "Why not . . . ?" "Did you . . . ?" "How did it feel . . . ?" "Where else . . . ?"

This is an incredibly powerful tool in the motivated-to-learn toolkit. Allow your students the freedom, the time, and the safe place to ask questions, even difficult questions, even impossible questions. But don't stop with just letting them ask the questions; begin to explore the possible answers. Explore whether your questions have knowable answers or merely speculative answers.

When I created the Digging Deeper world history study guides to go with my tape series, *What in the World's Going on Here?*, I included questions designed to get the mental juices flowing as students read the recommended

CHECK YOUR BRAINS AT THE DOOR!

DON'T CHECK YOUR BRAINS AT THE DOOR!

resources. Occasionally, I receive a telephone call like this one from a very distraught mother:

> *"Excuse me, but I think my curriculum guide is missing some pages?"*
> *"Really?"*
> *"Yes, you see, you've got these questions, but there are no answers at the back of the book!"*
> *"Ah, yes."*
> *"Well, I don't know what to do! I don't know the answers to those questions!!"*
> *"What questions are troubling you?"*
> *"Well, for instance, how am I supposed to know which of Adam's names for animals are still in use?!"*
> *"Excellent question. Can you think of any resource book that would give the answer?"*
> *"No!"*
> *"That's right. There is NO way to know what remains of Adam's names, since we don't know for sure what language he spoke. However, I wanted to get you and your children thinking and asking questions. If this helps them to consider the difference between what we can know for sure and what we can just imagine and speculate upon, I will have accomplished part of my purpose."*
> Silence. *"Um, but do you think you could add the answers to the back of the book?"*

Explore the possibilities! Ask the questions! Find out whether the answers are knowable or mere speculation! Take the time! It will pay rich dividends in your students' understanding and thinking skills.

The third step in this learning process is *discovery*. Discovering the answers is an amazingly fruitful moment in our education. Actually, when Bill was in teacher training at the university to become a public school teacher, he learned that the worst way to have a student learn was through the lecture method, while the best way to learn was to have the student *discover* the answers for themselves. (Notice that this information has not yet sifted through to most institutional learning structures!)

Discovery is powerful, memorable, and can even be life-changing. To show you what I mean, here are excerpts from an article entitled, "A Whole New World," written by Catherine Sandbrook of New Zealand about her experiences using *Ancient Civilizations and the Bible*:

147

REAPING THE HARVEST

Like Alice ducking down a rabbit hole and finding herself in a whole new (crazy, illogical) world, we ducked into our first unit for the year and were lost in a fascinating (wonderful, logical) world, which, unlike Alice, we didn't really want to get out of. It's become an investigation that will continue to intrigue and thrill us all our lives and, I suspect, into eternity. We started studying "Creation" . . .

It was a revelation to me to realize my children would have a far more accurate and tantalizing picture of the first people of history than I'd ever had. They could lay good foundations in theology and anthropology. They could wrestle with the origin and effects of man's sinfulness—moral issues. They could also have a more comprehensive grasp of science through Genesis and creation from the very first verse . . . In studying the Periodic Table, our older children got so excited (rather to my astonishment) in peering through the complexity to see patterns and connections that only an extremely brilliant and orderly mind could think of. Glimpsing God through the Periodic Table was an unexpected surprise for us all. (Shouldn't have been.) As were some of our chemical experiments, but we made good carbon, and we can make mothballs not only smell but also cover every piece of furniture in the living room with volcanic-like ash . . .

In their creative endeavors, our children show one of the wonderful attributes of their Creator, a characteristic not found in any animal. So in our unit we allowed space for creative activities—some formal, some independent. Creation, of course, is a fabulous topic for this. We dabbled in modeling clay, edible clay, plaster of Paris, and soap carvings . . . I allowed extra space for our own creative interests, mine included. Then we had delightful times with Diana Waring's suggestions in creative writing and games, puns and ideas, like renaming the animals. Can you guess what a yingying is, a houseback, or a hopdog, a beddybyefly, a thunderwalk, or a wise-guy? We also admired the creations of artists, craftsmen, sculptors, and composers. We all chose our favorite parts from Haydn's oratorio, The Creation. We learnt new hymns and grew to love best of all, This Is My Father's World.

Our 2–3 week unit study became 2–3 terms! I began to wonder how we would ever get out of this topic of Creation. Studying God's Creation is endless! . . . When we dived into our unit study on Creation, I had no idea of how much I'd learn myself and in such unexpected areas, nor of how exciting it would be.

Most of all, we never realized that the rest of our lives will be seen through a "looking glass"—this is our Creator's world.

Discovery takes . . . (can you guess?) . . . *time.* Discovery means time to think, time to research, time to experiment, time to consider.

Listen, explore, discover! Take the time! It's worth it.

The fourth step is **practice.** It might be restated as:
- *play with it*
- *work with it*
- *manipulate it*
- *draw it*
- *sing it*
- *act it*
- *dance it*
- *storytell it*
- *figure it*
- *cook it*

Do you remember copying in your notebook fifty times, *"I will not talk in class. I will not talk in class . . ."*

The reason why a teacher has a student write something fifty times is so they will remember it. It is not fun, but it is fairly effective at drilling something into our memory. By starting with the principle of doing something over and over and then adding our creative thinking, we arrive at this concept of *practice.*

Practice what you have just learned or discovered or explored through various means, like writing a newspaper article about it, composing a song about it to the tune of *Deck the Halls*, choreographing an interpretive dance that demonstrates the knowledge, producing a theatrical performance about it, rendering this information with oil paints, gathering a group of younger siblings and doing a puppet show to display what has been learned, coloring geometric forms to illustrate the subject, cooking foods to elicit the flavors of your newly-learned information. The more ways you find to practice something, the more your mind will retain the information. The more ways you find to demonstrate what you have learned, the more you will understand it.

Let it be interesting, enjoyable, and fun! *"Did you just say fun? Why does it need to be fun?"* There are very practical reasons. Recent research on the brain shows that there are actually positive chemical reasons for enjoying what you learn:

> "Pulitzer Prize-winning science writer Ronald Kotulak describes acetyl-choline as "the oil that makes the memory machine function. When it dries up, the machine freezes."
>
> —*The Learning Revolution* by Dryden and Vos

What causes acetylcholine to be released in our brains? Positive, happy emotions cause the release of endorphins, and they in turn trigger the release of acetylcholine. When a student is enjoying what is being learned, the brain has a greater ability to actually store the new information. Isn't that something to remember?!

OK. Listen, explore, discover . . . practice, practice, practice.

The final step in this effective recipe for successful learning is to *own it*. When you own information, you are able to teach others. Teaching someone else is one of the most effective ways of really learning something. (Could that be why so many homeschool parents are learning so much more than we did when we were in school?)

When you own it, you are also able to use the knowledge in various situations (without having to always look it up!). For instance, when you own the knowledge of how to spell "encyclopedia," you can not only teach it to someone else, but you can also write it confidently and test someone else on their ability to spell it. Once you own the spelling of that word, you won't easily forget it.

For me, "encyclopedia" was imprinted on my brain through Jiminy Cricket's song on the old Walt Disney show.

"ENC-YC-LO-PEDIA"

It takes no effort now for me to own the spelling of this word. And that is the goal we want our students to attain in spelling, mathematics, history, and all that they pursue. We want them to own the knowledge they are learning. Otherwise, they haven't really learned it, have they?

As we consider our curriculum, let us refuse to climb into the box, let us not be content to do unto our students what was done to us: lecture, study, test, pass/fail. Instead, let us use the marvelous brains God has bestowed on us all—breaking out of the box so that our students can actually learn, think, and create. May we use our critical and creative thinking skills and our understanding of worldview issues to build bridges rather than walls, while at the same time defending our position through careful attention to the standard of God's Word.

In other words, may we all grow to be more like the Bereans and less like sheep!

RECOMMENDED RESOURCES

Simple Tools for Brain Surgery (video) by Bill Jack
Learn the four killer questions to use in dialoguing with non-Christians. We have used this in group discussions with adults as well as our own family.

The Deadliest Monster by Jeff Baldwin
What do *Frankenstein* and *Dr. Jekyll and Mr. Hyde* have in common? They are both illustrative of worldviews! In Jeff Baldwin's wonderful book, he creates a pictorial understanding of worldview issues. Highly recommended!

Worldview and Apologetics Lecture Series by Worldview Academy
Listen to Bill Jack, Jeff Baldwin, Randy Sims, and Todd Kent as they talk to audiences of young people about worldview topics. It will be eye-opening.

The Fallacy Detective by Nathaniel Bluedorn and Hans Bluedorn
Subtitled, "Thirty-Six Lessons on How to Recognize Bad Reasoning," this excellent book by homeschoolers for homeschoolers will give an introductory taste of higher-level critical thinking skills. Great discussion tool!

How Should We Then Live? by Dr. Francis Schaeffer
As noted previously, this is the book and video series that gave many Christians their first understanding of the importance and historical impact that worldview has had on culture.

Understanding the Times (abridged) by Dr. David Noebel
Learn more about the worldviews listed briefly in this chapter. I highly recommend this book!

REAPING THE HARVEST

Worldviews of the Western World by David Quine
This high school-level curriculum is designed to give advanced students a thorough grasp of the way various worldviews have shaped the Western world. It includes philosophy, science, history, literature, and more.

Reasonable Faith: The Scientific Case for Christianity by Dr. Jay L. Wile
Written from a scientific basis, this is an excellent book for learning and understanding the debate that rages between those who think science disproves God and those who see that science affirms God's Word. Highly recommended!

The New Evidence that Demands a Verdict by Josh McDowell
Combining his earlier titles, *Evidence I* and *II*, this version of Josh McDowell's invaluable work is user-friendly, well-documented, and absolutely essential in the area of apologetics (knowing why we believe what we believe and being able to defend it). Highly recommended!

PART THREE
REAPING THE HARVEST

Who's in Charge Here?

Tom Bragg of YWAM Publishing is simply one of the most interesting folks I have ever met. He is a wonderful servant of God and a fantastic publisher to boot. Because of his work with an international missions publishing company, he travels to different parts of the world and communicates with people of many nations, who are all doing fascinating stuff in the Kingdom of God. Every conversation with Tom is an eye-opening, encouraging, make-you-think-big, bird's-eye-view of what's happening around the world. Every chat with Tom leaves one exclaiming, *"Wow! God is doing that?!"* You get the idea.

In one of these discussions, our talk turned to the homeschooling phenomenon in the U.S., Canada, and the growing interest around the world. Since Bill and I had chosen to follow this philosophy of parenting and homeschooling near the beginning of this movement, Tom was interested to ask us questions and gain insights. It was a fun dialogue—there is nothing like having an interested and sympathetic party ask you questions about your favorite subject!

Tom began to get really excited as we talked, and I could see that he had something significant to share.

> *"You know, I was just speaking the other day with Dave Boyd from the University of the Nations about homeschooling. In our conversation, it came out that both of us believe that God Himself is behind this, raising up a whole group of stable, discipled young people to go to the nations! This is powerful!!"*

For a brief moment, I had the most amazing sense that God had pulled back a bit of the "curtain," and that I was being given a glimpse into the eternal workings of His plans and purposes. This phenomenon was NOT merely the result of a group of folks coming up with an idea that snowballed. This was God's idea . . . not ours but His.

Wow! It was stunning! Just think—in our simple act of homeschooling, we are a part of a *move of God*. (I thought that only happened to people in history!!)

OUR JOURNAL

When Bill and I took our family to New Zealand to attend a YWAM Family Ministries DTS, I thought it was going to be a wonderful break from the merry-go-round of normal life, a wee vacation from the ordinary, a long time to sit and bask in God's presence. I was desperately in need of such a break, and I looked forward to it with great anticipation.

However, what I saw as "time off," God saw as time to deepen, change, fix, and heal. It was as if, according to our school leader, we had offered God three months of our undivided attention, and He wasn't going to waste a minute of it! The deep and penetrating work of God began the first day of class with the first speaker. Her name was Carolyn Chisholm, and her word to us that day was "relinquishment." Carolyn humbly and poignantly shared with the class her own life story, how God had taught her to relinquish to Him that which she held most dear. Relinquishment does not mean walking away from something, it means releasing in one's heart the ownership of the things we hold dearest—relationships, rights, material possessions, plans, goals—and then letting God be God, free to do what He pleases with what we have.

Oh, my. Her illustrations sent an arrow through my heart, and I wept as if I would never stop. This was the first day, mind you. There was much, much more to come. Over the course of the first ten weeks, the Lord dealt with all kinds of attitudes, memories, wounds, sins, and more in my life. It was almost normal to expect Him to put His finger on yet another heretofore unnoticed problem. But during the tenth week, God brought me face-to-face with the deepest motivations and fears in my life.

We were in the midst of a lovely time of worshipping the Lord. It was a precious moment, filled with the sense of His nearness and His goodness. I had never felt so loved by God in my entire life. At that moment, one of the leaders leaned over to me and whispered, *"Diana, it is safe to trust God with your treasures."* A bolt of lightning struck my soul, as I was confronted with the eternal God asking me to fully trust Him with my children and my husband. It was the breathtakingly clear consummation of the first day's message: would I relinquish into His loving care those I loved most in the world?

I couldn't even breathe. Every ounce of my being silently cried out in agony, *"No! You can't have them,"* because I knew that He was asking for a permanent transfer of ownership. As thoughts and emotions swirled around me in a cataclysmic storm, it suddenly became clear that my children were my source of identity, my source of career, my defense from being alone in this world. It wasn't just maternal love, it had become maternal pride and personal need, as well. God wasn't just asking me to relinquish my family, He was asking me to relinquish my identity, career, and buffer zone.

Agonizing moments passed as it became obvious that He was asking for *everything*. All of the messages and teachers from the previous weeks of class had shown us again and again and again that He was Love Incarnate, that He was trustworthy and true, that He was goodness itself. That weighed against my fears of losing everything, and it helped me to at last say, *"Yes, Lord."*

However, relinquishing did not bring rejoicing at that moment. I was left with the sense that everything in my life was in a little pile of ashes consumed by the request of God. I left the room empty and unaware of the freedom God was bringing to my life. Freedom, you ask? Yes, freedom from the overpowering, disabling fear I had always known. It is the freedom to let my children follow God, obey His direction, and drive their cars(!) without the worrying. It is the freedom to face their graduation from homeschool without the aching emptiness of "what will I do now?" It is the freedom to watch them apply to distant universities and travel to other nations without succumbing to the fear of "who will fill my time and keep me company." It is the life-changing freedom of recognizing who's in charge and of releasing my children into His loving hands.

In His great wisdom and mercy, God prepared me to let go.

YIKES! I DIDN'T KNOW IT WAS YOU!

What were you doing the day before the New Millennium? Were you busily collecting jugs of water and bags of freeze-dried celery? If we had been in the U.S., we would have probably been doing the same thing, but since we were at a Christian camp in New Zealand, we just sat back and waited to see what was going to happen.

This camp was happily situated in the beautiful city of Gisborne—the first city in the world to see the dawn of the New Millennium. The organizers had done a bang-up job of bringing world-class Christian speakers and musicians for this six-day event, and we were thrilled to be there. One of the speakers was a man I had heard speak twenty-four years prior, and even way-back-when he had been one of the best around. Winkey Pratney was at the top of the list of speakers I wanted to hear that weekend, and the message he brought changed my life.

The Scripture Winkey preached from was Psalm 24:1:

"The earth is the LORD'S, and all its fullness, The world and those who dwell therein."

As the audience sat on plastic chairs and the ground, he began to give us a picture of what this Scripture indicated.

"Everything in the WORLD belongs to God. All of it. Every atom of it. Every place in the world, every person in the world—they all belong to God. Whether they recognize it or not, this is the reality according to Psalm 24:1."

To help us understand a wee bit of the depth and breadth of this Scripture, Winkey took us to the Gospel of Mark (Mark 4:35–41) for an amazing look at how the earth truly is the Lord's. Do you remember the story about Jesus and His disciples sailing at night across a lake when a fierce storm arose? The disciples—several of them professional fishermen and well acquainted with the potentialities of storms—freaked!! They woke Him out of a sound sleep with the words, *"Teacher, do You not care that we are* perishing?!"

Winkey really brought this story alive for us, as he pointed out that these manly men would not have been so worked up if it had been a mere gust. Rather, the howling wind was wreaking destruction, the foaming water was already filling the boat to dangerous levels, and they knew that at any moment they would be going down. In absolute panic, they turned to Jesus. In their wildest imagination, they could not have known what He was about to do.

"The earth is the LORD'S, and all its fullness, The world and those who dwell therein."

Jesus rose up in the midst of that maniacal storm and *rebuked* the wind and said to the sea, *"Peace, be still!"* With the help of Winkey's spellbinding storytelling ability, we were able to see the scene as eyewitnesses.

Here was the Lord Himself, the Creator of that very same wind and sea. He had been peacefully sleeping, and as Winkey surmised, these two havoc-wreaking forces must not have seen Him—or else they wouldn't have tried to sink the vessel! When Jesus stood and rebuked it, we could almost hear this powerful wind—which moments before had done its very best to frighten the wits out of the insignificant humans in its power—say in a shocked voice, *"Yikes, I didn't know YOU were in the boat!"* The wind CEASED! It was gone. It fled the scene like a naughty dog caught in the act. As Jesus turned His eye on the sea and told it (as only a parent can), *"BE QUIET!"* the churning sea frantically said, *"Oops . . . Um . . . Sorry . . . Big Mistake!"* and went immediately calm.

In a moment, the forces of nature went from all-out attack to complete submission. The disciples looked at each other in *exceeding* fear and said to themselves, *"Who IS this guy?!"* You see, not one human on the face of the globe has this kind of power. *No one* can command the wind and the sea. But the earth is the LORD's. It all belongs to Him, and He *can* rebuke the wind and calm the sea. The earth is the LORD's.

Selah.

How did Winkey's teaching change my life? It helped me understand on a deeper level than ever before that God IS God, no matter where we go, no matter who we meet, no matter what we experience. And even more important for my perspective as a mom, God IS God, no matter where my children go, no matter who they meet, no matter what they experience. The same Lord who rebuked the wind and calmed the sea walks with us in our daily lives—in OUR DAILY LIVES!

This is the first of three foundational understandings of our faith and of our parenting:

❶ *We live in a world that belongs to God—the one True God, the Judeo-Christian God. In other words, He's in charge here.*

Hmm. So, if the entire world belongs to God, if our God is the Lord over heaven and earth, how does that impact our homeschooling endeavors? What changes in our attitude when our eyes are lifted to a higher altitude?

For me, it has put everything into perspective. The *really* important subjects are no longer math, science, history, literature . . . but humility, obedience, faithfulness . . . before the Lord. *This is not a case of "either/or." This is "both/and," though in the right order!* Restated, this is not a case of academics OR character. It is both academics AND character, but character changes position and takes the lead: character AND academics. For instance, character leading academics would mean to take a math test without cheating or lying about the results; to write a great language arts paper without plagiarizing the text; to redo an experiment until the results are accurate without being fixed; to read the entire book before writing the report. If sibling rivalry erupts during homeschool time, the homeschool mom can (and should) take the time to deal with the problem before getting back to the history lesson. Without the character, without the Christian discipleship, our children may end up educated fools. The *really* important goals of homeschooling are no longer an impressive university, a high-paying job, or an ability to impress people with big words used correctly but God-breathed Christianity lived out in a life of service to the Lord.

OK. To help firmly establish this in our brains, we will use a little exercise. I will shout the question, and you shout the response—kind of a "go, team, go" coaching technique. Ready?

As homeschooling parents, are we merely raising our children to:

Win a scholarship to a brand name university? **NO!**

Land a job with a six-figure income? **NO!**

Use six-syllable words that no one understands? **NO!**

Give us bragging rights? **Well, maybe!**

Is there more to life than this? **YES!**

What is it? **READ ON!**

YA GOTTA SERVE SOMEBODY

Over and over again in the Scriptures, we are given a God's-eye perspective on true truth and real reality. It tells us, in no uncertain terms, that we are not in charge. Though we would like to think we are "masters of our own destiny," the Bible flatly denies that this is the case. In fact, Jesus told many parables that illustrate the fact that, like it or not, rich or poor, young or old, male or female, black or white, educated or illiterate, we are all servants. SERVANTS? That's right—servants.

The question must then arise,

"Who is my master?"

For non-Christians, the answer is: whatever you idolize. Whatever you give yourselves to—money, power, fame, success, etc. We have all seen this: a workaholic filling every hour with an unmatched devotion to clawing their way to the top of the heap. They have been mastered by their desire. But the master is not a kindhearted, compassionate, wise, patient, loving, selfless master. Far from it!

For Christians, the answer is clear. We, too, are "mastered by our Desire"—the Desire of Nations, Jesus Christ. We are His servants. The King James Bible describes these two states of servanthood in Romans 6:16, 18:

"Know ye not, that to whom ye yield yourselves servants to obey, his servants ye are to whom ye obey; whether of sin unto death, or of obedience unto righteousness? . . . Being then made free from sin, ye became the servants of righteousness."

Praise the Lord! We are now servants of righteousness, servants of the Righteous One, servants to a Master who *IS* kindhearted, compassionate, wise, patient, loving, selfless, and good in every way! He is our Lord and Master in a personal, all-encompassing, all-of-life kind of way.

This leads us to the second foundational understanding of our faith and parenting:

❷ *As followers of Jesus Christ, we do not belong to ourselves—we belong to God. In other words, He is the Master; we are the servants.*

1 Corinthians 6:19–20 tells us:

"Or do you not know that your body is the temple of the Holy Spirit who is in you, whom you have from God, and you are not your own? For you were bought at a price; therefore glorify God in your body and in your spirit, which are God's."

We were bought with a price, an amazing price, the death of God's own Son. You know, in our society, we gauge the value of an object by what someone is willing to pay for it. Fourteen-carat gold rings are *far* more valuable than Cracker Jack-box rings and, therefore, cost *far* more.

Just sit and consider this for a moment: Jesus gave His very life to purchase us. What incredible value we must have in His eyes!! AND, of course, let's not miss the other significant point here: we've been bought.

Bought? Like a slave or something? Yes. Bought out of the slavery of sin and death, out of the kingdom of darkness and brought into the Kingdom of God. (The *really* incredible news is that we're not just servants, we've also been adopted into the Family—joint heirs with Jesus!)

REAPING THE HARVEST

Since most of us don't have a clue what it is to be a servant (or to have a servant for that matter), consider how Jesus described the normal course of events in the life of a servant.

> *"And which of you, having a servant plowing or tending sheep, will say to him when he has come in from the field, 'Come at once and sit down to eat'? But will he not rather say to him, 'Prepare something for my supper, and gird yourself and serve me till I have eaten and drunk, and afterward you will eat and drink'? Does he thank that servant because he did the things that were commanded him? I think not . . ."*
>
> —Luke 17:7–9

Whoa. That goes against the grain, doesn't it? Seems sort of unsporting, unchristian even! Isn't it interesting that those listening didn't let out a string of protests, form a "Servants Union," and hold up picket signs declaring, "Unfair Servant Practices!" after Jesus said this. The reason why they didn't was because He described servanthood as it truly was experienced in those days. This was not an earthshaking change of job description.

So from this portrait of servanthood what can we discover?

1) *Servants do what the master tells them.*
2) *Servants serve the master.*
3) *Servants don't pursue their own interests, they pursue the interests of the master.*

"Application?" you ask. *"For us as people and as parents?"*

1) *We need to do what the Master tells us. (obedience)*
   a) *We need to let our young adult children do what the Master tells them.*
   b) *We need to trust the Master to know what He's doing in their lives.*
2) *We need to serve the Master. (humility)*
   a) *We need to let our young adult children serve the Master.*
   b) *We need to trust the Master to know what He's doing in their lives.*
3) *We need to pursue our Master's interests, not our own. (faithfulness)*
   a) *We need to let our young adult children pursue the Master's interests, not OUR OWN!*
   b) *We need to trust the Master to know what He's doing in their lives.*

Finally, we must consider whether "what is good for the goose is good for the gander," so to say—whether what is true for us as servants was true for the Son of God Himself. Examine what Jesus told His followers in this important passage from Mark 10:42–45:

> *"You know that those who are considered rulers over the Gentiles lord it over them, and their great ones exercise authority over them. Yet it shall not be so among you; but whoever desires to become great among you shall be your servant. And whoever of you desires to be first shall be slave of all. For even the Son of Man did not come to be served, but to serve, and to give His life a ransom for many."*

What was good for Jesus is good for us—we also are here to serve.

To recap: everything belongs to God; we belong to God; and we are in the position of servants. Who's in charge here? God is. Who's in charge of our children? God is.

OK. Let's try our little "go, team, go" exercise again.

As homeschooling parents, are we merely raising our children to:
Win a scholarship to a brand name university? **NO!**
Land a job with a six-figure income? **NO!**
Use six-syllable words that no one understands? **NO!**
Give us bragging rights? **Well, maybe!**
Is there more to life than this? **YES!**
What is it? **SERVANTHOOD!**
Job Description? **READ ON!**

REPRESENTATION WITHOUT TAXATION

After the September 11th attacks on the United States, we were all in dry-mouthed shock and grieving disbelief. What on earth would the United States do in the face of such atrocities? How could it pursue a course of action in that area of the world where Americans are legislatively hated? Since Bill and I were travelling during that world-shaking time, we took the opportunity to watch CNN coverage every night in our hotel room. The international news poured forth like a faucet that had blown its gaskets. Every aspect of both the horror of overwhelming loss of life in New York, Washington, and Pennsylvania and the international maneuvering, both diplomatically and militarily, by all parties was recounted on the televised coverage. One of the significantly interesting bits of newsworthy news concerned the brand new U.S. ambassador to Pakistan, Wendy J. Chamberlin. After the terrorist attacks, this woman presented her credentials to the President of Pakistan, General Pervaiz Musharraf, and then proceeded to "deliver the goods" by requesting help for the U.S. plan to track down Osama bin Laden.

It was fascinating to see that a woman had such an incredible position of power to do her job in a culture that does not normally have a place for women in power! How was this possible? Why was she given access to the President of Pakistan? How on earth did she have the gumption to ask a Muslim leader to set himself against another Muslim? The answer is very simple: she did not represent herself, she was an ambassador who represented the government of the United States.

It is vital for us as Christians to come to an understanding of what it means to be an ambassador—since it is our job description!

2 Corinthians 5:20 tells us:

"Now then, we are ambassadors for Christ, as though God were pleading through us: we implore you on Christ's behalf, be reconciled to God."

The third foundational understanding of our faith and parenting is this:

❸ *We are ambassadors for Christ—in the home, in the marketplace, in the community, in the world. In other words, He is the "sending government;" we are the sent ones.*

What does that mean? What does that look like in *real* life? It means we don't have to cower in corners quietly mumbling, *"I am a Christian, really I am."* No, we can walk through the corridors of governmental power, through the neon-lit halls of commerce, through the brilliantly moving kaleidoscope of the media, through the antiqued frame of family with our heads held high, speaking of Jesus and His message wherever we are.

That's what ambassadors do. They don't represent themselves; they don't go in their own power; they don't push their own agenda. Instead, they *represent* another. Ambassadors go with one purpose and plan: to represent their government. They have the power of their government backing them, and they pursue the agenda their government has set. If someone has a problem with that, the ambassador merely refers them back to the sending government.

How effective are ambassadors? The truth is that they are only as effective as the government that has sent them. If you are an ambassador from a weak-kneed, wishy-washy, ne'er-do-well government, you will have a difficult time convincing the folks you have been sent to that they need to pay attention to your message. On the other hand, if you happen to be an ambassador of a world power, of a militarily mighty government, of a can-do and we-mean-business country, then the folks you have been sent to will sit up and take notice.

If we are the ambassadors of the King of Kings and Lord of Lords—the Creator of the Universe and the Centerpiece of human history, the Omnipotent Savior and Redeemer—then we represent the most powerful "government" in the history of the world! That means we have been given power in His name to do His works.

We see this ambassadorial power described in Daniel 11:32b:

> " . . . but the people who know their God shall be strong, and carry out great exploits."

People who *know their God*—people who know that they are not in charge but know that the One with all Authority is—these people do *fabulous* achievements, have *extraordinary* adventures, experience *wild* feats of faith—in the name of the One who has sent them.

Servanthood has just taken on a whole new complexion, hasn't it? Servant duties with a twist—representing the Creator God of the whole universe as His ambassadors, going to wild places and doing extraordinary things, sometimes on the other side of the globe, sometimes without leaving your neighborhood, but always in obedience.

The next time your child says, *"Mom, this is boring!"* you just remind them that they are in training to do GREAT EXPLOITS as God's ambassadors!!

Wow! Amazing!! Totally Cool!!! Hang on, though. Is it all sweetness and light? Power and success? Fame and fortune? Popularity and acclaim? Not according to our Master's words:

> *"Blessed are you when they revile and persecute you, and say all kinds of evil against you falsely for My sake. Rejoice and be exceedingly glad, for great is your reward in heaven, for so they persecuted the prophets who were before you."*
>
> *—Matthew 5:11–12*

And, how about this one?

"A disciple is not above his teacher, nor a servant above his master. It is enough for a disciple that he be like his teacher, and a servant like his master. If they have called the master of the house Beelzebub, how much more will they call those of his household! Therefore, do not fear them. For there is nothing covered that will not be revealed, and hidden that will not be known."

—Matthew 10:24–26

So, our job is Ambassador of the King of Kings, and the method is serving others as Jesus served. Our earthly reception does not look particularly good, but the heavenly reward is out of this world! Go, team, go!

As homeschooling parents, are we merely raising our children to:
Win a scholarship to a brand name university? **NO!**
Land a job with a six-figure income? **NO!**
Use six-syllable words that no one understands? **NO!**
Give us bragging rights? **Well, maybe!**
Is there more to life than this? **YES!**
What is it? **SERVANTHOOD!**
Job Description? **AMBASSADOR!**
What do we do? **READ ON!**

BECAUSE I SAID SO!

In this chapter, we have considered three foundational understandings of faith and parenting:

❶ *We live in a world that belongs to God, the one True God, the Judeo-Christian God. In other words, He's in charge here.*

❷ *As followers of Jesus Christ, we do not belong to ourselves—we belong to God. In other words, He is the Master; we are the servants.*

❸ *We are Ambassadors for Christ—in the home, in the marketplace, in the community, in the world. In other words, He is the "sending government;" we are the sent ones.*

Now we need to consider how this impacts our homeschooling and our teenagers. What are the implications, the applications, and the change-your-life issues? When we apply the answer to the question, *"Who's in charge here?"* to our families, we are confronted with the stark reality that these precious young people belong to Him. Though we have been given the unbelievable opportunity to live with them, nurture them, teach them, disciple them, clothe and feed them, laugh with them, work with them, yet, they don't belong to us.

The Biblical term for this is "stewardship." It means that though we can function with the authority of the master in day-to-day dealings with people and situations, we do not have ownership. Jesus described this in Luke 12:42–43:

> *"Who then is that faithful and wise steward, whom his master will make ruler over his household, to give them their portion of food in due season? Blessed is that servant whom his master will find so doing when he comes."*

Notice that there is no blurring of lines in this description. The servant was given rulership over the master's household, but the master was still ultimately in charge, and the servant remained accountable when the master returned.

It is true for us as parents. Our children say, *"But, why do I have to do that?"* We sometimes reply, *"Because I said so!"* meaning, *"I'm in charge here . . . I am the Boss."* The truth is that as parents, we ARE in charge until our children become adults. However, it is crucial that we remember that we are in charge the way a steward is in charge. We are in charge, because He gave us the opportunity and responsibility. We are in charge, but we are accountable to Him for those under us. There is a Master who is calling the shots, and He is watching very carefully.

What are *His* plans and purposes for our children? Do they coincide with *our* plans and purposes for our children? Who's in charge here?

Our plans and purposes might not be as extreme as the stories of parents who demand their children become doctors or lawyers in order to financially care for the parents when they become old. We might not be so uncouth as to demand our sons become athletes when they really desire to become artists. We might run from the image of controlling our daughters so that they live as second-class citizens. Good.

However, it goes much deeper than this—painfully deep. Jesus said,

> *"For everyone to whom much is given, from him much will be required; and to whom much has been committed, of him they will ask the more."*
> —Luke 12:48

Have your children been given much? Have they had the benefit of your attention, your approval, your love, your encouragement, your instruction, your prayers? Have they grown up straight and strong, full of faith in God? Are they articulate, intelligent, compassionate? Are they the most wonderful young people you have ever known? Aren't you proud of them?

Then, guess what? We are told that from these precious ones who have been given much, much will be required. What does that mean? It means that this life is about *more* than our children's "personal peace and prosperity." This is about God's plans, His heart for the world. Consider this Scripture:

> *"For we are His workmanship, created in Christ Jesus for good works, which*
> *God prepared beforehand that we should walk in them."* —Ephesians 2:10

God Himself has lavished His creative delight on our children, given them parents who are committed stewards to raise them up into healthy adulthood—for His plans, for His good works. He is the One who has been preparing them all along. Our task, our requirement ultimately, is to remain stewards. We need to recognize Who's in charge here. We need to relinquish ownership into the Master's capable hands. We need to walk in an awareness that God Himself is behind this parenting/homeschooling movement, raising up a whole group of stable, discipled, young people to go to the nations!

Friends, as an historian, I can tell you that to be part of a move of God in history is not a comfortable place, but it is powerful! May you have the grace to move out of your comfort zone and into His plan.

For the final time, "Go, Team, Go!"

As homeschooling parents, are we merely raising our children to:
Win a scholarship to a brand name university? **NO!**
　　Land a job with a six-figure income? **NO!**
　　　　Use six-syllable words that no one understands? **NO!**
　　　　　　Give us bragging rights? **Well, maybe!**
　　　　　　　　Is there more to life than this? **YES!**
　　　　　　　　　　What is it? **SERVANTHOOD!**
　　　　　　　　　　　　Job Description? **AMBASSADOR!**
　　　　　　　　　　　　　　What do we do? **RELINQUISH!**

Remember: This is all about Jesus—the Lordship of Jesus over all the earth—Jesus, just Jesus . . . This is not about us, but Him.

RECOMMENDED RESOURCE

Making Jesus Lord: The Dynamic Power of Laying Down Your Rights
This little book by Loren Cunningham will change your life and your world.

Becoming World Changers

Homeschoolers do the most amazing things. Travelling in the U.S. and internationally, we have had the opportunity to meet homeschooled young people who have a vision and a passion for doing "great exploits." With the incredible preparation and equipping that comes through having been trained, educated, and discipled by devoted parents, these young people are often ready and raring to go!

Jonathan Leedahl fits this description to a "T." He is a young man with God-given vision and a determination to pay the price to fulfill this vision. Jonathan was raised on a farm in North Dakota, homeschooled since third grade, and prayerfully discipled by his parents, Arlo and Cam. Growing up was filled with all the fun of healthy families and the ongoing responsibilities farm families share: hunting, fishing, church, camping with friends, theater productions, homeschooling, chores, working in the fields. When Jonathan was in his mid-teens, he felt a clear call of God to serve as a missionary pilot in a developing nation, and he eventually shared the news with his parents. They responded in a way I long to emulate—they began to focus his studies on aviation and missions. They helped him with the practical and technical aspects of what this might entail, and they encouraged him to go for it.

The first hurdle to jump was flying itself. Jonathan had to pay for his flying lessons, so he became an excellent steward of the earnings he made. As Jonathan attained his pilot's license, Arlo and Cam began praying for a Christian pilot to mentor him who would understand what it is like to be a missionary aviation pilot. They found their prayers answered at church one day when their pastor introduced them to a retired pilot who had flown for a missionary society! Jonathan went on to get his instructor's license.

His dad encouraged him to buy a plane rather than spend money on the constant rental of planes. They prayed about this rather daunting purchase, and the Lord worked another amazing blessing. They found a plane that the owners had just decided to sell and had undervalued in price. The value of Jonathan's plane has unexpectedly gone up $20,000 since that time.

After finishing his high school years at home, Jonathan enrolled in an aviation mechanic's school (after all, if you fly them into the jungle, you better know how to fix them so you can fly them out!) and a Moody Bible Institute correspondence course on the Bible. After finishing mechanic's school, Jonathan discovered that, on the mission field he was headed to, he really should know how to fly helicopters as well. Easier said than done, or perhaps, cheaper said than done. However, God continues to work His amazing ways in Jonathan's life and has provided the means for instruction. Jonathan now has his helicopter license and his helicopter instructor's license. More than that, the Lord opened up an opportunity for Jonathan to work alongside a master helicopter mechanic—and get paid for it!

The goal? New Tribes Missions. The pathway? Getting the best instruction and the best preparation possible. The chief cheerleaders? His parents. Jonathan Leedahl, a homeschool graduate, is on the road to becoming a world changer.

OUR JOURNAL

One of the most precious memories I have of our time in New Zealand is the opportunity my children and I had to interview Loren Cunningham, founder of Youth With A Mission. Loren has preached in every nation of the world(!), before kings and tribal elders and primitive farmers, on television and radio, in churches, and in small groups; travelled on planes, boats, trains, cars, on foot; and I longed to pick his experienced brain about his perspective on what God has done through different people groups both in the historic past and currently around the globe.

When Loren learned of my interest, he graciously agreed to an interview. However, there was only a brief window of opportunity in his packed schedule, so Isaac, Michael, Melody, and I sat and waited for his "between meetings" moment. Much to our astonishment, Loren asked us if we would mind having the interview in his car as he had to zip to the dry cleaners before the next speaking engagement! So, we all piled in, eyes and ears on high alert for the gems we expected to receive from this Christian statesman.

In the midst of sharing his thoughts on God's hand in history, Loren began to tell us of an insight God had given him years prior concerning the way He desires to impact people and nations far beyond the scope of an evangelistic message. While having a quiet week with his family in the Colorado Rockies, Loren received from the Lord seven "spheres of influence" that are like classrooms for discipling nations.

"It was totally out of the blue for me," Loren said. *"The following day, I was asked if I would go over and meet with Bill and Vonette Bright (of Campus Crusade for Christ) in Boulder, Colorado. As we met, Bill pulled out his list, which was almost exactly the same as mine, and he told me how God had spoken similarly to him."*

The seven spheres of influence that Loren shared with us were the family, education, the arts, the media, government, business, AS WELL as the church. We were amazed to consider how God wants to use all of us, in all of our varieties and uniqueness, to minister His Kingdom and His Heart through teaching and working in all of these areas. World changing is not limited to the evangelist or pastor; it is God's plan for all of us, wherever we live and whatever we do.

That quick trip to the dry cleaners was an encouragement to keep doing what we are doing with all of our might. And to teach our children to think strategically about what arena God would have them work within in order to change the world for His glory!

Seven spheres of influence . . . seven areas of impact for Jesus in the nations . . . seven ways in which we can become world changers.

PRESENTING PROVEN PATHWAYS TO
PROFOUND PERFORMANCE!

There are a few things to think about as we consider becoming (and raising!) world changers. Merely pursuing one of the seven spheres of influence will not mean you are a world changer for good. There is a path we must follow if we are to see godly impact as a result of the way we live our lives. We will describe the world-changing characteristics of these seven spheres of influence later, but first, here are some comments about the path. The Bible describes certain attitudes, certain characteristics, of those whose lives change the world around them: humility, faithfulness, and obedience. Let us consider each of these paths in turn and see how nurturing these attitudes in our lives will give us a platform from which God can truly use us.

Pathway ❶ *Humility: serving the Master*

We need to define humility—first what it isn't, and then what it is—so we can understand the importance of nurturing it in our lives.

Many folks believe that being humble is to speak badly of oneself: *"Oh, I don't know much of anything . . . I'm just a homeschool mom."* Or, *"I don't do anything right, but God's not finished with me yet."* It seems to be humble and to show our spirituality when we deny any ability, any right doing, any positive action on our part. To be truly humble, in some folks' opinion, would be to hold your head at half-mast, never lifting your eyes to meet anyone and expecting doormat status.

Humility to many Christians is a will-o'-the-wisp, unattainable attribute that one can only hope for in heaven. Perhaps it could be stated like this:

"Humility is something that when you think you have it, you have most certainly lost it!"

But is that true? Is that what the Scriptures teach us about humility? When Peter wrote, *"Therefore humble yourselves under the mighty hand of God, that He may exalt you in due time,"* (1 Peter 5:6), was he telling us to do something we are incapable of doing? Was he telling us to go to our neighbors, friends, and enemies berating ourselves and putting ourselves down? Is this just a cosmic "Far Side" joke?

Hmmm. Obviously not.

Let's try another apostle, another Scripture. Paul wrote in 1 Corinthians 15:10:

"But by the grace of God I am what I am, and His grace toward me was not in vain; but I labored more abundantly than they all, yet not I, but the grace of God which was with me."

Was Paul, who elsewhere calls himself the chief of sinners, being proud and not humble in this statement about his labor? Or, in fact, was he displaying for us what true humility looks like: *"by the grace of God I am what I am . . ."* AND *"yet not I, but the grace of God which was with me."*

There is something very profound about being honest about ourselves and at the same time seeing that whatever we do is by the grace of God. We need to recognize that God gives each of us grace and gifts, and that not acknowledging God's gifts of talent and ability and character and activity in our lives shows our ingratitude toward Him.

"Oh, you know, I don't have any creativity; I don't have any talent; I am ugly; I am a hopeless case . . ." (Can't you just picture God's heart breaking over our total ingratitude for what He has done in us?)

The trick here (and, oh, the line is very fine at this point!) is to both honestly acknowledge who we are (good and bad) AND to give God all the glory for the good.

"You know, I CAN sing that song on Sunday if you would like. The Lord has given me real joy in singing songs that direct others to Him."

If we remember that this is all about Jesus, not about us, then we can be truthful, honest, AND humble. This is NOT about impressing others, or trying to make a name for ourselves, or finding our sense of identity through our accomplishments. This IS about being transparent, being open, not trying to impress . . . so that through our lives the light of Jesus shines.

Humility. It is the first pathway toward becoming a world changer. Remember, the Bible tells us that if we will humble ourselves, God will, in His time, exalt us—which is a great platform, a high-altitude vantage point from which to impact the world for Jesus!

Pathway ❷ Faithfulness: pursuing the Master's interests

Faithfulness is a critical part of becoming a world changer. Jesus, in the Parable of the Talents, described the end result of one who is faithful:

"Well done, good and faithful servant; you were faithful over a few things, I will make you ruler over many things. Enter into the joy of your lord."
—Matthew 25:21

Wow! Being a "ruler over many things" sounds like an excellent place from which to change the world, doesn't it? So, what does faithfulness mean? How does it work in real life? Where do we begin?

Faithfulness means doing what is expected, being dependable, living the reality of faith in every day life. It is to be a person of integrity—doing what is right even when no one is watching.

In real life, faithfulness looks like this:

"He who is faithful in what is least is faithful also in much; and he who is unjust in what is least is unjust also in much."   —Luke 16:10

We begin by being faithful in the small things that we need to get done—being careful to satisfy the person in charge, being focused to supply the effort required. It's amazing how small things can add up to huge opportunities!

We experienced that the year Isaac was thirteen. His voice dropped from a high-pitched, squeaky boy's sound to a luscious, velvety-rich man's sound. Isaac would answer the phone, then when I came on, the caller would say, *"Who on earth is that?!"* They thought he was about thirty-five years old! One day, in the midst of the joy of a newfound baritone voice, Isaac asked me if he could get a job at KSLT, our local Christian radio station. I started to point out to him that he was only thirteen years old, but the Lord showed me that this was going to be a growing experience for him and that I should keep quiet and see what happened. A few minutes later he came to me and announced that he had an interview on Tuesday!!

"Did you tell them that you were only thirteen years old?"

Puzzled expression. *"No, Mom."*

So, the growing experience was getting more interesting! I thought briefly (and feverishly) about calling the radio station and telling them this interview had been scheduled under false pretenses since Isaac was only thirteen years old, but the Lord gave me wisdom to see that he would never learn if I "pulled the plug." So, I drove him to the interview on Tuesday (since he was too young to drive himself!). Expecting it to be no more than a five-minute "interview," once they saw how young he was, I was flabbergasted to be waiting for nearly an hour. When Isaac showed up in the car, he turned to me with a mischievous smile and said:

"Well, I start tomorrow."

"WHAT??!!"

I was electrified into near silence, apart from incoherent sputterings.

"Do they know you are THIRTEEN YEARS OLD?!"

"Yes, Mom."

"Are they going to pay you?"

"No, Mom."

Okay, Diana, get a grip. *"So, what is going on?"*

"Well, I told them that I was homeschooled and very interested in the ministry of Christian radio. They got all excited and told me that they would like to have me apprentice in all of the different departments at the station, so I start tomorrow!"

Well . . . I was thankful that I had kept my mouth shut and gone along for this adventure! Thus began a year or so of Isaac doing all the things that nobody else wanted to do. He cheerfully licked stamps and envelopes, filed CD's, answered the telephone, and more. He helped collect the trash at an event the radio station sponsored. He was sort of a gopher—you know, "go-fer this, go-fer that." After eighteen months, though, Bill and I asked Isaac if this was what he had had in mind in the beginning. He thought about it for awhile and said that he really had wanted to learn to be a DJ. We asked him what we should do to help him accomplish this endeavor. He told us that he would go by himself and talk to Kerry Liebelt, the morning DJ, to explain the situation.

It was so gratifying to learn that Kerry's response was, *"Isaac, I've been watching you for a long time. You have been faithful to do whatever was asked of you. It would be my pleasure to teach you how to be a DJ."*

So the experience grew some more as he began the odyssey of learning to multitask at the DJ's soundboard. Isaac learned to enter the weather forecast, report the news, do the commercials, play the music, pray for the needs phoned in, and all of the myriad tasks DJ's do. After three months of training, at fourteen years of age, he found himself in the situation where they needed him to actually broadcast live on the radio. We gave him our blessing, and at the top of the hour, we heard him say over the airwaves to a listening audience of 100,000 people:

"This is KSLT, the Word in music. Thanks for listening. I am Isaac Waring. I've got you for the next two hours, playing the best music in the Black Hills..."

And nobody knew it was a fourteen-year-old kid on the air for the first time!

Faithfulness. It is the second pathway toward becoming a world changer. Remember, the Bible tells us that if we will be faithful, God will, in His time, make us ruler over many things—which is another great platform, another high-altitude vantage point from which to impact the world for Jesus!

Pathway ❸ *Obedience: doing what the Master tells us*

Obedience is the third and final pathway we will consider. The Bible describes the impact of Jesus' obedience:

"And being found in appearance as a man, He humbled Himself and became obedient to the point of death, even the death of the cross. Therefore God also has highly exalted Him and given Him the name which is above every name, that at the name of Jesus every knee should bow, of those in heaven, and of those on earth, and of those under the earth, and that every tongue should confess that Jesus Christ is Lord, to the glory of God the Father."
—Philippians 2:8–11

The Kingdom of God is not like the kingdom of men. God's ways are higher than our ways, and His thoughts are higher than our thoughts. He took Jesus'

humility and obedience unto death and *transformed* them into the Resurrection, into the Name above all names, into the One to whom every knee will bow.

In the same way, God will take our obedience to Him—even cleaning toilets and changing diapers—and transform it into a place of influence, a world-changing platform.

"Oh, really?" you say. *"Can you prove that?"*

Yes. Reflect for just a moment on the story of Amy Carmichael—one of the most significant Christian authors in all history. Though she had training and experience as an evangelist to women in the British Isles, when she came as a missionary to India, she had to let go of this training and expectation in order to spend her days taking care of children. Amy was tucked away in an obscure village in India where she started an orphanage to care for the wee ones God kept bringing to her, those who had been rescued from temple prostitution. She lived for many years at a place called Donhauver caring for the needs of these precious children—laughing with them, changing their diapers, caring for them in their sicknesses, racing around the garden on a tricycle. When she broke her hip at age 64, her life changed dramatically. This lively woman was confined to bed where she remained for the next twenty years. We should be thankful and grateful to the Lord for that last twenty years, as it was mainly during this season of her life that she had the time to write about her experiences.

Amy Carmichael is considered by some, such as Elisabeth Elliot, to be among the most influential of Christian writers. Amy's obedience to the Lord to care for children in relative obscurity rather than ministering as an evangelist, was *transformed* by Him to world-changing stature through the insight that she shared in her books.

Obedience to God *is* powerful. It will change the world, one life at a time. However, there is one more thing that needs to be said in this area. It is one thing for us to obey God. It is another thing entirely to release our children so they may obey God, especially if God is calling them to do something that seems dangerous or far away or difficult. As parents, we must continue to obey God by releasing our adult children into His hands so that they may follow His call on their lives.

I am in the process of living this out. Michael, our middle child, has been called of God to missions since he was seven years old. At that time, he had a vision of a city and knew that God was calling him to minister in that place. As we have walked this out over the past dozen years, God has been gently dealing with my heart over the issue of letting him go. A few years ago, as we rode a ferry across Lake Champlain, I said to Michael that his mission field was a very dangerous place and that working there could actually result in his martyrdom. His answer stunned me.

"Mom, I've not only given Jesus my life; I've given Him my death, as well. If He can use my death to bring glory to His name, then it's okay."

Truthfully, I wondered if I would ever be able to view it from this perspective. Some time later, I had the chance to process this some more. On September 9, 2001, two days before the unthinkable occurred, a close friend told me about a very dangerous trial some Christians were facing at that moment in Afghanistan.

"Diana, the situation is grim. Some foreign workers have been arrested along with sixteen nationals who worked for them. The nationals will most certainly be put to death by the Taliban, and it may be the same sentence for the foreign workers. Please pray for them."

This tore my heart apart as I realized in that moment that it could have been my son jailed in a hostile land with death an imminent possibility. I cried out to God, not only for these workers and their families, but for my own heart as well. I didn't think I could survive if Michael were ever found in the same situation.

Then, two days later, America changed. 9/11 rocked our country, while the nation of Afghanistan and the Taliban regime suddenly came to prominence before the entire world. As we prepared for war, I kept crying out to God for these foreign and national workers and their families, knowing that if military action reached Kabul, these people would certainly die. Day by day, I watched to see what bits and pieces of information were available about the trial and what was happening to these prisoners.

The day we picked up a newspaper and read that the foreign workers were released unharmed in a field outside Kabul, I broke down and wept. But more was coming: we later learned that the sixteen national workers had ALSO been released unharmed. Praise the Lord! That was *miraculous* and *divine intervention* in their lives. It was also, in my own heart, a wondrous display of God's ability to work miracles in the midst of impossible circumstances, in hostile countries, with God-defying governments! He showed me categorically that I can trust Him with my son, even as he goes to a dangerous place. Whether in life or in death, my son is safe in Jesus.

As parents, we must take our own step of obedience—trusting all the while in God's amazing love and power—to allow our children to obey the Lord. No matter where He leads them—whether missions, business, politics, education, family, or any other endeavor—obedience is the wisest, safest, and best course when viewed from the perspective of eternity.

Obedience. It is the third pathway toward becoming a world changer. Remember, the Bible tells us that if we are obedient, God will, in His time, take our obedience to Him and use it to transform the world around us. What an incredible opportunity we have been given! All we need to do is follow Jesus in obedience.

Humility. Faithfulness. Obedience. They seem like such tiny steps—so obscure, so different than the normal means of wielding influence. Yet, God will take these qualities and use them to change the world!

DISCIPLING NATIONS

Matthew 28:18–20 gives us the commission:

"Then Jesus came and spoke to them, saying, 'All authority has been given to Me in heaven and on earth. Go therefore and make disciples of all the nations [disciple nations], baptizing them in the name of the Father and of the Son and of the Holy Spirit, teaching them to observe all things that I have commanded you; and lo, I am with you always, even to the end of the age.'"

God's heart is that everyone in every place would know the goodness and grace and mercy poured out through Jesus Christ. He has commanded us to take the Good News of redemption throughout the earth to every people, tongue, and tribe. However, the Gospel brings not only salvation to individual hearts, it brings transformation of villages, cities, even countries. There are numerous examples of this in history:

- *The Reformation, begun when Martin Luther nailed the ninety-five theses to the Wittenburg Door, unleashed a dramatic change in government;*
- *Florence Nightingale's desire to obey God during the Crimean War led to a transformation of health care, nursing, and hospitals;*
- *Elizabeth Fry, a devout Christian woman, attained the humane reform of the prison system in England;*
- *George Frederick Handel, under the inspiration of God, feverishly composed* The Messiah, *which continues to sway hearts toward God, especially in the triumphant "Hallelujah Chorus;"*
- *Susannah Wesley worked diligently to raise her children in the Lord. Many historians recognize that her son, John Wesley, through his preaching of the Gospel during the Great Awakening, saved England from a Reign of Terror similar to what had occurred in France;*
- *The Welsh Revival in 1903–04 so changed the local people that the police*

and judges in many towns throughout Wales had nothing to do, AND the pit ponies in the mines could not understand their masters' commands since they no longer included swear words!!

When we consider soup kitchens, relief work in Albania, Mother Teresa's homes for the dying in Calcutta, evangelistic-motivated movies, orphanages, Christian universities, and even a family inviting neighbors over for dinner, we see the heart of God expressed like a rainbow. Though we see many colors—red, orange, yellow, green, blue, indigo, and violet—each one comes from the same pure source of sunlight, which is reflected like a prism through many raindrops. In the same way, God's heart of love is reflected like a prism through His people in many varied and even colorful means. God cares for every aspect of life, for all of the issues that affect people. Though some may argue whether we should feed people's stomachs or their souls, in truth, it is God's heart to feed BOTH stomachs and souls! This concept—bringing the Lordship of Jesus over every human setting, which is referred to as "discipling nations"—is simply applying the Christian worldview to every avenue of life. When we catch the vision of discipling nations, we are set free to work and excel (and to release our children to work and excel) in a number of different areas, no longer feeling like part-time Christians if we work outside of the local church. Understand that God intends to send His people *throughout* the world, into different arenas, to declare His Lordship in every sphere of influence: family, church, education, media, the arts, government, and business. Remember, this is all about Jesus, not about us. This *discipling of nations* is to bring His Lordship over every person in every place.

So, let us consider each of these seven spheres of influence and see how they can be used to *disciple nations*.

THE SEVEN SPHERES OF INFLUENCE

1) FAMILY

As we look around our culture, or at almost any culture in the world, it is obvious that the *family* is in trouble. Divorce, child abuse, spouse abuse, rebellious teenagers, generation gaps, all show just the tip of the iceberg. Through the media, the arts, the local coffee shop, even many churches, we discover that the prevailing attitude in our culture is that marriage is an iffy business, and child-rearing a gamble, at best.

REAPING THE HARVEST

Into this morass of confusion, heartache, and despair, the Christian family with God-graced vision and healthy relationships, displays the goodness of God like the powerful beacon of a fog-enshrouded lighthouse. As people see our families laughing together, working together, getting along in day-to-day situations, they can not help but ask, *"How do you do that?"* In that precious moment, as the family acknowledges God's goodness, the reality of the Lordship of Jesus invades the conversation and impacts the understanding.

Bill and I have recently witnessed an example of this in the Witek family of Indianapolis. Bill and Michelle Witek are wonderful homeschooling parents who have made significant choices for the sake of their family. Bill left a corporate job in order to have more hands-on time with his family. They now run a campground where the whole family works together, including the youngest boys who roar about in golf carts to lead RV's to campsites (which is quite a delight!). As soon as we arrived at their campground, it was obvious they had to be a Christian homeschooling family—there was such a sense of the involvement of mature, helpful, and fun children. Within a short time, we had the opportunity to visit with the parents and discovered that they were, indeed, Christian homeschoolers. Bill and Michelle shared with us that guests are constantly questioning them about how their children can get along so well. Their answer?

"It's Jesus."

Their family, by just being a family, is displaying the Lordship of Jesus to thousands of campers every year. The doors for meaningful conversation, profound witness, and practical ministry are open for them through this sphere of influence.

We must not downplay the significance of being healthy, grace-filled families. For many of us, just living in our neighborhoods as Christian families will have a tremendous impact on those around us. However, for some, the calling will be to an even larger audience, as it was for Edith Schaeffer. For me, her transparency and honesty in sharing the realities of living as a Christian family—warts and all—offered not only inspiration but a very practical understanding of a Christian family operating in love and grace. It changed my life, and eventually my own family. Multiply this one reader by the tens of thousands of books printed, and we begin to see the extent of her influence. Edith, through her writings on the family (*What is a Family?* and *The Hidden Art of Homemaking*), has helped to *disciple nations* and bring the Lordship of Jesus over the earth in the area of family.

2) CHURCH

Let the Church be the Church. As we function as the Church, as we *"love one another as I have loved you,"* we display the Lordship of Jesus before a watching world.

We attend Countryside Community Church in Spearfish, South Dakota. Since it meets in the gym of the local university, lots of people are involved each week in hours of set-up and tear-down. It is amazing to be around these folks, because they are having fun at 7:30AM on Sunday mornings(!), fellowshipping with one another as they set up chairs, the platform, and the sound equipment. It is not only amazing; however, it is a witness of the reality of Jesus displayed in the local church. One man recently reported that his twenty-something son had come to visit during a break from the military. As the son observed these people in action, in their obvious care for each other and their joyful service, he was completely undone. After returning to the military base, he called his dad and tearfully told him that he had rededicated his life to Jesus, *because* he had seen the reality of God's love through the service of our church folks.

Let the Church be the Church. As we all function as members of the Body of Christ, we will change the world. Many of us think, however, that it is only the "big names" that have a real impact for the Church. It's not true! Each of us, even the "little people" are significant in bringing the Lordship of Jesus over everyone in every place. Let us consider for a moment a case in point:

Most of us are familiar with D.L. Moody. In the late 1800's, D. L. Moody turned the English-speaking world on its proverbial ear! He was a simple man who preached the Gospel with fire. England was especially astonished at this plain-talking American preacher impacting the young and old of their nation in such dramatic ways. His name is one we know well. But how many of us know the name of Edward Kimball? He was a normal Christian man who served the Lord faithfully. Part of his service to the Lord was in being a Sunday School teacher. As it happened, he had D. L. Moody in his class. Observing over time that Moody was not converted, he took the time to go to the shoe shop where Moody worked and talk with him earnestly about salvation. The timing was right, and Moody surrendered to the Lordship of Jesus.

You see, in the wonderful ways of God, it was the influence of Edward Kimball in Moody's life that led to the influence D.L. Moody had on the world! So, he who sows and he who reaps (or, you might say—he who has a "big" name and he who has a "small" name) have a *significant* part of God's work in the kingdom!

3) EDUCATION

When you consider all the people in this world who experience some form of education, whether primary, secondary, undergraduate, or graduate level, it becomes obvious why this sphere of influence is so important. Regardless of what form of education is given to students (public, private, homeschool), the students are being greatly influenced both by *what* they are taught and by *whom* it is taught. Through the method of teaching and the worldview of the teacher, far more is communicated to the students than merely names, dates, and places. Students are also taught their worth, their value, and their relationships to others.

There are countless stories from the past of students who were significantly impacted by one good teacher who went beyond mere communication of material to communicating a commitment of relationship: *"I care about you, and I want you to succeed."* Perhaps this is one of the major reasons homeschooling is so successful, regardless of the parents' level of education.

It is through education that we can either open students up to the wonder of God's world and His personal care, or close them up in a meaningless, mechanistic universe. It is through education that we can display the reality of a student's worth and value by teaching them in a way they can understand, or manipulate and destroy them by rigid, unyielding methods that leave them feeling stupid. It is through education that we can broaden a student's horizon and inspire them to greatness, or train them to do mindless work with no questions asked. Education is powerful.

Certainly, the most significant teacher in my life has been Rosalie Pedder. As I have described before, she is an energetic, seemingly tireless Kiwi, who travels around the world teaching adults about the wondrous way God made their minds. Through years of study, teaching, and experience, Rosalie has learned a lot about the various learning issues: modalities, eight intelligences, right brain/left brain, convergent/divergent, and more. And she is quite effective in the way she is able to communicate this liberating material through the use of three-dimensional objects, storytelling, pictures, song, movement, and anything else you can imagine! But that is not the reason Rosalie is such a powerful teacher. It is because she has made a commitment to bring the Lordship of Jesus back to the classroom—to teach in a way that honors Him and honors the people He has created.

When the *Lordship of Jesus* is directing the behaviors and attitudes in a classroom (whether at home or in a huge auditorium), the teacher no longer resorts to manipulation, playing favorites, exerting a self-centered control, self-aggrandizing pride, laziness, or any of the other sins that so easily beset us. Instead, the focus is on serving the needs of the student in a way that brings glory to the Lord Jesus and true help to the student. Education is no longer separated from the Lordship of Jesus—they walk hand in hand. The results are incredible! In Rosalie's classroom, adults around the world are being restored and healed in their attitudes about learning. She enables them to actually accomplish academic work, which they never believed they were capable of doing! The ripple effect is that these people often go and teach others in this God-honoring way.

Remember, *"The earth is the LORD'S, and all its fullness"* includes all areas of learning and education. This sphere of influence touches almost every life on the globe. May the Lord raise up many of us to bring His glory to this area.

4) MEDIA

In our modern day technology, we have indeed become a "global village." With media reporters stationed all around the world, we can have almost instant access to fast-breaking news stories in Afghanistan, Bosnia, Zimbabwe, London, New York, and every place in between. Most people get their version of what is occurring in politics, royalty, fashion, morals, and vacation spots from reports in the media: newspapers, television, magazines, and the latest media source—the Internet.

We are becoming increasingly *programmed* to believe what we are told in the media. It is expected that we will receive the news report as thorough coverage, completely true and utterly reliable. One now finds television in most restaurants, airports, waiting rooms, hotel lobbies, and the channel is usually broadcasting the news. It is almost inescapable, and the majority of people seem to accept the viewpoint being expressed as truthful (amazing how naive we are!). If you question someone about what they are relating in a discussion, they will say in their defense, *"But I heard it on the news!"* End of argument. As most Christians know, however, the worldview of the producers of the media is generally not in keeping with a Biblical worldview. These media producers are able to control what we see through the judicious "cutting and pasting" in the editing room and by giving the storyline a particular *spin* through the sixty-second blip of information read by the reporter. In that sixty seconds, we believe what we have seen and heard, but we are NOT aware of all that they very carefully did not show us or tell us. It feels like firsthand information, but it's often more akin to secondhand gossip. And few seem to know it.

REAPING THE HARVEST

So, the media is both globally pervasive and culturally persuasive. This medium is extremely powerful in its ability to mold the perspective of a whole generation of people, and it seems to have a big banner emblazoned across the door:

"NO CHRISTIANS ALLOWED"

However, referring back to Psalm 24:1, we know that the banner has no meaning. *"The earth is the LORD'S, and all its fullness"* certainly includes the media centers, the television producers, the newspaper cubicles, and the Internet sites. As I recall, Jesus told His followers that the gates of Hell shall not prevail against the Church. As we boldly march into this sphere of influence, I believe we need to have this confidence. If we feel like complaining to God, as Elijah did, that no one else in this area believes in Him, then remember that God told Elijah He had 7,000 others who had not bent a knee to Baal! Persevere in your calling: you plus God make a majority.

Dr. James Dobson is an excellent example of Christians who effectively do battle in and through this sphere of influence. In his radio program, "Focus on the Family," Dr. Dobson offers a distinctly different perspective on Christian and family issues than what is normally found on the airwaves. However, because he is utilizing this powerful medium, he has informed, educated, and blessed millions of listeners.

May the Lord raise up thousands, ten thousands, and more to fill the airwaves, the Internet, the newspapers, and the magazines with His truth and His glory. May we go not only into "Christian radio," "Christian TV," "Christian magazines and newspapers," but also to secular radio, CNN, Good Housekeeping, the Wall Street Journal, and all the rest. That which the enemy has intended for evil can certainly be used by God for good!

5) ARTS

The arts, perhaps more than any other sphere of influence, have the ability to touch the hearts, souls, and minds of people. They express a perspective; they display a way of thinking; they communicate the worldview of the artist and those who have influenced the artist. All these have a powerful impact upon the audience. Whether we speak of paintings, sculptures, theater productions, movies, music, dance, tapestries, poetry, or literature, these creative offerings give us far more than a momentary glimpse of beauty (or ugliness!); they also speak to us of the artists' view of the world—a worldview which they would have you share.

There are many examples of art being used to display the artist's message to the world. Pablo Picasso, a genius in this arena, very effectively communicated to the early twentieth century world that life makes no sense. For example, Picasso's painting, *Nude Descending a Staircase,* has neither a recognizable human being nor a set of stairs. John Cage, a well-known composer in the twentieth century style of music, did an impressive job of communicating that the world is a random jumble. Much of what is expressed in modern dance, modern literature, modern poetry, modern movies, modern music, modern art share this element of meaningless, random, ridiculous, amoral communication. And, if we consider what the general population believes about the world today, we discover that artists in this sphere of influence have been very effective in communicating that worldview.

However, once again, we need to remember that, *"The earth is the LORD'S, and all its fullness."* Art, in all of its many expressions, has such a power to bring to all the earth the message and reality of the Lordship of Jesus. For example, Rembrandt, the famous Dutch painter, created a masterpiece of both art and Christian worldview when he painted, "The Raising of the Cross," because he showed that he himself was guilty for putting Jesus on the cross. This painting has spoken truth through the centuries—that we are all guilty and in need of the Savior. Just as Picasso's painting influenced culture, so Rembrandt's painting has influenced the world.

The Lord is gifting men and women everywhere today in this sphere of influence; we have but to bless them and release them. One artist we know, Alexis Wilson, has a gift for communicating the heart of God through paintings. For Michael's graduation from high school, we commissioned Alexis to paint a picture with a focus on the mission field to which Michael has been called. When we received the painting, I was dazed by what I saw. Alexis had painted the beauty of a very old place of worship with the central focus of a man on his knees. The painting, through Alexis's skill, cries out that we should pray for these people whom God loves. It shows them in their beauty and in their need. It is powerful beyond this meager word description, like all great art.

We have been drawn to worship God as we have seen dance performed for His glory. We have been challenged to live more fervently for Him through literature displaying His character. We have been awed and amazed at His greatness and goodness through music created for His pleasure. We have been deepened and quieted through poetry that reflects His heart.

Art is powerful, and God is worthy of our best efforts in this area. Christian artists need excellent training, excellent discipleship, and excellence as a standard. Whether in the Church or in the galleries of the world, artists have an important part to play in discipling nations. May He raise up many to display to the world the truth of His Lordship and His love.

6) GOVERNMENT

"Power corrupts. Absolute power corrupts absolutely."
"Politicians are two-faced, money grubbers who will promise one thing before election day and vote entirely the opposite when in office."
"Christians should stay out of politics. It is a dirty business."

Hmmm. There are lots of old sayings about politics and government, and there is a lot of truth in some of these old sayings. However, *"The earth is the LORD'S, and all its fullness"* includes this sphere of influence. If Christians abdicate their position of influence in civic leadership, government will have no salt slowing down the rot!

Perhaps my favorite example from history in this sphere of influence is William Wilberforce. He is the man who almost single-handedly accomplished:

" . . . one of the greatest moral and social revolutions in history."
—P. Coupland, in an article about Wilberforce

Who was he? And what gave him the strength to take on the British Empire and win? Wilberforce was born in Yorkshire, England, in 1759, to a wealthy family. His privileged upbringing allowed him a position of rank, and he easily won a seat in Parliament. At this point in his young life, politics was a pleasant pastime for a wealthy dilettante. However, God reached down and gloriously saved him in the midst of his ease. As he began to walk out the reality of the Christian life, he wanted to withdraw from the pollution of public life. He understood, perhaps better than most of us, that politics was "dirty." Wisely, however, he consulted with John Newton (the composer of *Amazing Grace*) who told him, *"It is hoped and believed that the Lord has raised you up for the good of His church and for the good of the nation."*

Wilberforce, in praying about God's work for him to accomplish in the sphere of government, realized that slavery and the slave trade were abhorrent to God and were the issues He would have Wilberforce struggle with in the political realm. Thus began an incredibly arduous, uphill fight for the next forty-six years. At the end of it, both the slave trade and, as he learned on his deathbed, slavery itself were abolished in the British Empire.

This one man determined to bring the Lordship of Jesus over the mightiest government of his day. And as Scripture has promised, *"If God is for us, who can be against us?"* We are, Biblically, in league with the God of the universe. And, as has been often observed, *"If you read the back of the book, we win!"*

May the Lord raise up many disciples who will strive mightily with Wilberforce as their model to bring the Lordship of Jesus into this sphere of influence. And may we, as parents, release our children to this sphere of influence as God directs their paths!

7) BUSINESS

Of all the areas of life, the one least connected in our minds to the Lordship of Jesus might be the business world. How often have you heard someone say,

"Yeah, he is a Christian, but his business sure doesn't know it (or show it!) . . ."

There is an attitude of a dog-eat-dog world when it comes to business, a top-of-the-heap mentality, a king-rat-at-the-head-of-the-rat-race philosophy. We learn from top authors about such items for *business leaders* as the leadership secrets of Attila the Hun, the military secrets of Sun Tzu, Machiavelli's formula for success, and worse.

Where, oh, where does the Lordship of Jesus fit into this arena? Where do memo-minded CEO's, the bottom line, edging out the competition, accounts payable, payroll, taxes, and all of these concerns of business connect with the Kingdom of God? For many, they don't. Business is business—church is church.

However, *"The earth is the LORD'S, and all its fullness"* means that in this sphere of influence, world-changing Christians can have a tremendous impact that will ripple outward into many parts of the globe. Two areas of *discipling nations* in this sphere are, first, in the personal witness of a Christian businessman to his employees, his customers, and his competition and, secondly, in the strategies of Christian businessmen to start businesses in countries closed to the Gospel.

An example of the first is Robert Laidlaw. He was an astute businessman in New Zealand, who saw a need in the market for products and filled it. He was extremely successful in his business venture, but he longed to share with his employees the most important "success" in his life—that of being the servant of Jesus Christ. He wrote his testimony and a basic outline of Christianity in the booklet, "The Reason Why," which he distributed to his employees. The booklets began to circulate throughout the country, bringing the Gospel to many. Several years later, when our family visited New Zealand, our hostess/tour guide/friend, Barbara Smith, shared that it was this booklet that had brought her to an awareness of Jesus Christ and His saving grace. One businessman's testimony had a tremendous influence across an entire nation.

The second area, that of Christian businessmen going into places where no missionaries could ever hope to go, is absolutely dynamic! Think about it: developing nations that want nothing to do with Christianity open their arms wide when someone can bring legitimate business opportunities to the nation, giving the people honest work and the country healthier economics. When this is done for the cause of Christ and not for the coffers of the businessman, it can have a powerful influence upon that nation.

Business is NOT about us. Business is about Jesus—accomplishing His goals, fulfilling His plans. The profit made by successful Christian businessmen can be used for His purposes, to minister to the areas of His heart. Successful businessmen are often key players in funding Christian projects at home and abroad. So, if God is calling you or your child to be a leader in business, do it with all your heart—and remember that you are not your own; you belong to Jesus!

Remember the Seven Spheres of Influence:

- *Family*
- *Church*
- *Education*
- *Media*
- *Arts*
- *Government*
- *Business*

"The earth is the LORD'S, and all its fullness."

RECOMMENDED RESOURCE

Prisoners of Hope by Dayna Curry and Heather Mercer
Imprisoned by the Taliban regime in Afghanistan in 2001, Dayna and Heather share their first-hand account of God's work in the midst of impossible circumstances.

Da Money Will Follow!
(Do what you love and . . .)

Matt Harris has an unusual job for this day and age. He is a blacksmith—not your ordinary, garden-variety blacksmith, however. Matt is an architectural blacksmith, designing and creating wrought iron gates, stair railings, and more. He also seems to specialize in doing things few other people nowadays have the knowledge to do, sort of a connoisseur of the metallic past. And the really wild, delightful part of all this is that he is making a living doing it.

Matt is the homeschooled son of Ronnie and Maxine Harris, good friends of ours in Maryland. Growing up, Matt loved Royal Rangers (a Christian boy-scout-type organization), especially when it came to the activities that had to do with historic campouts. When we first met Matt, he was very excited about participating in Revolutionary War reenactments and was especially thrilled with his new black-powder musket. There was a draw, an allure even in those teenage days, toward the historic past and the implements of times nearly forgotten.

When Matt graduated from his homeschool high school, he thought long and hard about what he really wanted to do. In the midst of pondering and praying, he was offered the chance to enter an apprenticeship with an elderly Dutch man who was a master blacksmith. It was incredible timing and an incredible opportunity. This man patiently and carefully taught Matt the rudiments of blacksmithing and then began to take him to all of the blacksmith shops in the area so he could see the various possibilities in the field of blacksmithing. One shop was that of a master knife and sword craftsman who offered Matt the incredibly rare opportunity to study this craft with him. Matt jumped at the chance. Through those classes, he became one of a very small, elite group of knife makers in this country who can make a composite Damascus sword—a collector's item made from one piece of steel that is heated, pulled, stretched, laid over, pounded, and then heated again. This process is repeated time after time after time, resulting in a sword with one hundred to five hundred layers and beautiful, intricate patterns.

On a visit to a shop in Philadelphia, Matt was introduced to a seventy-year-old Italian man who was about to retire. His specialty was in tempering and reshaping stone mason hammers. Matt requested a chance to learn how to do this, and the elderly man graciously agreed. Though he had difficulty understanding the man's English, Matt took copious notes as he carefully watched the process. Shortly after, the man returned home to Italy. Amazingly enough, some stone masons are learning that he has the skill and the knowledge to do this work. His mom told me in some astonishment that people from Pennsylvania have begun showing up at Matt's door, asking him to temper and reshape their stone mason hammers. In fact, one gentleman told Matt that if he truly had mastered this, he would never lack for business, since there were only a handful of blacksmiths on the east coast who knew how to do the work. The customers have indicated their satisfaction, and they are now giving good reports to others.

Matt has his own forge behind his parent's home, where he does much of his blacksmithing. If you can picture the fire and the bellows and hear the ting of steel shaping iron and the hiss of hot metal touching cool water, you will be envisioning his normal work day. It is indeed like stepping back in time to watch him work—a young man with a passion to do well, evidencing the Master's touch.

OUR JOURNAL

We never set out to own a business/ministry devoted to homeschooling families. All we really wanted was to be together as a family, to have both parents be able to spend vast amounts of time with our kids, and to eventually work together. When we moved back to Bill's hometown of Belle Fourche, South Dakota in 1992, we had no idea what kind of work he would find as I stayed home to continue homeschooling our three children. It didn't really matter to us, though, since at that point the goal was to simplify our lifestyle and devote more time to our family.

The Lord, however, knows the desires of our hearts and knows His plans for His children. He began to lead us down an unusual path that looked bizarre to outsiders but seemed right to us. After the move to South Dakota, a door opened up for us to travel around the country selling materials for a homeschool resource company. We loved having our family experience life on the road and work in the booth! We treasured the moments with our children, the homeschool families we were meeting, and the other vendor families who lived out of a suitcase like we did. Eventually, as I started sharing some of the wild things I had learned while teaching my own children world history, people began to ask me for tapes of these stories. We recorded *What in the World's Going On Here?* an audio overview of world history from a Judeo-Christian perspective. Though it was thrilling to have accomplished that project, we found our funds running extremely low. We also realized we were not making enough money to feed our family by working for someone else. So we began to earnestly pray about what the Lord would have us do.

"Um, Lord, could Bill go back to work as a teacher? It's better money than this!"
"Um, Lord, could Bill work as a truck driver? It's better money than this!"
"Um, Lord, can we do ANYTHING else? It's got to be better money than this!"

The answer in our hearts to all of these requests continued to be a steadfast, *"No."* Our parents and our friends did not understand why on earth we didn't just go out and get real jobs, but there was a quiet confidence that, though the path looked scary from a financial perspective, God was calling us to walk it with Him.

We officially started our own business, Diana Waring—History Alive!, in April of 1996. It was a true case of starting on a shoestring budget, but we were hoping that the old adage was true, *"Where God guides, He provides."* Step by step, book by book, tape by tape, our company began to pay its bills. It was an incredibly exhilarating sensation when our company began to pay us as well! Though no one I know is in this business for the money(!), there is a real joy in being able to do what you love, work with your family, and put food on the table. It just doesn't get any better than this!

LIFE IS LIKE A TREASURE HUNT

Have you ever been on a treasure hunt, map and all? If so, you may remember the frustration of trying to figure out what the clues on the map indicate. Several people standing around, scratching their heads, and puzzling over clues can be funny to the casual observer but absolutely brain-draining for the participants.

In many ways, life is like a treasure hunt. We are all seeking the treasure of joy, satisfaction, and fulfillment in life, and for most it appears to be hidden in an unknown place. So people spend energy, time, and money hunting around in unusual spots, looking under rocks and digging up dirt in an effort to discover their treasure.

The Christian philosopher, Blaise Pascal, once described this treasure hunt as a God-shaped vacuum. Only God Himself can fill this void in our lives, and until we come into relationship with Him through Jesus Christ, we will be unable to fill the void (or find the treasure!). So the first and most important part of the treasure hunt is found in God, Himself.

That is not the end of the treasure hunt, however. It is only the beginning. As Christians, we need to discover what God's thoughts are concerning us—His plans and purposes for our lives. Why did He create us with these specific giftings and desires? Why did He set us in this nation at this point in history? Is it, Esther-like, *"for such a time as this?"* Amazing! Not only are we on a treasure hunt, but the map is written in Hebrew and Greek! The Creator of the Universe, the Author and Finisher of our faith, the God of the Bible has a plan for each of our lives. He is calling us to a work that is uniquely ours to do. Whether that work is being a stay-at-home mother who homeschools her children, a missionary translating the Scriptures in Papua New Guinea, a film director creating movies to challenge our culture with the Judeo-Christian worldview, President of the United States during a world crisis, or a caring piano teacher, He has something special designed just for us, for this particular moment in history, in our specific locale—a job for us to do.

When it comes to finding out what God's call is on our lives, there appear to be four responses:

❶ People who seem to know for sure:
"God called me to the mission field when I was seven years old, and that call has never wavered."
❷ People who aren't sure:
"Um, I think God might want me to be a dentist, but I haven't really figured it out yet."
❸ People who don't have a clue:
"God has a plan for my life?"
❹ People who want (fill in the blank) to be God's call:
"I am SURE God is calling me to be a NASCAR driver!"

Since there are numerous books, tapes, seminars, and more that will give helpful information about knowing God's will in your life, I would like to simply share two things we have learned about this subject: *pray* and *wait on the Lord*.

To the first group of people, who seem to know what God's call is, I would encourage them to pray and wait on the Lord to confirm the timing, the provision, and the pathway.

I learned this lesson the hard way. When I was twenty-one, I heard a clear call of God in my heart to go to the nation of France. Though I wanted to leave college at that moment and go, there was a strong sense that God intended for me to finish my studies, so I changed my major to French and began learning all I could about that mission field. When I graduated, an opportunity arose to work in Europe for a summer with French-speaking university students. It looked good on paper, but the experience was totally devastating. I ended up back in the U.S., knowing I would never be able to go to France as a missionary by myself. In the midst of pastoral counseling, I realized that the primary desire in my heart was to be a wife and mother. Shortly afterward, Bill (my best friend from college days) and I were married. Since 1976, I have been waiting on God about this call to France. He has continued to lead us in paths that don't seem to lead to France, but there is a certainty in my heart that God has used this in my life to direct my steps. A wise missionary, who recently returned home from France, told me that God's timing is perfect. She said, "Diana, God knows that you were probably not ready for the French people AND the French people were not ready for you. In His time, it will be perfect."

To the second group of people, who aren't sure what God's call is, I would encourage them to pray and wait on the Lord to give them clear direction.

We experienced this just prior to starting our business. We had tried to get Bill back into teaching, but the doors kept shutting, and it was obviously the hand of the Lord. We wanted to find a permanent job, but the Lord impressed Bill with the thought that we needed to do another season of homeschool conventions. Since we did not know what was going to happen after that season finished, we began to fast twice a week and pray constantly, seeking the Lord for His plan for us. Six months into this state of crying out for God's wisdom, He suddenly made our path very clear. That was the beginning and the reason for our own business.

To the third group of people, who don't have a clue that God has a plan, I would encourage them to pray and wait on the Lord to show them what He wants them to do.

As a young Christian, I had no concept that the God of the universe had a plan for my life. I thought it was all up to me to figure it out, so I started out in college with what I loved best: theater. That was a rather weird experience, which definitely drew me away from a relationship with God, so I tried again. This time I chose music for a major, since I love to sing almost as much as I love acting. It was fun to learn music theory, to sing twentieth century choral music, and to attend the student recitals, but it wasn't the right "fit" for my personality. After the call to France, I really began to pray about how to proceed. Much to my amazement, He showed me I was to return to college and change my major, yet again, to French. Though I have not yet been to France, God has used what I learned in that degree program in mighty ways in my life and our business. Once I understood that I should ask Him, God showed me the best path to take.

To the fourth group of people, who want what they want to be God's call on their life, I would encourage them to pray and wait on the Lord to show them His ways and His thoughts, remembering that His thoughts are not the same as ours.

When we first started working for the homeschool company, we were thrilled with the opportunity to travel the nation, selling fabulous books to wonderful people. We loved the folks we worked with, we loved the books we sold, we loved meeting all of the homeschoolers. What could be better? Unfortunately, we assumed that God wanted us to do what we wanted to do, so we never asked Him. This came home to us in a powerful way after the second year, when I ended up in the hospital with pneumonia. We had struggled through that year financially, relationally, "vehicle-ly" (our motor home broke down in almost every town we visited), and physically. Lying in that sickbed, I cried out to the Lord, "Why is this happening?" To my amazement, He began to show both Bill and me that we had never asked Him if we should do what we were doing! Though we were in the basic area of gifting, talent, and passion, He had something different in mind for us than working for another company, selling other people's books. We were amazed to discover that we had missed what He really wanted us to do—create our own products and sell them. Getting in trouble because we ran off in our own direction, without letting God show us His, was a lesson we hope never to forget!

So, as we consider how to conduct our personalized treasure hunt—to do what we love and "da money will follow"—we need to remember these things:

❶ *Ask the Lord.*
❷ *Wait for His direction.*

DREAMS AND PASSIONS

Laura Kolb is our friend. She is a gifted piano teacher with an ability to pass on not only her knowledge of the piano but also her passion for the piano to her many students. Her story is astonishing.

Laura has loved music since she was a young girl. She played piano, gobbling up all of the instruction that came her way, always eager to know more. In her first year of college, she studied piano seriously with great enthusiasm and joy. However, her parents were greatly concerned that Laura would never be able to make a living playing the piano, so they counselled her to go into another field—a more lucrative career. She bowed to their wishes and transferred to another school, where she studied chemical engineering. After graduation, Laura found work with an international chemical manufacturer, where she quickly rose through the ranks to a position of supervisor. Though the money was great, Laura missed the joy of music in her life, so she resumed her piano studies on the side. After many years of "working for the man," Laura became very sick. As she struggled for months to recover from this debilitating illness, she contemplated her life and began to pray earnestly about what she was seeing.

Laura realized that the longing of her heart was to teach others how to play piano. Though she had been very successful in her chemical engineering career, it had not satisfied her heart. Though this career was very lucrative, she was not happy. And after all, money isn't everything! So, this very brave lady took an immense step. She quit her job and used her savings to move back to our little town in South Dakota to set up a piano studio. We are personally very, very glad she did, because she is the one who helped Melody go from being a fair student to a serious student of the piano.

Does Laura miss her other job? Not for a moment. Does she miss the security of a well-paid position? Truthfully, it has been quite a change, quite a stretch of faith, to own her own business, to make just enough to cover her bills. However, Laura has expressed to me that it is well worth it. There is a joy, a tremendous satisfaction in teaching piano. Laura has learned the truth of this saying:

"A person who loves what they do will never work a day in their life!"

REAPING THE HARVEST

In contrast to Laura and the joy she now finds in her teaching, think about some of the people you have seen working in fast food joints. You know the ones I am talking about. They stand around with bored expressions on their faces. If you need help, they reluctantly shuffle over and halfheartedly take your order. If given half a chance, they will gladly tell you all of the complaints associated with their jobs. They are miserable, and you are not happy with their service . . . It is a common occurrence.

Misery in a job is not limited to fast food employees, however. You can find it in high-rise office buildings, in professionals with impressive letters after their names, in people with six-figure incomes. It is seen in department stores, hotel lobbies, post offices, libraries, and accounting offices. Job dissatisfaction is one of the more serious issues in the business world today. Many people are locked into jobs they don't like with debts and obligations that make it seem impossible to change careers. They are in the rat race, and they are tired of being rats.

From personal experience, let me tell you that is much easier to make thoughtful, well-counselled career choices as a young person than to change midstream when you are in your 30's or 40's or 50's. So here are a few ideas for you as you prayerfully consider your options:

List your dreams/passions/talents.
- *What giftings, talents, and passions do you have?*
- *What relationships in your life might be part of the puzzle?*
- *What background and experience do you have?*
- *What are your weaknesses?*
- *How is your self-motivation?*
- *What gets your attention?*

Next, write out careers that fit your dreams/passions/talents. Use creative thinking skills to brainstorm the possibilities! For example:
- *"Love to cook"—caterer, chef, stand-in for Julia Child, mom*
- *"Can whinny like a horse"—horse trainer, clown, father who amuses his children*
- *"Pretty good storyteller"—history teacher, used car sales, fiction writer*

I would strongly encourage you to sit down with family members and friends and discuss these questions openly with them. The Bible speaks great wisdom when it declares, *"The wounds of a friend are better than the kisses of an*

enemy." *(para.)* Having someone you trust speak loving truth about your strengths and weaknesses, though it may burst a few unrealistic bubbles, will give great clarity and realistic wisdom, which will help you succeed in your endeavor. *"Diana, I know you love to arrange your furniture and keep your house tidy. I just don't think you are going to be the one to bump Martha Stewart off her pedestal."*

Now, look for an opportunity to test out your selections.

It is far easier to *try before you buy* if you are not yet married with children. Try to pursue learning opportunities before enrolling in a university, relocating, getting married, or other major long-term commitments. Squeeze in some chances while still in school. Try different approaches like these. If you have a hankering for catering, seek a short apprenticeship with a caterer and see if you like the hours and the pressures. If you have a yen for doctoring, ask a local doctor if you can shadow him or her for a few days, weeks, or months to discover whether the sight of blood makes you faint! If you have a longing for singing, take some choir courses and find out whether your throat can endure. If you desire a zoo vet career, volunteer at a wild animal attraction and learn about the realities of fangs and claws. If you have always dreamed of being a Bible translator to a people group with no written language, go on a short-term missions trip to find out if you have the right stuff.

All of these short apprenticeships, courses, and volunteer positions will help you understand whether your dreams are what you had expected. If you love it and come back for more, then there is a high probability that you will love that particular career for a long time. If, on the other hand, time drags, and you can't wait to be finished, you need to do an about face and find a different option.

For some, the door to the dream career is a lengthy apprenticeship, like Matt Harris. For others, the door opens while they are living at home, as they start up an entrepreneurial business, or find a job that is really enjoyable. For still others, the door opens at college or tech school.

So, as we consider how to conduct our personalized treasure hunt—to do what we love and "da money will follow"—we need to remember these things:

❶ *Ask the Lord.*
❷ *Wait for His direction.*
❸ *Consider your dreams and passions.*
❹ *Try before you buy.*

197

COLLEGE? NO SWEAT!

One of people I most enjoy hearing describe the benefits of homeschooling is Dr. Jay Wile (Ph.D. in Nuclear Chemistry). He was, at one time, a science professor at Ball State University in Muncie, Indiana. One day, while driving to work, Dr. Wile pondered what characteristics his top three students had in common and realized that they had all been homeschooled. Since Dr. Wile and his wife, Kathleen, had no children at that point, they knew very little about this modern-day phenomena. However, he was quite good at researching (one of the skills you learn in graduate school!), and he began to research in the library all of the studies, statistics, and current information available on homeschooling in the U.S. and Canada. His research led him to regional, state, and national studies—most of which were done by educational researchers, not homeschoolers. The studies overwhelmingly showed that homeschoolers scored significantly above the norm in academic AND social tests, which meshed with Dr. Wile's experience of teaching freshman-level, science courses. There is something about the homeschooling environment which, regardless of parental income and academic achievement, produces excellent academic students who are quite skilled at getting along with others.

Dr. Wile, as he tells this story to enthusiastic crowds of homeschoolers, points out that colleges and universities are more and more receptive and appreciative of homeschoolers who seek to attend their schools. In 1999, 68% of U.S. universities accepted a parent-prepared transcript (which means homeschoolers) *at the same weight* as public school transcripts. Also, in 1999, Stanford University accepted 27% of the homeschoolers who applied, which is twice the rate of what they usually accept from public and private school students (13%). A major study at Boston University shows that homeschoolers continuing in college have a grade point average of 3.3, while the grade point average of the college population as a whole is 2.0!

So, if you are homeschooled and interested in attending college, you have a good reputation already. I was fascinated to learn that a former U.S. Department of Education researcher, Patricia Lines, was quoted as saying:

> *"If I didn't know anything about someone other than their educational background, I'd rather hop into a foxhole with a homeschool kid than one from public school. The homeschool kid will be a little better educated and dependable."*

College? No sweat. Well, maybe a little sweat.

Let us ask at this point, what should one study in college? Environmental engineering was the recommendation a few years ago, because that was where the big bucks and the guaranteed jobs were going to be. If environmental engineering is the stuff of your dreams, then go for it! However, if you have talents/passions/giftings in other areas, I would encourage you to NOT go into environmental engineering—to not "follow da money." Instead, carefully consider what a college experience can do to help you prepare for your dreams. You need to ask the right questions.

First, why am I doing this?

College is an investment in your future. It may be one of the doors to unlocking your talents/giftings/passion, but you need to really consider why you want to go. If it is only to mark time, there may be better ways to spend it preparing for your future. Have you thought about various options, besides college? You might also consider: correspondence schools, military service, volunteering to gain experience, foreign missions, apprenticeships, mentoring, or vocational or specialty schools.

Secondly, what studies will further my education and help me to accomplish my goals?

One of the wisest bits of advice I received as I contemplated going to college was to study subjects that would broaden my horizons. There was so much about the world that I didn't know existed, and taking wide-ranging courses helped me discover answers to questions I hadn't even asked yet. Because of this advice, I took African history (one of my favorites!), Anthropology, Logic, Philosophy of Science (a watershed course, where I learned to defend my faith even though I was the only female and the only non-Science major in the course!), and more. Though I ended up as a French major where these courses were not required, they broadened my awareness of knowledge and the way people think, which continues to be of use to me today. Please don't settle for courses in just one area—stretch out and discover an amazing world of learning!

Thirdly, how can I wring every last bit of value out of this very expensive education?

Carpe diem—seize the day! You are the only one who can take your college courses beyond the bare minimum required into an actual learning experience.

Ask questions, talk to the prof about his background and worldview, interact with the material, set up discussion/study groups with other students. In essence, this is not about getting a degree, this is about learning as much as you can. The degree is just a byproduct.

College? It may be the wisest investment of time and money you ever make. Or it may be a waste of time. You are the one who determines the end result.

Once again, as we consider how to conduct our personalized treasure hunt—to do what we love and "da money will follow"—we need to remember these things:

➊ *Ask the Lord.*
➋ *Wait for His direction.*
➌ *Consider your dreams and passions.*
➍ *Try before you buy.*
➎ *Invest in your education, broaden your horizons, seize the day.*

KEEP IT SIMPLE, SWEETIE!

The final thought I would like you to ponder in this issue of doing what you love and "da money will follow" is the question of how much money is enough? Some of us, in doing what we love, might have lots of money follow. Others of us, doing what we love, may have to depend on the Lord's supernatural provision in order to continue (much like Hudson Taylor, founder of the China Inland Mission in the 1800's). But in order to be free to do what we love, we must thoughtfully consider what our goals are in this area and why we have set those goals.

Today, there are books on the market that promise to teach you how to become millionaires, how to make killer investments, how to become rich with a handful of dollars and the book's secret strategies. All around us is a culture that defines success in life by how many toys you acquire, how early you can retire, and the size of your annual income—which they admire.

Is that it? Is this all about how much wealth I can acquire? Is my net worth determined by my bank account and possessions? Is this the path to happiness? Does the Bible have any answers to this area of life?

"Now godliness with contentment is great gain. For we brought nothing into this world, and it is certain we can carry nothing out. And having food and

clothing, with these we shall be content. But those who desire to be rich fall into temptation and a snare, and into many foolish and harmful lusts which drown men in destruction and perdition. For the love of money is a root of all kinds of evil, for which some have strayed from the faith in their greediness, and pierced themselves through with many sorrows." —1 Timothy 6:6–10

Godliness with contentment is great gain. That is not how our culture defines great gain, is it? The Bible speaks truth, however. If we are in Christ, walking obediently to Him, and if we can be content with what He has given us, THAT is great gain! Contentment is one of the most precious treasures we can find in our personalized treasure hunt. The Apostle Paul found it:

"Not that I speak in regard to need, for I have learned in whatever state I am, to be content: I know how to be abased, and I know how to abound. Everywhere and in all things I have learned both to be full and to be hungry, both to abound and to suffer need. I can do all things through Christ who strengthens me."
—Philippians 4:11–13

Contentment is not having everything I want. It is not having the means to buy anything that catches my eye. Contentment is being satisfied with what the Lord has put in my life—and it takes Him working His strength in me to accomplish it! Once again we see that this is not about us; it's about Him.

While in New Zealand, we met a precious, young woman named Moana. Moana is Maori, the indigenous people of New Zealand. She had the elegance and looks of a princess, the graceful mannerisms of royalty. I was astonished to learn in conversation with her that this beautiful, elegant, gracious woman served the poorest of the poor in Sudan. She had come home for a short time to recuperate, and that is where we met. Moana is a successful woman; her life has incredible net worth; she has joy (in the midst of suffering); yet she is a missionary, who lives by faith and has very little of this world's treasure.

Success and worth and joy in the Kingdom of God are not equated with dollars in the bank. As we seek to know God's plan for our lives, as we try to discover the clues to the treasure in our giftings and talents and passions, as we work hard to prepare for a lifetime of service, we need to keep the Apostle Paul's words about contentment continually before us. We need to strive to remember that with eternity in view, our success and net worth have a different definition than what the world uses.

As we consider how to conduct our personalized treasure hunt—to do what we love and "da money will follow"—we need to remember these things:

◆ *Ask the Lord.*
◆ *Wait for His direction.*
◆ *Consider your dreams and passions.*
◆ *Try before you buy.*
◆ *Invest in your education, broaden your horizons, seize the day.*
◆ *Be content.*

A final story. Rich Jeffus, cofounder of Visual Manna, was a man we called, "friend." Rich was an incredible artist, an amazing storyteller, a comfortable bear of a man who encouraged everyone he met. Rich and his wife, Sharon, were fellow homeschool vendors who travelled around the U.S. to conventions and to support groups to do art workshops for kids. They drove older vehicles; they lived in an older house; they were always struggling to make the various ends meet—much like many of the homeschool vendors we know.

In March of 2002, Rich Jeffus was killed in an accident while working on his van in preparation for a convention. We were shocked and grieved to lose this beloved friend. After the funeral, we were amazed to learn that Rich had led more than 3,000 people to Christ in his lifetime! Everywhere he went, Rich engaged people in conversation, leading them to the subject of the Lord who had so changed his own life. He had lively debates with evolutionists and atheists—many of whom attended his funeral. He was a man whose life had touched thousands upon thousands of people with the reality of the Living God. Rich had also inspired countless young people in their art, leaving a legacy of creativity and encouragement.

Though Rich was not rich in the things of this world, he was one of the richest men I have ever known. He had served the Lord faithfully, loved his family dearly, taught children enthusiastically, strove for excellence in his paintings and sculptures, and walked as a pilgrim on this earth. With all my heart, I believe that heaven resounded with these words on his arrival: *"Well done, good and faithful servant . . . Enter into the joy of your Lord."*

RECOMMENDED RESOURCES

The Guidance Manual for the Christian Home School by David & Laurie Callihan
An excellent resource! It's like having a guidance counselor in your home!

Finding a Job You Can Love by Ralph Mattson and Arthur F. Miller, Jr.
A fabulous book that will help in your treasure hunt!

Let My People Go!

In April of 2000, we had the privilege of attending the Massachusetts homeschool convention (known by the lovely acronym, HOPE). Our family had been asked to sing on Friday night after the graduation ceremonies, so we had a chance to watch one of my favorite sights—homeschool graduates! Well organized with a steady flow of young people marching across the stage, when each student was presented, the emcee read a description of their homeschooling experience and plans for the future.

We sat, amazed and delighted, as the litany of accomplishments and goals was recited. It was as if we were seeing the cream of America's crop crossing the stage, and indeed, we were. Fully one-third of these young people had been involved in short-term missions, one-third had started their own entrepreneurial businesses, many had contributed significant volunteer activity throughout their high school years. As the goals rolled out, we heard that many were planning to attend a university while others were planning to go into the military or missions. The wide-ranging interests, the varied activities, the servant-heart expressed that evening gave us great hope for the future of our nation's leadership.

As parents and grandparents cried, as graduates warmly thanked their parents for making it all possible, as the audience basked in the glow of flashbulbs and a job exceedingly well done, I realized that we were witnessing a golden harvest of healthy, ready-to-serve, well trained, educated young people about to take on the world. It was one of the most comforting sights I have ever seen.

OUR JOURNAL

When Craig and Barbara Smith wrote to us that their oldest two wanted to spend some time in the United States, we jumped at the chance to show them our nation. After all, the Smith family had gone to great lengths to show us New

Zealand, and we felt that this was a delightful opportunity to reciprocate in kind. E-mails flew back and forth across the Pacific as we considered dates and arrangements. At last, it was decided that Genevieve and Zach would join us in March of 2001, and travel with us until the end of June. In that time, we would travel through thirty states, giving them quite a taste of America. After leaving us, they would work for another homeschool business, visit friends around the U.S., and end up at their grandmother's house in California for the winter. (Craig is from California, so not only do Genevieve and Zach have U.S. family, but U.S. citizenship.)

It was difficult for Craig and Barbara to say goodbye to these two children, helpers, and friends. When Genevieve and Zach embarked, it was uncertain how long they would be away, and at this writing, it has been nearly a year and a half! However, the Smiths were willing, for their children's sake, to let them go for this once-in-a-lifetime overseas experience.

Because of their parents' willingness and sacrifice, Genevieve and Zach have had amazing opportunities to see another nation, meet thousands of homeschoolers, work at homeschool conventions, visit museums, go to ballets, listen to concerts, visit churches, hear thought-provoking speakers, make new friends, and prepare themselves for the rest of their lives. We've had the privilege of observing them on this adventure, listening to them process the experience and praying for them.

Their plans for applying what they have learned are fascinating, as well. They are storing up wisdom and insight that will help their parents' business, that will strengthen their service to New Zealand homeschoolers, and will bless their own families someday. Zach has examined possible apprenticeship and career choices, which are helping clarify his direction. Genevieve has been processing how she can aid her parents when she returns to New Zealand, gaining knowledge that will better serve them in their marvelous homeschool magazine, *Keystone*. Craig and Barbara made an amazingly difficult choice to release their children, and it is resulting in a blessing for them all.

These lessons have not been lost on us. As we contemplate the upcoming moments of releasing our own children to their adult futures as the Lord leads them, we remember what we have learned from Craig and Barbara Smith, *"Let them go and grow."*

ROOTS

One of the most valuable aspects of homeschooling is that parents can give children a rootedness, a sense of belonging, a connectedness to family. As they grow into young adults, our homeschooled children know who they are, they know where they come from, and they have a deep sense of family identity, which is increasingly rare in today's culture.

Our relationship is not institutional, not just that of caregiver/bill payer to a dependent. It is instead a deep and abiding friendship between parents and children. We have stepped outside the norm of our culture, where the attitude seems to be, *"Just survive till they're eighteen. Then they'll be gone, and you'll be done!"* Instead, we homeschoolers are grateful for each day with them and consider our children's departure from home as a gaping hole that will require the Lord Himself to fill. We work long and hard to give them "roots" of traditions, memories, and identity.

It takes commitment nowadays to give roots to your child. It takes time. It takes sacrifice. It takes energy. It takes selflessness. At the same time, in the mystery of how God formed the creation, roots grow naturally. Consider this: a farmer has to work and put out his own effort to plant the seed, yet he wisely knows that only God can grow the plant, only God can give the increase, only God can give the plant roots. Similarly, in our families, it takes work on our side, effort that we expend, but it is God who truly grows the roots in our children. These roots spring out of having shared experiences, like a camping trip when you spent all your time huddled in sleeping bags due to the cold rain, insider jokes that only the family knows and appreciates, memories of spontaneous fun or of unexpected difficulty, and conflicts resolved. Roots grow naturally living day by day in a family that cherishes each of its members.

Root growth can also be encouraged, as I learned in my early twenties when I joined a friend for a day in her class at Regent College in British Columbia. Regent is designed to train college graduates to think Biblically, act Christianly, and change the world. My friend was especially enjoying this particular class. I gladly went along for the ride, anticipating hearing something special that day, but little knowing it would be a pivotal message for my life.

The professor spoke about the importance of traditions in the life of a child and for the health of a family. He described in great detail the elaborate Christmas traditions his family had instituted, like waiting to open presents until breakfast had been served and cleaned up! He told us of birthday traditions and harvest traditions and Easter traditions and patriotic traditions. It was not the specific traditions that he was seeking to impress on us; in fact, he told us we needed to create our own. What he was endeavoring to show was the incredible value, the glue-that-holds-us-together function, and the precious and unique impact of family traditions.

REAPING THE HARVEST

Traditions are one of the God-given ways we can use to encourage roots in our children. One of the Waring family traditions is that of singing for our invited dinner guests. We think of it as "singing for YOUR supper!" We also attend the parade and rodeo on the 4th of July in Belle Fourche, South Dakota, with a picnic lunch sandwiched in between. These and other traditions have given our children a sense of what it is to be part of the Waring family. It has helped give them a rootedness in who they are and where they come from.

I must confess, however, that we have not always kept our holiday traditions intact. There have been years where, due to sickness or travelling or exhaustion, we have let them slide. This concept of creating and maintaining traditions is not to put a heavy burden on your shoulders. It is simply something to consider, something to examine to see how your family is doing and if there are a few traditions you can regularly and joyfully do that will help give your children a sense of belonging and identity. Fortunately, traditions are not the ONLY means of giving our children roots.

Good memories are another wonderful way to encourage roots. As we seek to give our children special memories, as we take time to create a memorable moment, as we expend the energy to give them a precious experience, we are giving our children roots. Some of my favorite memories with Bill, Isaac, Michael, and Melody are the times when we were focused on being together—singing on stage at the Buffalo Round Up in Custer State Park, walking the Freedom Trail in Boston during a misty rain, cooking a special, candlelit dinner of turkey crepes, reading *Laddie* by Gene Stratton-Porter, going to see *Lord of the Rings* at an historic theater in Seattle. We have delightful memories of friends joining us on the road for a taste of the Waring lifestyle—Genevieve and Zach, Lani and Nadia, Christy, and Nick. There are precious friends who have visited us in the Black Hills and allowed us to play tour guide—Rod and Alexis, Craig and Barbara, Dave and Nanci, John and Marsha, Jesika and Catriona, Ashley, and Tanice. All of these people and places and events bring an ongoing blessing to us as we view them in our memory.

What does it take to create a memory? An attitude of joy and delight is foundational. To that, add a bit of fun and food. If you have a view, so much the better. And of course, there are always the ants, mosquitoes, bees, and other momentous challenges to be conquered, which add to the memory! In essence, it is mostly about sharing an experience together.

A sense of identity is crucial to growing roots. You are already giving a huge chunk of that by wandering off the crowded path of normalcy in order to home-school your children. They understand fairly quickly that one of their identifying traits is being homeschooled. As you share your ethnic background, your hobbies, and your memories of growing up, you will be giving them a true sense of where they come from, to what family they belong. As you eat the foods of your culture, listen to the music, dance the folk dances(!), read the stories of your nation's history, you will be establishing a cultural identity for your children. As you go to church, worship with them in music, talk about God's present reality in your life, read the Scriptures, and pray with them, you will be helping them find their identity in the Body of Christ.

The Bible speaks of the importance of being rooted in Jesus:

> *". . . that Christ may dwell in your hearts through faith; that you, being rooted and grounded in love, may be able to comprehend with all the saints what is the width and length and depth and height—to know the love of Christ which passes knowledge; that you may be filled with all the fullness of God."*
>
> *—Ephesians 3:17–19*

> *"As you therefore have received Christ Jesus the Lord, so walk in Him, rooted and built up in Him and established in the faith, as you have been taught, abounding in it with thanksgiving."*
>
> *—Colossians 2:6–7*

This business of giving our children roots is ultimately about assuring that they are rooted in Christ. That is where our true sense of belonging and our true identity comes from. Without this solid foundation, the house will eventually fall. So, I would like to encourage you to take the time, take the effort, create the climate to share with your children frequently and significantly about the goodness of God, pray for them without ceasing, and open God's Word to their hearts. Give them the roots of belonging to your family, and encourage their roots in belonging to God.

STAY OR GO?

OK. We are diligently working and praying to establish healthy roots in our children. That, however, is not the end of the story, as these children have the indefatigable habit of growing up to adulthood.

There are various ideas floating around the homeschool community concerning whether children should remain with their parents when they reach adulthood.

REAPING THE HARVEST

Some feel that these wonderful, young adults need to continue working alongside the parents, living close by, and forming an extended family unit, especially when grandchildren arrive. Others believe that these well-prepared, young adults have been raised up by God, *"for such a time as this,"* that they might go out (away from the parents) and serve the Lord in another location. In our travels, we have met strong proponents for each side.

Boiled down to its simplest components, the question is, *"Stay or go?"* The answer from history is twofold: *"Stay."* OR *"Go."* For Christians, the real question is, *"Would the Lord have me stay or go?"* And His answer could be either one, based on the plans He has for you—the good works He prepared before the foundation of the world for you to walk in. We will look at two recent examples of people who made opposite decisions and whose paths were obviously blessed by God.

An example of someone who stayed comes from the story of the von Trapp family (remember *The Sound of Music*?). At the FPEA homeschool convention in Orlando in May of 2000, we were thrilled to learn that Rosemarie Trapp (the family dropped the "von" when they left Austria) had come to speak to homeschoolers. Rosemarie was accompanied by Bill Anderson, a writer we had collaborated with in the past. Bill had recently finished a marvelous book on the Trapp Family Singers, and it had been his suggestion to the convention organizers to bring Rosemarie to speak. Though I had talked with Bill on the phone many times, we had never met in person, so we were delighted to have the opportunity to finally connect.

"Bill! It's so nice to meet you in person! We would love to have dinner with you one of the nights of the convention."

"Oh, that would be great, but, is it all right if I bring Rosemarie with me?"

Shock. Cough, sputter, sputter. Disbelief in the face of great fortune!

"That would be FABULOUS!!"

Imagine, if you will, sitting around a hotel room with Rosemarie Trapp, hearing the stories of her childhood and singing songs together, including songs from *The Sound of Music* and from New Zealand! Rosemarie was the first child born to the Captain and Maria, and though she was not portrayed in the movie, she was in the thick of things during the escape from the Nazis in Austria and the subsequent time in the U. S. As Bill Anderson encouraged her reminiscing, an amazing perspective surfaced. The Trapp children as young adults had made a carefully reasoned decision to continue working with their family, travelling as the Trapp Family Singers. This incredible music group travelled all over the U.S., as well as many nations of the world, bringing delight to the ears of music lovers and joyous encouragement to families everywhere. They spent nineteen years of

208

their adult lives in this way before the touring was finally discontinued. Bill told us that the Trapp siblings had shared with him, during the research for his book, that they had enjoyed unusually long and productive lives, well past the normal age for such things. It seemed to them that God had given them at the end of their lives an extra nineteen years of health and productivity to enjoy.

We were riveted by the thought. This was good news, indeed! What an example for our own ready-to-leave offspring! Here was a family that homeschooled (on the tour bus and at the hotels), that travelled around the nation in order to do the family business, and whose young adults chose to continue working with the family. And God certainly blessed them.

Lesson examined and noted.

We need, however, to turn the coin over to the flip side. From the same era, an example of one who goes is the story of Jim Elliot. He was raised in a Christian home by devout parents. He went to a Christian college, Wheaton, where the Lord began to speak to his heart about tribal people who had never heard the Gospel. After graduating from Wheaton, Jim sensed God's call to South America as a missionary and was given his parents' blessing. Perhaps, you know the story. He, along with several other men, sought an opening for communication with the Auca people, a fierce tribe that killed all outsiders who ventured into their territory. The missionaries, having dropped gifts from their plane, landed on a beach in Auca land. They made tentative contact with three members of the tribe and were elated at this first opening into a closed culture. The next day, the Auca warriors attacked, and the missionaries chose not to defend themselves though they had rifles and could have done so. The world was shocked by the martyrdom of these missionaries, and many people began to question what was so significant about Christianity that someone would give his life to bring the Gospel to a stone-age tribe. As a result, many people came into the Kingdom of God; many offered their lives as missionaries, and the door was eventually opened to bring the Gospel to the Aucas. (Elisabeth Elliot's book *Through Gates of Splendor* tells this part of the story. The incredible conclusion of how the Lord broke through the closed doors of this tribal group is found in *Dayuma*.) Let me restate. Jim Elliot's life and death were used by God in unbelievably powerful ways all over the world, and his influence continues to this day—we constantly meet people who mention Jim Elliot's death as the turning point in their own lives.

We were gripped by the thought. This is a much harder road to follow, and I was less anxious to point out this example to my own children. Here was a Christian young man, raised by Christian parents, a world changer called by God, who lived a short life of service in a remote location of the globe. Though his death seems tragic on this side of eternity, we know from the fruit it brought that God certainly blessed him, both his life and his martyrdom.

Second lesson examined and noted.

We must walk very carefully in this area. Our children *might* be called by God to work along side us for the rest of their lives. Our children *might* be called by God to serve Him in another location, even a dangerous one. We might have one called to remain with us, while another is called to the ends of the earth. Brothers and sisters, it is not OUR choice! We need to be openhanded with their futures, holding them up to God for His use and His pleasure.

A UNIQUE PORTRAIT

Have you ever heard the fable of the villagers who all complained that they each had the *greatest* amount of problems in all the village? Each one was convinced that his was the worst lot in life, until a stranger suggested that they each put all of their troubles into a bag and hang it on a clothesline. They were to then choose the smallest bag of troubles for their very own. Amazingly, when they looked at each other's bags, their own bag of troubles was discovered to be by far the smallest and most easily borne. Gladly, they took up their own bag of troubles, and in all tellings of this tale, they lived contentedly ever after!

This story has great application for our own lives, whether we consider our troubles or our joys. Have you ever looked at someone else and wished you could change places with them? Seeing their success, their affluence, their fame, their family, etc., have you thought that perhaps God has particular favorites, those upon whom He lavishes better stuff? I certainly have. More than twenty years ago, I looked at the fairy tale life of Princess Diana and longed for the ease and provision reported by the press. She had two beautiful children, governesses, chefs, housekeepers . . . while I, another Diana, labored at home with my three children, playing the part of governess, chef, and housekeeper to the point of exhaustion! I wondered at that point why some people got to live the fairy tale life while others where denied that pleasure. Over the next few years, however, it became obvious that no one lives a fairy tale, no matter what it looks like to outsiders. It taught me in a very real way to be thankful that God made me to live my life and no one else's.

Psalm 107 describes how the circumstances of our lives should give rise to great thanksgiving to God:

"Oh, give thanks to the LORD, for He is good! For His mercy endures forever. Let the redeemed of the LORD say so, Whom He has redeemed from the hand of the enemy. And gathered out of the lands, From the east and from the west, From the north and from the south. They wandered in the wilderness in a desolate way; They found no city to dwell in. Hungry and thirsty, Their soul fainted in them. Then they cried out to the LORD in their trouble, And He delivered them out of their distresses. And He led them forth by the right way, That they might go to a city for a dwelling place. Oh, that men would give thanks to the LORD for His goodness, And for His wonderful works to the children of men!"

—Psalm 107:1–8

1 Thessalonians 5:18 says about the circumstances in our lives: *"In everything give thanks; for this is the will of God in Christ Jesus for you."*

What amazing freedom comes to us when we begin to give thanks to God for what He's done in our lives. What incredible joy begins to flow through us when we quit complaining about how so-and-so has it so good, or how we have it so bad. What delight we have when we can gladly thank the Lord for the path He's leading us on.

OK. Here is principle ❶ Be thankful.
Principle ❷ is walk the path.

God has specifically designed a path for you, a journey where He will call you, send you, lead you, and carry you if you agree to go. We often have conversations with our children about the incredible journey God has for each of them and how thankful they need to be for it. Though they have much in common—salvation in Christ, Bill and Diana Waring as parents, homeschool, travelling, and more—they are each going to walk out their lives in ways unique to themselves. One might go to a university straight through. One might start and stop. One could travel around the world instead. Or they might do something entirely different. One could marry at age twenty-two, one at age forty, while one never marries. Or they might all get married on the same day at the same church! One might live close to us; one might live on the other side of the world; one might have several homes in various locations. Or they could do all three at some point in their lives. One might work for us, one for himself, one for a corporation. Or they might all become carpenters! Their lives will not look just like ours, and they will not look just like each other. God has a specific path for each one of us. And we need to be thankful.

Reaping the Harvest

When it comes to areas such as marriage, family, career, or ministry, God wants to paint a one-of-a-kind portrait in you. For instance, though you may read a wonderful book describing someone's recent courtship, or unusual marriage, or family size, or career accomplishments, or ministry endeavors, don't assume that you should make your life look just the same.

> *"Lemme see. Alan and Imogene courted for six months, spending fifteen minutes a day with each other in the company of their parents. Their courtship turned out pretty good. OK. That's what I am going to do."*
>
> *"Lemme see. Billy Bob married a girl named Jessie Sue and they are happy. I guess I better find myself a Jessie Sue."*
>
> *"Lemme see. Carter and Kaitlin had fifteen babies in fourteen years and they are happy. That's my plan, too!"*
>
> *"Lemme see. Dougie works for Legos, Inc., and he is happy. I should get a job there."*
>
> *"Lemme see. Edward and Mindy went to India as missionaries, and they are being blessed by God. Hmm. That's the happening place in ministry. I guess I'll go, too."*

Oops! Don't forget—God is uniquely leading you through life—your story will NOT be a carbon copy of someone else's. God is far more creative, far more lavish, far wiser than that. He is looking to show His greatness through us in wonderfully unique and powerful ways.

When the Apostle Paul wrote, *"Imitate me, just as I also imitate Christ,"* he was not telling the people of Corinth to become travelling missionaries. He was not asking them to start making tents. He was not setting up a role model for all who would read his words through the ages to be beaten, stoned, shipwrecked, handcuffed to Roman guards, and executed by Nero! The imitation he was describing had to do with heart and attitude issues that spill over into daily actions.

Similarly, we need to imitate those who have hearts and attitudes pleasing to the Lord, but that is not the same as trying to live exactly, to the dot and tittle, just the way they do. You do not have to live in the same town, wear the same clothes, eat the same food, use the same curriculum. They have a unique walk, designed by God. And so do you.

OK. Principle ❶ Be thankful.
Principle ❷ Walk the path God specifically designs for you.

What kind of unique portrait is God painting on the canvas of your life? What one-of-a-kind, adventure story is He writing on the pages of your life? What magnificent melody has He chosen to play, in which you will ring out His goodness and grace to a watching world? He has carefully designed the recipe for you; He has lavished His love and His creativity upon you; He has thoughtfully prepared the way for you to walk. It is not anyone else's story that He desires to write in you—it is uniquely your own.

As parents, make sure your expectations for your young adults is in line with this concept—that they are free to walk a unique path. As young adults, recognize that God is calling you to walk something special, a never-before-seen life, which will result in God displaying His glory through you in a unique way. We must teach each other to be thankful with who and how God made us and encourage each other to walk the path God has set before us.

WINGS

To everything there is a season, A time for every purpose under heaven:
A time to change diapers, A time to give diplomas;
A time to chauffeur, A time to hand over the car keys;
A time to call them in for a nap, A time to take a nap yourself;
A time to discipline, A time to let the Lord correct them;
A time to hold on, A time to let go;
A time to give roots, A time to grant wings.
—Diana Waring, 2001

I would like to leave you with two pictures and a final challenge.

The first picture is that of a mother eagle with her just-about-to-fly offspring. I have been told that the wise mother nudges the young eagle out of the nest, when it is ready to use its wings. Though the young eagle may take its time, eventually it leaps out of the nest and starts plummeting to the bottom of the world!

"Oh, no! What did I do that for?!"
"Never fear, Dear, Mother is here."

Gracefully, the mother eagle positions herself under the young eagle and gently slows it down. Back up to the nest to try again. Nudge, nudge. Hesitate, leap. Plummet, catch. Over and over again. Until . . .

REAPING THE HARVEST

"Hey, everybody, look at me! I can FLY!!"

We need to understand that the time will come when God asks us to be like eagle mothers to our fledglings, nudging them to test their wings, carefully overseeing them while they learn to fly—neither throwing them out before it is time, nor overprotecting restrictively.

The second picture: as loving parents, we often hold our wee ones' hands as they toddle down the street. We love to hold their hands as they say grace at a meal. We give a quick squeeze to our child's hand as we hear wild tales of harrowing bicycle adventures. We gently hold our teen's hand while he or she pours out an emotional hurt. Picture holding their hands. Do you see how your hand is on top, fingers closed tightly, and their hand is underneath? It is a picture of comfort, of security, of safety.

The time comes when God asks us to change our hand position. He asks us to become the hand below, open and supporting, while our child's hand is free to lightly rest on ours for balance and support.

Throughout these growing years, you have stepped out in faith to homeschool them. You have given them the best of your life, the best of your heart, the best of your mind. You have poured out time and money and prayer into raising these precious young people. Well done.

Psalm 32:8 has an amazing and directing word to us and for our children: *"I will instruct you and teach you in the way you should go."*

Our part in being the primary teachers, the primary instructors, draws to a close. There is One who is even more loving, even more faithful, even more willing to teach our precious children now.

Here is the challenge, dear ones: take the next step. There will come a time to take the next step. Take the step with the Lord, under His wings, in His timing, yes, but still you must take it. We must step out in faith to release, to bless, to liberate our homeschool graduates. With the Lord's gracious help, may we have the grace to change our hand position. Let them go to the university; let them start their own businesses; let them move to other cities; let them go to the mission field. In essence, release them to be adults. Though it seems difficult beyond belief, though it seems lonely, scary, and like an ending to family life as we have known it, we must take the next step and grant our children wings. Taking our courage firmly in hand, may we as parents and stewards of these precious gifts do what we have been designed by God to do. May we grant our children wings.

For, you see, they were designed by God to soar like eagles!